DATA ANALYSIS, INTERPRETATION, AND THEORY IN LITERACY STUDIES RESEARCH

Data Analysis, Interpretation, and Theory in Literacy Studies Research

A How-To Guide

EDITED BY

Michele Knobel, Judy Kalman, and Colin Lankshear

Myers Education Press

Gorham, Maine

Myers Education Press

Published by Myers Education Press, LLC
P.O. Box 424
Gorham, ME 04038

Myers Education Press is an academic publisher specializing in books, e-books, and digital content in the field of education. All of our books are subjected to a rigorous peer review process and produced in compliance with the standards of the Council on Library and Information Resources.

LIBRARY OF CONGRESS CATALOGING-IN-PUBLICATION DATA AVAILABLE FROM LIBRARY OF CONGRESS.

13-digit ISBN 978-1-9755-0213-3 (paperback)
13-digit ISBN 978-1-9755-0212-6 (hardcover)
13-digit ISBN 978-1-9755-0214-0 (library networkable e-edition)
13-digit ISBN 978-1-9755-0215-7 (consumer e-edition)

Printed in the United States of America.

All first editions printed on acid-free paper that meets the American National Standards Institute Z39-48 standard.

Cover design by Sophie Appel.

Contents

Dedication

To all our chapter authors,
for the work you do and the way you do it.
We esteem your generosity and goodwill.

Acknowledgments

The editors wish to acknowledge the generous contributions of different kinds made by individuals and publishers to create and produce this book.

We owe particular thanks to our fellow chapter authors for all the time, energy, effort, and goodwill they have dedicated to this project. We know they all lead busy and demanding lives, and truly appreciate all they have done and the warm and expansive manner in which they have gone about the work. In the process we have learned a great deal from them all.

Jason Toncic undertook considerable behind the scenes work with indexing and proofreading. We are very grateful for his rapid, efficient, and accurate responses to requests, all of which were undertaken with an unceasing cheerfulness and attention to detail.

Thanks also go to our many research students for questions and conversations that helped us conceive this book and motivated us to realize this project.

We wish to thank Jon M. Wargo and Kara Clayton for their personal permission to reproduce Figure 4.1.

We thank the universities and institutes who employ our contributing authors for supporting their research and publishing activity. As editors we thank the following institutions for their ongoing support of our own work: Montclair State University, el Centro de Investigación y Estudios Avanzados del Instituto Politécnico Nacional, and Mount Saint Vincent University.

We also sincerely thank those at Myers Education Press for taking a chance on this book and making it such an easy job to administer. Particular thanks go to Chris Myers, Stephanie Gabaree, Wendy Jo Dymond, Emily Janson, and Sophie Appel. Their patience, goodwill, good humor, and talent are greatly appreciated.

Finally, thanks are owed to the following publishers and journals for granting permission to reproduce previously published material: Designs for Learning; Learning, Media and Technology; Linguistics and Education; Peter Lang Publishing; Routledge/ Taylor and Francis; Sage. Specific permissions details are appended to the relevant material in the text.

CHAPTER 1

Data Analysis, Interpretation, and Theory in Literacy Studies Research

Michele Knobel, Judy Kalman, and Colin Lankshear

Background to the Book

This book has emerged from two quite different, but complementary, kinds of experiences shared by the editors over the past 20 years. The first comprises our respective experiences of working with research students and early-career researchers doing qualitative research on aspects of literacy in our roles as advisors, supervisors, candidate committee members, and collegial mentors. Despite working in somewhat different contexts and under different conditions from one another, we have found a large degree of overlap with respect to the kinds of challenges novice qualitative researchers seem to have genuine difficulty getting their heads around in the course of learning how to conduct their studies as rigorous (social) research marked by well-thought-out design and logic of inquiry.

Our collective experience as qualitative researchers and as teachers and mentors of novice researchers suggests four key things to us:

1. Many students struggle with knowing (a) what methods are available to use to analyze their data, (b) how to implement their chosen analytic method, and (c) what to make of—or how to interpret—the results

of their analysis. In particular, many students experience serious difficulty with issues arising at points of connection among theory, data analysis, and meaningful interpretation of analytic results or findings.

2. This is often associated with a shaky sense of overall research design, that is, not quite understanding how one's research question, theoretical framing, location within a field or fields, and analytic methods need to cohere with each other and how to pursue coherence. This can include misunderstandings regarding what constitutes and informs data collection design too (e.g., thinking about interviews but not about how they are informed by a study's framing theory and research question).
3. Those responsible for advising and supervising research students often find themselves having to work on studies outside their areas of theoretical and methodological strength. They may be able to advise students on the kinds of theoretical and methodological options that would cohere with their research purposes but not feel confident in providing expert, hands-on guidance.
4. Becoming good at analyzing data and interpreting the results of data analysis are tasks best and most easily mastered through guided, hands-on activity in authentic research contexts and by practicing them until they become fluent. In this respect, the learning in question is much like other forms of learning that have been talked about at length during the period in which resources available on the Internet have enabled novices in diverse social practices to learn how to do things they would otherwise have found difficult to master if they had had to depend on conventional kinds of manuals and texts.

Often the consequence of novice researchers lacking a strong sense of research design and logic and/or a sound understanding of how their framing theory will inevitably shape their data collection and analysis but should not *drive* their outcomes becomes most apparent at the writing-up stage—by which time it may be getting too late to do much about it. Our experiences of working with students during write-up, and of directing them to other people's dissertations, theses, and published articles, indicate a range of common recurring pitfalls novice researchers face and, in many cases, do not overcome. These include the following specific examples:

- "Tails wagging dogs" issues. There are many kinds of ways in which novice research can fall prey to some form or other of a research "tail" wagging the research "dog." These can range from such things as deciding on a research site before understanding clearly just what it is that one wants to investigate or collecting data in advance of thinking sufficiently about one's research purposes and theoretical and conceptual frames all the way through to using one's research questions to report findings by matching patterns to the questions rather than analyzing the data as much as possible on its own terms.

- Adopting an "I know what I'll find" orientation. This is where the researcher has the outcomes in mind prior to the study, and simply sets out to "prove" some preexisting claim or viewpoint rather than posing genuine questions, letting the data speak to them, and adopting an open approach to analysis and interpretation.
- Adopting an "everything but the kitchen sink" approach. In some cases, novice researchers throw all kinds of theories and methods into the mix, as though the point is to cite as many theorists as possible, rather than seeking to understand whether multiple theories are even needed to serve their research purpose and/or whether those selected actually fit together in some useful and illuminating way. A second variant—and often both are evident in the same study—involves trying to combine diverse methodologists and methodological approaches within their data collection and analysis, again without pondering whether they are all necessary and/or fit together coherently in the interests of a logical and elegant research design.
- Engaging in "throat-clearing theory work." This is when the researcher understands that theory plays a very important role in framing a study and spells out the theory or theories that shape the study at hand but leaves it at that—without revisiting the theory to explicate and justify the data collection and data analysis techniques or to discuss and interpret findings. This denies the novice researcher the opportunity to refine theoretical understandings or to contribute new theoretical insights and/or theoretically informed innovations at the methodological level to the field.
- Confusing description given for analysis or for interpretation. In such cases, researchers describe interesting things that happened in the study and stop short of reporting *analytic* outcomes (e.g., in the form of patterns, categories of things, themes). This also occurs when the researcher describes patterned outcomes of some kind but fails to broach the "So what?" of these patterns in light of their research question or framing theory and literature (including identifying new insights gained along the way or challenges to be made to existing knowledge).
- Failing to provide a sufficient "audit trail" to establish the *quality* of a qualitative research study. Qualitative researchers have developed concepts and criteria designed to shore up confidence in the quality of

> the research process and the claimed results of research. They do not aim for "truth," "proof," or approximations to "certainty" so much as for ideals such as communicative validity, trustworthiness, and defensible interpretation. These ideals build on the belief that reporting the conduct of a research project should be, in part, a kind of *conversation* between the researcher and the reader and not merely an act of *delivery*. This means that researchers should provide the kind of detail that allows readers to be able to think (or say) things like, "Okay, I can see how you got here, and why you have claimed or concluded the things you have. I might not agree with you, but at least I can follow your line of reasoning and can take it on board as being defensible or, at least, arguable. From my perspective, however, and on the face of the evidence you provide, I might be inclined more toward claiming X or arguing Y . . ." In the case of reporting on *data collection*, the researcher should demonstrate how the data they collected was appropriate to the research purpose, why and how this was decided, and what some typical examples of data of various kinds look like. In the case of *data analysis*, this involves drawing on some typical and significant stretches of data and demonstrating in close-up detail how the analysis was done such that the reader can make informed judgments about whether to go along with such things as the codes the researcher developed for particular slices of data and/or with their process of identifying particular patterns among the codes as a basis for claiming the development of certain categories, themes, and so on. Failure to do this audit-trail work sufficiently well is an unfortunate feature of all too many reports of literacy studies research.

These material signals of misalignment or misunderstanding can be minimized and, ideally, avoided altogether by paying careful attention to the logic of research design and conduct. This book is an attempt to develop a supportive resource for novice researchers and their advisors that would help with pragmatic and meaningful decision making regarding research design, choice of theoretical approach, and the processes of data analysis and interpretation of results. It is based on our shared conception of a "bottom line," according to which for inquiry to count as bona fide *research*, rather than some form of information gathering or a general form of data-based inquiry, it must aim to generate robust and defensible claims to knowledge. This means there has to be a coherent chain of reasoning that runs all the way from the research purpose and questions to the research findings via appropriate and adequate data collection, data analysis, and interpretive processes that are informed by relevant theory and concepts. This is the approach we advocate and that this book tries to model for novice researchers and their mentors so far as bringing a theoretical perspective to bear on data analysis, making the analysis explicit, and arguing cogently for the interpretation of findings are concerned.

The second kind of experience that directly informs this book involves a mix of personal activities, observations of other people's activities, and reviews of an extensive body of literature broadly concerned with how everyday people in everyday contexts learn how to do things by accessing peer guidance and expertise online. As examples of such guidance, shared and distributed expertise, and explicit modeling, we took as our model for authors the kinds of online learning resources, such as Instructables, walk-throughs, demonstrations, models, and the like, that come as close as possible to "stand-ins" for an expert, someone being right there alongside you, teaching you how to do something well when there is no immediate alternative to working alone.

The sharing economy online has resourced all kinds of affinity spaces with explanatory and how-to guides designed by expert others to help scaffold newcomers' understandings of how to do or be something or other. On YouTube, for example, the comments appended to step-by-step videos for how to complete small, do-it-yourself home repairs show that novices watch these videos all the way through and then follow the video how-to guide step-by-step as they work through resolving a particular repair. Watching these videos also shows us that the makers typically include things newbie do-it-yourselfers should take extra care with (e.g., make sure the water mains are turned off, do not tighten the nut too tightly, take care you do not strip the screw). The same applies for photo-based guide sites, such as wikiHow and Instructables. Typically, a series of in-process photos with commentary from the poster guides a newbie through a particular process (e.g., how to sew a cushion cover, how to sew a zipper into something, how to sew knitted squares together). Close-up photographs of the task in process act as though an experienced other is right there, showing how something is done in a clear and infinitely patient manner. Models for scaffolding newbie learning also are found in video game walk-throughs, where players record their gameplay for others to watch and to see for themselves how the game mechanics work in this new-to-them game world, greatly facilitating subsequent play. These gameplay walk-throughs can include spoken hints and tips for guiding play, too, and give a sense of "being there" alongside the gamer. Readers will no doubt be familiar with these kinds of how-to procedural resources and almost-in-person guides. The concreteness and "insiderliness" of these logically ordered tutorials that pull back the curtain on the inner workings of things are precisely the kinds of resources that have shaped our idea of this book and its format.

The Idea of the Book

These two sets of experiences generated the idea for a book that addresses some of the most difficult aspects of learning to do robust qualitative research within the field of Literacy Studies, where the chapters approximate as closely as possible to the kinds of modelings, walk-throughs, step-by-step guides, and so on, that we have encountered so widely within nonformal online learning settings and resources. The idea was to first identify some established researchers with demonstrated expertise in theory-informed approaches to data analysis and interpretation of results that often are used in Literacy Studies research. The second part of the idea was to work with chapter authors to identify specific projects they had undertaken that we regarded as good examples of their research craft and that have been written up as published research articles or reports. Although this was not a formal requirement, it has been followed in all cases, in line with the book being designed, in part, to provide a degree of interactive experience among readers, the authors' book chapters, and a series of originating texts that the chapters explicate in terms of overt and behind-the-scenes theory framing, analysis, and interpretation or discussion. The original sources pertaining to the various chapters and that are readily available for readers to access are listed in the references to this and subsequent chapters.

Authors were invited to take a self-consciously didactic approach to spelling out key dimensions of their study, homing in on *how* they analyzed their data, *why* they took this approach, and how they *translated or interpreted* the results of their analysis as findings. This would involve, crucially, spelling out the role of their adopted theory in guiding how they did their work. At each point, the emphasis would be on *showing*, rather than simply *telling*, so far as possible, but outside this, authors were free to choose the kind of format and register they would adopt.

So far as the substance of each chapter was concerned, we suggested that authors focus as they think best on four key elements. One was to identify and elucidate the main data analysis method or methods showcased in the chapter. With reference to the study each chapter was based on, authors were invited to identify the research question(s) and research design, describe the study's theoretical framing and key concepts, and explain why they chose their particular analytic method for the study. Against this broad background, each chapter would detail what the analytic method looks like when applied to the data collected in the study. Finally, authors were invited to describe and explain how they interpreted (i.e., made sense of) their analytic results and wrote them up and to suggest two to three texts they would recommend to readers for learning more about the analytic methods in question.

Field and Audience

This book addresses theoretical, analytic, and interpretative approaches that are particularly appropriate for qualitative inquiry in Literacy Studies research. This field of inquiry, often called the New Literacy Studies, dates from the early 1980s (e.g., Heath, 1983; Scribner & Cole, 1981; Street, 1984). It is characterized by an explicitly social and cultural/anthropological approach to studying literacy as *literacies,* conceived as social practices and conceptions of meaning-making and exchange mediated by tools and techniques of inscription. We speak of Literacy Studies here, rather than the New Literacy Studies, for two reasons. First, the field is now long established and, in that sense, is no longer "new." Originally, the "new" was used to mark off emerging social-cultural approaches to investigating and understanding literacy from psychological approaches that had previously dominated the research into reading and writing almost exclusively. "New" announced a new kind of paradigm, but that paradigm is now thoroughly consolidated and widely subscribed.

Second, with the emergence of digital-electronic technologies and the explosion in digitally mediated practices of communicating and negotiating meanings, distinguishing "new" literacies (digitally mediated) from conventional print-based (typographic) literacy practices became common. With this increased use of "new literacies," the distinction between the New Literacy Studies and the study of new literacies was often blurred. Equally, of course, the so-called "new literacies" are also, by now, thoroughly embedded in everyday life throughout the world.

At the most general level, literacy studies research begins from understanding literacy as multiple—as so many *literacies*. These literacies are, in turn, understood as complex situated social practices. Reading, writing, and other forms of representation and their related semiotic systems are located within contexts of wider social practices and the importance of social relationships, institutional arrangements, material circumstances—including tools, techniques, purposes and tasks, and participant knowledge and skills—and issues and configurations of power are emphasized (see Barton & Hamilton, 2000; Scribner & Cole, 1981; Street 1984, 1995; as well as Kalman, Valdivia, & Rendón, this volume; Rish, this volume). As situated social practices, literacies are framed *ideologically* by the social and cultural contexts in which they play out, contextualized by situated activities, and vary to a greater or lesser extent from one social or institutional arrangement (e.g., family or school) to another (e.g., church or workplace).

Ryan Rish (this volume) identifies literacy studies research as being grounded in two key theoretical constructs: literacy events and literacy practices. Proceeding from Shirley Heath's (1983) seminal work, Rish (this volume) defines literacy *events* as "observable situations in which reading, writing or related semiotic systems play a nontrivial role in the actions taken by people" (p. 55) participating in the wider activities that make up the contexts in question. Literacy studies researchers identify, describe, and explain literacy *practices* "by observing comparable literacy events and making inductions about how people enact, adopt, adapt [and] resist literacy practices extant within particular social arrangements" (Rish, this volume, p. 55).

Broadly speaking, literacy studies researchers go into situations where people are doing things that involve some kind of purpose-driven activities, and where the pursuit of these ends is mediated by texts of one kind of another (and the kinds of tools, techniques, knowledge, and resources required for creating, communicating, exchanging, and negotiating these texts) and try to make sense of what is going on in terms of the dynamic between the literacy components and the larger activities in which they are embedded.

Scribner and Cole (1981) described and analyzed these uses in terms of social practices that always involve technologies, know-how for using them, and social knowledge. Situations of use can be anywhere: online, off-line, inside, outside, in a fixed location or across locations, at some circumscribed time or over time, and so on. Researchers observe, ask questions, collect artifacts, and may participate more or less centrally or peripherally but always with a view of trying to make some kind of sense based on evidence of what is going on and how it is playing out.

This book presents a range of approaches in terms of research designs, methods, and theoretical perspectives that researchers can take to doing this kind of work. As Rish notes, while there is broad agreement about the theoretical, conceptual and methodological parameters of literacy studies research, there is nonetheless plenty of variation among researchers around matters such as how to define literacy events; how inductions are made to identify, describe, and examine literacy practices; the kind of scale on which literacy practices as conceived and understood; and the roles played by tools, techniques, and materials within particular literacy practices.

The point, of course, is not to aim at reduction to some single correct or pristine version of "a" literacy practice but, rather, to recognize a variety of approaches that complement and fruitfully interact with one another in wide and constructive conversations that generate rich understandings of literacies as situated cultural and social phenomena and to employ these approaches in robust and rigorous ways in the name of good quality social and cultural *science*. The chapters in this book provide many guides, resources, and examples for doing precisely that. They are by no means exhaustive, but they are certainly representative.

The primary audience for this book is honors, master's, and doctoral students enrolled in formal university programs and working in the field of Literacy Studies, academics responsible for advising and supervising them in their research, and other early-career researchers who may still be finding their way in qualitative inquiry. We hope this collection will also appeal to many qualitative researchers outside literacy studies because many of the methods and approaches demonstrated in the following chapters travel usefully into other areas of inquiry. For example, microethnographic analysis of classroom language practices can be applied as readily to mathematics as to literacy (see Chapters 2 and 6 in this volume); conversation and discourse analysis can be applied to a wide range of conversations and research foci—from doctor–patient interactions through to teacher–student interactions. And approaches such as the kind of collaborative participatory research described by Larson and Moses in Chapter 8 can be applied to a diverse range of community-based issues and phenomena. We are also hoping that the book will be relevant for teacher researchers and workplace-based researchers—all too often sidelined by academic researchers—who want to inform or hone their research expertise. In short, this book is aimed at novice and practiced researchers alike who wish to ensure that their work meets the criteria and standards of qualitative research as a form of deeply logical and coherent empirical inquiry.

Overview of the Chapters

In Chapter 2, Sanghee Ryu and David Bloome address microethnographic discourse analysis research for transforming classroom education. They identify the theoretical basis of microethnographic discourse analysis in the understanding that culture—the worlds in which we live—is created primarily in and through "languaging": how we use language. When employed in classrooms, this approach explores how educational concepts and "ways" are *languaged* into being. Consequently, using microethnographic discourse analysis to explore classroom education "inherently involves a transformative perspective" because it "calls into question how people have been defining knowledge and learning, what it means to be human, and the context of schooling in such definitions" (p. 17). The authors identify six of the foundational principles of conducting microethnographic discourse analysis and argue that the approach is complex and varies from research situation to research situation. Learning how to do such research, then, is an "abductive" process, based on seeing how other researchers have applied the foundational principles and theoretical constructs in concrete situations. They provide an illustrative example of how such learning can proceed by reference to a study of two language arts classrooms in which Ryu (2016) collaborated with two teachers to explore the use of an arguing-to-learn approach in their classroom. The study design as a series of intervention/research—data interpretation and reflection—redesign sequences through four cycles is spelled out, explained, and summarized. The authors then illustrate in rich and graphic detail how data collected during an intervention phase was analyzed and interpreted. They conclude by observing how microethnographic discourse analysis brings ethnography and discourse analysis together to frame what happens in educational settings as "cultural and languaging processes," that is, in a way that differs from dominant research and practice frameworks that focus on "individuals and their psychological states." In so doing, it provides a way for collaborating teachers and researchers to simultaneously address complex pedagogical situations and contribute to the educational research base.

In the third chapter, Aaron Hung models using conversation analysis methods to study social interaction in the context of a group of teenage boys hanging out in private group chats using the Xbox 360 party chat (see also Hung, 2017, 2019). He begins by explaining the relationship between Conversation Analysis and Ethnomethodology and the nature and role of conversation analysis as one tool that can be used in ethnomethodological research to understand how people make sense of their world in and through social interaction. Some basic premises (e.g., "the social world is orderly" and "context is fluid") shared by Conversation Analysis and Ethnomethodology about the social world are spelled out in ways that make clear the kind of data conversation analysts work with. Hung then describes his approach to and preferences for collecting data in the form of (naturally occurring) talk in interaction, outlines some of the main conventions employed in the prevalent conversation analysis transcription format developed by Gail

Jefferson (2004), and identifies the kinds of things conversation analysts focus on in data analysis. In the second half of the chapter, Hung presents transcriptions of eight substantial excerpts of the boys' talk and shows how he analyzes their interactions. His explication brings alive the theoretical and methodological elements of Conversation Analysis discussed at length in the first half of the chapter. The chapter concludes with Hung's response to some common critiques of Conversation Analysis research and his view of what studies like his own can contribute to understanding social phenomena in everyday life.

In Chapter 4, Ryan Rish explains mediated discourse analysis as both an overarching methodology for literacy studies research and a specific approach to analyzing data. Against the background of a succinct and carefully crafted account of the New Literacy Studies, Rish draws on his study of student collaborative writing in an elective high school English class (Rish, 2015) to walk us through an example of using mediated discourse analysis to investigate literacy practices of adolescents using digital tools. Mediated Discourse Analysis—as a methodology—brings together methods for closely examining actions people take to make inductions about how those actions aggregate into individual and shared social practices over time. Mediated Discourse Analysis also includes methods for examining the relationships among social practices within and across contexts. Rish explains how micro- and macro-level methods can help literacy researchers understand how and why people take certain social actions in a given context and how those actions may be enacted differently or be regarded differently across contexts. This approach is particularly helpful for accounting for the significance of digital tools in the enactment of literacy practices within and across multiple contexts of meaning-making and learning. Rish draws on the work of researchers and theorists instrumental in conceiving and developing Mediated Discourse Analysis to identify and explain the key concepts and research logic underlying this approach to making sense of literacy events and practices.

Ingrid K. Jakobsen and Elise Seip Tønnessen address multimodal literacy in language teaching and learning in Chapter 5. The research context is a Year 10 classroom in Norway where students were learning English as a foreign language. In the study, Multimodality served as both an analytical method and an object of investigation. The chapter draws on data from Jakobsen's doctoral research and focuses on key aspects of the data collection, data analysis, interpretation of results, and the writing up process. Multimodality had been introduced into the Norwegian language curriculum subject in 2006, partly prompting their research interest in multimodality within a foreign language learning context. The study was informed theoretically by currents within the New Literacy Studies, including the New London Group's (1996) account of multiliteracies and work by Gunther Kress and colleagues, along with the distinction between the teacher's design *for* learning and the student's design *in* learning advanced by Selander and Kress (2010). Jakobsen and Tønnessen describe site selection and the ethnographic approach taken to collect data across a 4-week unit plan during which students studied a novel that included images in a significant way. The multimodal analytical focus and analytical approach are carefully described. Particular attention is paid to literacy *events*, how the design *for* learning and design *in* learning distinction played out empirically, and the ways theory informed and guided the analysis. The authors spell out their procedures for making sense of their analytic results and how they structured the writing up of their interpretation. They conclude with reflections on what could have been done differently in the research and the contributions their research could make to the intersecting fields of literacy studies, multimodal studies, and educational studies.

Interactional Ethnography as a logic of inquiry and analyses is the focus in Chapter 6, by Maria Lucia Castanheira, Beth V. Yeager, and Judith L. Green. They describe in close detail how archived ethnographic records generated during fieldwork in a microethnographic study of a bilingual fifth-grade class as culture-in-the-making were collected and analyzed. The data used in the chapter were collected in Yeager's class during the first morning of the school year, at the very outset of constituting the class as a "community-of-inquiry." The focus on Interactional Ethnography of a logic-of-analyses involves showing how Castanheira constructed multiple levels of analytic scale of the morning's data in the role of ethnographer-as-learner of the culture of the classroom. By means of a "telling case study" (Mitchell, 1984), the authors recount Castanheira's development of a "reflexive logic of analyses" to reconstruct, analyze, and display how Yeager, the teacher, "proposed and discursively and interactionally engaged the students in developing ways of knowing, and being a student in the class" (this volume, p. 95). They identify and describe the theory that informed their particular approach to conducting Interactional Ethnography of classroom culture. They explicate how Castanheira moved from being a cultural outsider to attaining an insider appreciation of what was "entailed by being a student in the class, and of who had access to what kinds of learning opportunities" (this volume, p. 95). Castanheira, Yeager, and Green show how Interactional Ethnography constitutes an epistemology (or way of knowing) rather than a method. They demonstrate their multiple levels of analyses by means of distinctive kinds of transcription methods that make their analytic moves visible—for example, by identifying subevents within larger events, focusing on transitions between events, and homing in on an individual student to show more clearly how the culture of the class was constructed moment by moment.

In Chapter 7, Judy Kalman, Patricia Valdivia, and Victor Rendón walk us through how they use Excel spreadsheets to generate a flexible and study-specific database of coded data as part of their analytic and interpretive process. Managing large qualitative data sets can be daunting for any researcher—and especially so for new researchers. Software designed to help manage complex descriptive data and its coding or tagging can, however, be costly for individuals or institutions in countries where public education funding is stretched thin. Furthermore, because it is predesigned, why or how these commercial programs do what they do is often not clear, so researchers must "trust" the epistemological decisions made by the designers. The authors explain how they took more of these design decisions into their own hands and how they set up their spreadsheet workbooks, label key columns (and explain why), and demonstrate how they develop and refine codes or tags that capture key elements and patterns emerging in the data as they work through it (see also Kalman & Rendón, 2016). These tags are informed by their framing theory while, at the same time, grow directly out of what they are seeing in their data. They also show how to rearrange and/or select columns and rows for closer scrutiny to help identify patterns that have gone unnoticed and discover contextual conditions key for understanding the data. They conclude by showing how they move from tagging the data to developing patterns to interpreting key patterns for understanding complex literacy practices and how the spreadsheet is also useful for retrieving concrete patterns for using in the write-up of a study.

Chapter 8, by Joanne Larson and George Moses, is based on an ongoing, long-term, and collaborative research partnership between residents of the Beechwood community in Rochester, New York, and faculty and graduate students from the University of Rochester. It describes a complex case of community-engaged scholarship in which community members participate as authentic research partners and research activity proceeds from recognizing the important role played by community-defined problems of practice in designing and conducting "research that matters." This research collaboration takes the form of participatory ethnography, in which all participants are simultaneously researchers and researched. It builds on the tradition of Community-Based Participatory Research, informed, in part, by an ideal of liberatory/emancipatory cultural practice through which community members can determine their own futures and "be free" and, crucially, live by the seven principles of *nguzo saba*: unity, self-determination, collective work and responsibility, cooperative economics, purpose, creativity, and faith (Karenga, 2018; Larson & Moses, 2018). The chapter describes the complex evolution of this collaboration in terms of building research roles and relationships grounded in mutual trust and respect that can build productively on "generative frictions" and pursue "attunement" in the course of expanding the front of research activity from collaboratively managing a community market to helping to meet the challenge of inhabiting "a food desert" to addressing wider issues and sites of practice across the community at large, including formal education in community schools. The authors describe processes and challenges associated with learning how to collaboratively collect observational and interview data, transcribe interviews and field notes, code data, construct categories, build descriptive and explanatory models, and negotiate theory, positionality, and competing values and perspectives. With reference to a collaboratively authored book (Larson & Moses, 2018), the authors describe in rich detail the main dimensions of an entire research process that goes all the way to co-authorship of academic, peer-reviewed work and co-presentation at conferences.

Allison Dziuba, Rebecca W. Black, and Jonathan Alexander use an interview approach in Chapter 9 to spell out conceptual, theoretical, data analysis, and interpretive aspects of a recently completed study of representations of autism in *Harry Potter* fanfiction (Black, Alexander, Chen, & Duarte, 2019). The study focused on how people with autism, their friends, families, and advocates represent autism in fanfiction writing and generally construct meaning around autism. The authors explain the grounding of the original study around broad professional interests in participatory cultures and "sponsored"—including self-sponsored—forms of literate and multiliterate practice. In this case, their focus homed in on participation and difference, and how participatory cultures sometimes "extend themselves . . . to include the marginalized and underrepresented" (this volume, p. 165). The site selection and its rationale, strengths, and limitations are discussed in association with some logistical challenges concerning data collection. Successive phases of reading and rereading fan-fiction stories, coding and recoding, and collapsing codes are described. Concrete instantiation of the process is provided by reference to examples, and the authors identify the main themes they believe were important to the story writers. The dynamic between inductive, bottom-up and deductive, top-down coding and tensions between analytic results that seemed to work well for some examples and not so well for others are addressed. The fact that most of the authors of the stories analyzed did not identify as being on the autism spectrum, and the significance of this for future work, is taken up as a key discussion point. The authors also address aspects of the journal review process for their original study's publication in helpful ways and close with some thoughts about some possible implications for working with students critically and creatively around what participation means, how to encourage it, what we can learn from it, and its potential to enhance personal and collective agency through literacy.

In Chapter 10, Jason Lovvorn and Kevin Leander present their approach to thinking about literacy from the perspective of Actor Network Theory. They observe that educational theory and research remain largely "people-centric" and typically emphasize "stability, sorting experience, and creating order out of disorder' (p. 181). By contrast, Actor Network Theory recognizes the integral role that nonhuman "actants" assume within robust descriptions and explanations of social phenomena. Researchers taking an Actor Network Theory approach learn to live with complexity and messiness as a price to be paid in trying to get as close as they can to phenomena. Lovvorn and Leander explain their understanding of Actor Network Theory as "part theory, part method"—more like a sensibility than a theoretical technology that is applied to understanding the world scientifically. They draw on a case (Brian) from a larger study of several youth across school and online settings (Leander & Lovvorn, 2006). Having problematized at the outset the idea central to Literacy Studies research that literacies are *situated*, the authors describe how they used Actor Network Theory to conceptualize and analyze literacy networks and consider how this might help inform thinking about literacy practices and their relations to "space-time." Their original research also sought to explore whether an analysis of literacy networks might help with understanding Brian's engagement, agency, and identity across a range of his different literacy practices, including classroom-based practices such as note-taking and researching, as well as playing a massively multiplayer online game at home. They present five analytic dimensions developed from Actor Network Theory and describe in detail how they thought about their data through the lens of the analytic dimension of "heterogeneity of space-time representations." (Leander & Lovvorn, 2006, p. 305) They also indicate how this, in turn, led them to think about the data through the lenses of "translation" and "movement and position of texts in circulation." (Leander & Lovvorn, 2006, p. 306) They end the chapter by identifying five broad "stances" they believe are useful for researchers using Actor Network Theory.

The book concludes with Colin Lankshear and Michele Knobel revisiting an exploratory study of early Internet memes to address aspects of research design, theory, data analysis, and interpretation in qualitative inquiry (Knobel & Lankshear, 2007). They identify the study's research purposes and how these centered on trying to identify characteristics that might be associated with the success of a diverse pool of English-language Internet memes from 2001 to 2005 and developing a provisional typology of these memes. Key components of informing theory, drawn from Literacy Studies theory, Richard Dawkins's (1976/2006) foundational account of memes and their defining characteristics, and some early work in the field of memetics are briefly surveyed. The authors then show how these theoretical elements and the study purposes were brought together in the study's research design, with particular reference to how concepts such as social practices, affinity spaces, language-in-use, and discourse were drawn on to develop cumulative sets of prompt questions designed to analyze the memes and build a typology. They briefly explicate the prompt questions with reference to three "systems" for exploring meaning, loosely adapted from the work of Michael Halliday (1978) and heavily inflected by James Gee's (2004) approach to discourse analysis. This is followed by some worked examples of applying the prompt questions to the memes data set and a summary of the main analytic results claimed in the original study. The results are briefly discussed by way of comparison with Dawkins's (1976/2006) concepts of "fidelity," "fecundity," and "longevity," with a focus on how Internet memes vary from the classic memes of cultural evolution as theorized by Dawkins. The chapter concludes with a brief interpretation of the study results in terms of their possible significance for literacy education and how they might help to further inform the theoretical orientation that underpins the study.

References

Barton, D., & Hamilton. M. (2000). Literacy practices. In D. Barton, M. Hamilton, & R. Ivanič, (Eds.), *Situated literacies: Reading and writing in context* (pp. 7–15). New York, NY: Routledge.

Black, R., Alexander, J., Chen, V., & Duarte, J. (2019). Representations of autism in online *Harry Potter* fanfiction. *Journal of Literacy Research, 51*(1), 30–51.

Dawkins, R. (2006). *The selfish gene* (2nd ed.). Oxford, England: Oxford University Press. (Original work published 1976)

Gee, J. P. (2004). *Situated language and learning: A critique of traditional schooling.* New York, NY: Routledge.

Halliday, M. (1978). *Language as social semiotic: The social interpretation of language and meaning.* London, England: Edward Arnold.

Heath, S. B. (1983). *Ways with words.* New York, NY: Cambridge University Press.

Hung, A. C. Y. (2017). Hanging out on Xbox Live: How teens enter and open conversations in party chats. *Language@Internet, 14.* Retrieved from https://www.languageatinternet.org/articles/2017/hung

Hung, A. C. Y. (2019). Political socialization on Xbox Live: A sociocultural linguistic approach to adolescent identity. *Journal of Youth Studies,* 1–17. Advanced online publication. https://doi.org/10.1080/13676261.2019.1636009

Jefferson, G. (2004). Glossary of transcript symbols with an introduction. In G. H. Lerner (Ed.), *Conversation analysis: Studies from the first generation* (pp. 13–31). Amsterdam, the Netherlands: John Benjamins.

Kalman, J., & Rendón, V. (2016). Uso de la hoja de cálculo para analizar datos cualitativos. [Using spreadsheets for analyzing qualitative data], *Magis Revista Internacional de Investigación en Educación, 9*(18), 29–48. https://doi.org/10.11144/Javeriana.m9-18.uhca

Kalman, J., Valdivia, P., & Rendón, V. (2020). Examining qualitative data using spreadsheets: Constructing analytical narratives around talk, action, and practice. In M. Knobel, J. Kalman, & C. Lankshear (Eds.), *Data analysis, interpretation, and theory in literacy studies research: A how-to guide* (pp. 123–147). Gorham, ME: Myers Education Press.

Karenga, M. (2018, December 20). Annual founder's Kwanzaa message 'Reimagining and remaking the world: A Kwanzaa commitment to an inclusive good.' *Los Angeles Sentinel,* A1. Retrieved from https://lasentinel.net/annual-founders-kwanzaa-message-reimagining-and-remaking-the-world-a-kwanzaa-commitment-to-an-inclusive-good.html

Knobel, M., & Lankshear, C. (2007). Online memes, affinities and cultural production. In M. Knobel & C. Lankshear (Eds.), *A new literacies sampler* (pp. 199–227). New York, NY: Peter Lang.

Larson, J., & Moses, G. (Eds.). (2018). *Community literacies as shared resources for transformation.* New York, NY: Routledge.

Leander, K., & Lovvorn, J. (2006). Literacy networks: Following the circulation of texts, bodies, and objects in the schooling and online gaming of one youth. *Cognition and Instruction, 24,* 291–340.

Mitchell, C. J. (1984). Typicality and the case study. In R. F. Ellens (Ed.), *Ethnographic research: A guide to general conduct* (pp. 238–241). New York, NY: Academic Press.

New London Group. (1996). A pedagogy of multiliteracies: Designing social futures. *Harvard Educational Review, 66,* 60–92.

Rish, R. (2020). Using mediated discourse analysis to investigate literacy practices. In M. Knobel, J. Kalman, & C. Lankshear (Eds.), *Data analysis, interpretation, and theory in literacy studies research: A how-to guide* (pp. 55–76). Gorham, ME: Myers Education Press.

Rish, R. M. (2015). Researching writing events: Using mediated discourse analysis to explore how students write together. *Literacy, 49*(1), 12–19.

Ryu, S. (2016). *Teaching and learning of sophisticated argumentative writing based on dialogic views of rationality in high school language arts classrooms: A formative and design experiment* (Unpublished doctoral dissertation). The Ohio State University, Columbus.

Scribner, S., & Cole, M. (1981). *The psychology of literacy.* Cambridge, MA: Harvard University Press.

Selander, S., & Kress, G. (2010). *Design för lärande: Ett multimodalt perspektiv* [Designs for learning: A multimodal perspective]. Stockholm, Norway: Norstedts.

Street, B. (1984). *Literacy in theory and practice.* New York, NY: Cambridge University Press.

Street, B. (1995). *Social literacies: Critical approaches to literacy in development, ethnography, and education.* London, England: Longman.

CHAPTER 2

Microethnographic Discourse Analysis Research for Transforming Classroom Education

Sanghee Ryu and David Bloome

MICROETHNOGRAPHIC DISCOURSE ANALYSIS is a philosophical and theoretical perspective for exploring how people use language together to construct the worlds in which they live. People act and react to each other primarily through their languaging (their use of language), and as they do so, together they construct knowledge, social relationships (including power relations), histories and futures, rationalities, morality, and what it means to be human together. People act and react to each other within social, cultural, and historical contexts, and these social, cultural, and historical contexts both influence and are constituted by people acting and reacting to each other. In this sense, microethnographic discourse analysis is multi-leveled, addressing the local event (such as a face-to-face interaction) and broader, more macro levels of social, cultural, and historical processes.

The theoretical foundations of microethnographic discourse analysis derive, broadly considered, from what has been called the linguistic turn in the social sciences (cf. Clifford & Marcus, 1986; Rorty, 1992), the understanding that it is through language that people define the worlds in which they live, knowledge and knowing, and give meaning to what they do. More specifically, the theoretical foundations of microethnographic discourse analysis derive from cultural and linguistic anthropology (e.g., Agar, 2013; Duranti, 2009; Heath & Street, 2008; Spindler, 1987), sociolinguistics (e.g., Agha, 2007;

García, Flores, & Spotti, 2017), the ethnography of communication (e.g., Hymes, 2013; Saville-Troike, 2008), interactional sociolinguistics, (e.g., Castanheira, Crawford, Dixon, & Green, 2000; Green & Castanheira, 2019; Gumperz, 1982), humanistic linguistics (e.g., Becker, 1988; Tannen, 2007), linguistic ethnography (e.g., Copland, Shaw, & Snell, 2016), essays on language associated with what has been called the Bakhtin circle (e.g., Bakhtin, 1935/1981; Volosinov, 1929/1973), the study of classroom discourse (e.g., Barnes, Britton, & Rosen, 1971; Cazden, 1988; Green, 1983; Markee, 2015), and the more recent area of languaging relations (e.g., Beach & Bloome, 2019; Becker, 1991; Jørgensen, 2004). Taken together, these intellectual foundations focus attention on the inseparability of language and culture, the particularity of language, and the centrality of the use of language in defining and constructing social relationships, social institutions, knowledge and knowing, social institutions, and social and cultural ideologies.

When microethnographic discourse analysis is used to explore classroom education (and other educational locations) it inherently involves a transformative perspective. To recognize that the basic concepts of education are languaged into being is to recognize that those basic concepts are not givens or inherent but, rather, are the historical products of what people together have socially constructed through their languaging.

Foundational principles of microethnographic discourse analysis include the following:

1. People act and react to each other.
2. People act and react to others both near and at a distance in space and time.
3. There is no separation between people and the events they create and within which they act and react to each other.
4. There is no separation between language and people's use of language (we use the term *languaging* to capture this principle).
5. Languaging always invokes social, cultural, and political ideologies that implicitly impose definitions of what it means to be human (including what kinds of humans there are in the world and what attributes different kinds of humans have).
6. All actions, including the responses and refractions people together make through their languaging to what has happened before, construct personhood (a shared definition of what counts as a person, what kinds of people there are in the world, and what attributes people have).

Because the foundational principles of microethnographic discourse analysis require framing what happens in educational settings as people responding to and refracting what has happened before, educational concepts need to be understood as existing in a tension between change and stability. The key question is not *whether* people (students) will change but, rather, *how* events will change and how people's participation in evolving and changing events will change over time and to what degree that change involves reflection and deliberation (see Lave's [1996] definitions of teaching and learning). More simply stated, when microethnographic discourse analysis is used to explore educational settings, it is inherently transformational because it calls into question how people have been defining knowledge and learning, what it means to be human, and the context of schooling in such definitions.

Our own uses of microethnographic discourse analysis always involve close collaboration with teachers. It is not just that we spend long periods in their classrooms but more so that we are interested in exploring with them how classrooms can become spaces where teachers and students can language new and more powerful ways of reading, writing, academic learning, enacting inclusion, and envisioning worlds of human dignity and civil and social justice. Sometimes our collaboration with teachers takes on the features of formative and design research (sometimes called design experiments; e.g., Brown, 1992; Reinking & Bradley, 2008). In other cases, the collaborative relationship is less formal but nonetheless is focused on making change in ways informed by engagement in microethnographic discourse analysis.

Illustrating Microethnographic Discourse Analysis

In order to provide a sense of doing microethnographic discourse analysis research, we share a brief description of a research project conducted by Sanghee Ryu (2016). We discuss microethnographic discourse analysis in terms of illustrations, in part, because the conduct of microethnographic discourse analysis is complex and varies from use to use depending on the research situation. That is, although principles and theoretical constructs guide the conduct of microethnographic discourse analysis (as discussed earlier), in our view, learning to use microethnographic discourse analysis is an abductive process. One learns by examining what others have done and how they have applied principles and practices associated with microethnographic discourse analysis in particular situations. Looking across cases, one can identify patterns and practices and how they are adapted and recontextualized from situation to situation. Thus, one learns both patterns and practices and ways to adapt those patterns and practices that can be informative to how one might use microethnographic discourse analysis within a particular situation.

In the following, we briefly describe one microethnographic discourse analysis study. We have chosen this particular study because it was embedded in a formative and design research framework. Indeed, we find that it is often the case that microethnographic discourse analysis studies are embedded in (or layered with) other research frameworks and theoretical frames. Therefore, given that in our view, learning about microethnographic discourse analysis is an abductive process, we would recommend also examining other illustrations of microethnographic discourse analysis in educational contexts and how they are layered with other methodological frameworks and theoretical perspectives (e.g., Bloome, Brown, Kim, & Tang, 2019; Boyd, Mykula, & Choi, 2009; Carter, 2007; Castanheira, Green, Dixon, & Yeager, 2007; Hikida & Lee, 2018; Hong, 2018; Lee-Johnson, 2017; Rowe, 2019; Seymour, 2018).

In 2013, Ryu began a microethnographic discourse analytic study of two high school language arts classrooms. Her interest, and that of the two teachers as well, was exploring how students might be taught to compose argumentative essays grounded in what has come to be called arguing-to-learn (cf. Newell, Bloome, & Hirvela, 2015). The way that argumentation has traditionally been taught in U.S. language arts classrooms has focused on students making a claim and then seeking evidence and developing warrants, or chains of reasoning, to support that claim. Arguing-to-learn asks students to explore the data (evidence) on a particular topic and then to ask what claim(s) might the collective evidence and set of warrants support. Arguing-to-learn then asks students to engage others in dialogue and serious listening so that the arguments that might be made evolve and take into consideration the arguments, perspectives, and rationalities of others. Arguing-to-learn is grounded in what Newell et al. (2015) call dialogic rationality (derived from Habermas's [1984, 1987] communicative rationality, and Gadamer's [1976] philosophical hermeneutics).

Based on their experiences, Ryu and the two teachers (hereafter, the Team) knew that moving students to write arguments grounded in arguing-to-learn would not be easy and that it would take a long time, at least the whole academic year. Although the Team had some initial ideas about teaching argumentation grounded in arguing-to-learn, they were uncertain about what made the most sense in how to teach arguing-to-learn to their particular students. They knew that students needed more than a recipe or procedural knowledge; they knew that the students needed to shift their paradigm for what counted as a high-quality argumentative essay.

The Team decided to create a series of intervention/research–data interpretation and reflection–redesign sequences (see Figure 2.1).

In brief, they designed an instructional unit involving student argumentative writing oriented to arguing-to-learn. The Team studied what happened during that unit by video recording classroom lessons, interviewing students, and analyzing student written work. Then, together they analyzed the data they collected and interpreted it. They were less interested in whether the teaching was good or whether the students wrote well; they were more interested in how the students took up what they were being taught (and what they were reading) about arguing-to-learn and then how they translated that into what they wrote. This was followed by the team designing the next intervention cycle, taking into account what they had learned from the first cycle. Although not of specific concern to the teachers, the data analysis and interpretation were also used by Ryu to consider what contributions might be made to the research-base and theory in the fields of argumentation, composition, literacy studies, and the study of teaching.

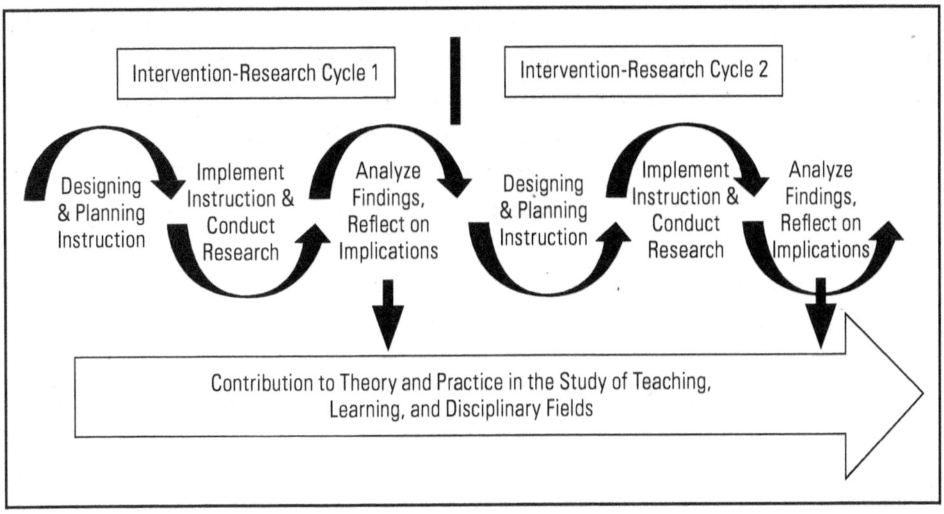

Figure 2.1. Research sequences

The Team went through three cycles of intervention/research–data interpretation and reflection–redesign. Please note, as indicated in Figure 2.1, the findings from the analysis of the data collected during each intervention–research cycle not only informed the next intervention–research cycle but also may make a contribution to the research-base in the field of the study of teaching and learning as well as to disciplinary fields.

In the next section, we share an illustration of how the data collected during an intervention phase of the cycle were analyzed and interpreted.

The Complex, Recursive, and Reflective Praxis of Microethnographic Discourse Analysis

As shown in Figure 2.1, the research study begins with the Team discussing together what they need to know to design and implement effective instruction for the particular students in the class. After some discussion, Dr. Ryu, Ms. Vale, and Mr. Moon all agreed that from their teaching experiences in previous years, an important issue in teaching argumentative writing as arguing-to-learn was helping students address the tensions that arise from different claims, from different perspectives, and from the inherent complexity of human beings interacting with other human beings. Rather than students engaging each other in a dialogue that would allow students with different arguments to appreciate other arguments, learn from others, and gain more sophisticated and complex insights that might require revising their claims, many of the students kept repeating their own positions and showed limitations in seriously considering different points of view. Dr. Ryu also knew that this was an important area of research in literacy studies and that what they learned would inform both how Mr. Moon and Ms. Vale taught argumentation in their respective classrooms and the broader research field. Thus, they all agreed that the first intervention–research cycle would focus on making warrants visible. Their reasoning (perhaps better labeled a hypothesis) was that by making warrants visible, the students could then explore the basis of the reasoning and the rationality behind it.

It may be helpful to know that video recordings were made of every class session during the first intervention–research cycle and similarly so with all subsequent cycles. Student-written work was also collected, and students were informally interviewed.

One of the instructional activities they designed for the first intervention–research cycle was the "lifeboat" activity. In brief, there is a lifeboat with too many people in it and a few of the people need to be kicked out of the boat. The students are given brief biographies of each person and then have to decide who to kick out of the boat. Ms. Vale and Mr. Moon required their students to craft arguments regarding who to kick out. Given the emphasis of the first intervention–research cycle on making warrants visible as a way of engaging students in a discussion of tensions, the classroom discussions during the lifeboat activity were targeted as a beginning place for discourse analysis.

After considering the various lessons and activities in their classrooms, the Team decided to begin the detailed discourse analysis by examining the discussion in Ms. Vale's classroom. The students had discussed whether an elderly man should be saved or kicked out of the lifeboat. The biography of the elderly man was "a retired man, formerly a professor of literature who has a great sense of humor, showed courage in the Korean and Vietnam Wars, and was in a concentration camp for three years, age 82." Kevin argued for saving him, but Kelly argued against saving him.

What we describe in the following is a discourse analysis and interpretation of one small bit of the classroom discussion embedded in a larger ethnographic study. We caution that little can be known about the quality of teaching from a very brief instance of classroom life, and therefore, judgments of the teacher and the students should be avoided.

The analysis here is only partial and illustrative (for detailed descriptions of discourse analysis compatible with an ethnographic approach see, for example, Bloome, Carter, Christian, Otto, & Shuart-Faris, 2005; Bloome et al., 2008; Erickson, 2004; Rymes, 2015). In this bit of classroom conversation, the teacher—Ms. Vale—is pushing Kelly to make visible how she warranted her position to kick the old man out of the lifeboat (see Table 2.1).

What is missing from the transcript in Table 2.1 is the prosody with which the utterances were rendered, nor are the nonverbal actions noted. In addition to words, prosody and nonverbal behavior constitute what Gumperz calls "contextualization cues" (Gumperz & Berenz, 1993). "Roughly speaking, a contextualization cue is any feature of linguistic form that contributes to the signaling of contextual presuppositions" (Gumperz, 1982, p. 131). Interlocutors in an event, including a classroom event,

Table 2.1. Transcript excerpt

1	Teacher	Because what do you believe
2		Do you believe what↑
3	Kelly	As you become old| you become weaker | like senses |||| sight becomes worse
4	T	And your evidence for that is+↑
5	Kelly	Do I need evidence for it↑
6	T	Where do you know that from
7	Kelly	Experience
8	T	Okay | cite something from your life
9	Kelly	Okay |||| my grandfather was in World War II
10		He won't talk about war or anything like that
11		And | as he became older |||| he became like mentally disturbed
12	T	Because
13	Kelly	Because things that happened during the war
14	T	And therefore
15	Kelly	And therefore he is not capable | probably of navigating someone xxxxx
16	T	Good good good

signal their interactional intentions, framings, and meanings not only through an explicit meaning of words but also through an implicit system of semiotic tools, including prosody and nonverbal behavior. Prosodic contextualization cues include volume shifts, tone shifts, rhythmic shifts, velocity shifts, pausing, stress patterns, intonation patterns, stylizing patterns, and so on. Some of these cues are indicated using the following conventions, but they always remain partial indicators of actual prosody (see Table 2.2). Nonverbal contextualization cues include gesture, facial expression, eye movement, eye gaze, posture, body movement, and so on.

Table 2.2. Transcription symbols

↑ = Rising intonation
+ = Elongated sound
| = pause
|||| = longer pause
xxxx = indecipherable

Contextualization cues provide a material basis for how interlocutors act and react to each other, how interlocutors interpret what others are saying and doing, and how interlocutors collectively construct social meaning and relationship (cf. Bloome et al., 2005). Contextualization cues are derivative of the cultural and social context within which the conversation is occurring as well as the cultural and social backgrounds of the interlocutors. Thus, how a particular intonation pattern should be interpreted cannot be predetermined but depends on the interactional context in which it is produced as well as the cultural and social contexts within which the interaction takes place.

We conducted the discourse analysis of the transcript in Table 2.1 while also watching the video recording of the event so that we could also take account of the prosodic and nonverbal contextualization cues. We also note that our attention is not so much on an utterance per se as it is on how that utterance is taken up subsequently. This is merely to say that the meaningfulness of an utterance is not in the utterance itself but in how the meaningfulness of that utterance is socially constructed within the ongoing interaction of the people in the event.

Prior to the transcript excerpt, Kelly states that she did not want to keep the old man in the lifeboat. Ms. Vale, in Line 1, then shifts the conversation to how Kelly is warranting that position. Ms. Vale begins with the word *because*, and that word requires a rationale; it places a burden on the interlocutor. However, Ms. Vale renders Line 1 with a flat prosody, and thus, she responds herself to the utterance in Line 1 with a question whose prosodic contour would seem to place a burden on Kelly to respond with a reason for her position. We feel confident in our interpretation that Line 2 was taken up as an obligation to respond because, in Line 3, that is what Kelly does and she does so in a prosody associated with giving an explanation. Notice the structure of the explanation: A (getting old) leads to B (becoming weak). There is no explicit connection between becoming weak and being kicked out of the lifeboat, and subsequently, it is not questioned by Ms. Vale or anyone else, so it seems to us reasonable to infer that Ms. Vale, Kelly, and the rest of the class view the connection between weakness and being kicked out of the boat as obvious, common sense, natural, and taken-for-grant.

Notice that Kelly's response in Line 3 is formatted similarly to a general rule (generally, as people get old, they get weaker). We know from our field research that in earlier lessons Ms. Vale had discussed with the students that warrants were often general rules. Thus, we suspect that Kelly's formulation of "As you become old | you become weaker" reflects those previous lessons. We cannot be sure that this is the case; if we had had the time and opportunity, we might have asked Kelly about this.

In Line 4, Ms. Vale asks Kelly about her evidence. We note that the prosody of the utterance (the elongated s sound accompanied by a rising intonation) would seem to place an obligation on Kelly to respond. Inasmuch as Ms. Vale and her class have been talking about the need for evidence in their previous lessons and instructional units, we suspect that the reference to evidence reflects those previous lessons and the shared assumption that students should have learned that they need evidence.

Kelly responds by asking if she needs evidence for her position. This suggests that Kelly has taken up Ms. Vale's question in Line 4 as if she and Ms. Vale had different views on the genre of argument at stake. That is, Kelly's response to Ms. Vale's question indicates that she had had a view of position-taking with regard to the lifeboat exercise as the kind of argumentation that did not require evidence. Regardless, that Kelly responds to Ms. Vale by questioning the need for evidence suggests that Kelly is pushing back against a demand that Ms. Vale is making, being oppositional, although, as the subsequent interaction suggests, her oppositional stance is not at a level that causes disruption, nor is her opposition stance continued.

Ms. Vale's question in Line 4 placed the lifeboat argumentation task into the genre of arguments requiring evidence. Ms. Vale's response in Line 6 suggests that she had recognized that there had been a minor miscommunication between herself and Kelly. Line 6 suggests that Ms. Vale was referring to evidence for the warrant ("As you become old, you become weaker") while Kelly was defining evidence as referring to the lifeboat situation itself. In Line 6, Ms. Vale responds to this miscommunication by making clear the reference is to the warrant. Kelly's response in Line 7 makes clear that Ms. Vale's utterance in Line 6 was a repair and that it was a successful repair.

In Line 8, Ms. Vale asks Kelly to expand her response in Line 7. As such, Ms. Vale has made visible that Kelly's response was inadequate. Ms. Vale's utterance in Line 8 provides Kelly with direction for how to respond. She provides a category of experiences, "something from your life," for her to use as "evidence." She does so in Lines 9, 10, 11, 13, and 15. Her response is validated as accepted by Ms. Vale in Line 16 ("Good good good"). There is also a subtle prosodic pattern that indicates that Ms. Vale and Kelly are in agreement. As Kelly tells the story of her grandfather, Ms. Vale interrupts her in Lines 12 and 14 but in ways that are rhythmically integrated. As such, labeling what Ms. Vale has done in line 12 and 14 as an interruption is not accurate; it is better referred to as joint storytelling or as scaffolding. The rhythmic integration is visible to all in the class and is likely to have suggested to all the students paying attention to the conversation between Ms. Vale and Kelly that Kelly and Ms. Vale are in agreement about the evidence for the warrant Kelly had used.

The discourse analysis of Kelly's interaction with Ms. Vale focused on warranting. As we noted earlier, the teaching of warranting was a major concern of the teachers. It is also a concern expressed in the research literature on the teaching of argumentation. That said, the Team was also concerned with how to help students productively engage each other in the kinds of dialogue that would lead them to more sophisticated arguments that embraced complexity and contradiction. The Team designed activities with the specific goal of exploring tensions with a focus on the use of evidence and warrants. They also wanted the students to understand that differences in experience and differences in cultural and social backgrounds might lead to different arguments with different sets of evidence and different warrants. One of the activities that the Team decided to try was labeled "Detachment Questions." "Detachment questions" refer to questions that provoke students to critically reflect on the controversial aspects of their warrants and reconsider their arguments by detaching from their own warrants. The teachers asked students to reconsider their arguments by detaching from their own warrants.

The transcript in Table 2.3 captures one such classroom conversation that was subjected to discourse analysis. As we noted earlier, Kevin disagrees with Kelly. Kelly argues to kick the old man out of the lifeboat; Kevin argues to keep him in the boat.

The teacher—Ms. Vale—begins her conversation with Kevin by noting that Kevin has a different position than Kelly. The rising intonation pattern in Line 101 is taken by Kevin to indicate that it is his turn to talk and he uses the word *because*, which was highlighted by Ms. Vale in her conversation with Kelly. We cannot be absolutely certain that Kevin's use of *because* is a response to the highlighting of *because* in previous conversations; however, there is increasing use of *because* in the argumentative conversations that students are having with Ms. Vale and with each other. Therefore, arguing that students are being socialized to use *because* and similar terms in warranting their arguments seems reasonable.

Kevin uses *So* in Line 102, which would indicate he plans to connect his position and his warrant ("Because he has a great sense of humor") with a possible conclusion or thesis statement. However, Ms. Vale interrupts Kevin before he is able to do so. Ms. Vale explains at length in Lines 104 to 112 that Kevin needs to address what Kelly has argued. This reflects a concern that the teacher had about students not seriously listening to each other and just offering their own views without actually engaging the views of others.

Kevin responds to Ms. Vale by referring to what he would have said had he not been interrupted ("I was gonna say"). The way this utterance is rendered and the too informal register (*gonna*) seem to us to be a rebuke to Ms. Vale's interruption of Kevin when he was beginning to explain his position (in Line 104). It would seem to be a restating of what Kevin had been trying to say in Line 103. Just as clearly, it is an ignoring of what Ms. Vale had said in Lines 104 to 112. When we label Kevin's utterance as an "ignoring,"

Table 2.3. Transcript excerpt

101	T	What you said counter that is↑
102	Kevin	Because he has a great sense of humor
102		So
104	T	Hang on++
105		How do you come back at
106		Now you are making a completely separate argument
107		But if you're gonna change her mind
108		You've got to address her thinking | okay↑
109		So how do you counteract
110		Um |||| her viewpoint
111		She believes this because her grandfather
112		She experienced this with
113	Kevin	I was gonna say
114	T	So what's her warrant↑
115	Kevin	the warrant is that |||| he is too old to work
116	T	So what does she believe about people have fought in a war and their age
117	Kevin	Kinds of incapability
118	T	Yes | so

we do not mean a passive action, as if Kevin did not hear what Ms. Vale had said. Rather, the ignoring here is an active response to what Ms. Vale said—it is almost as if Kevin has said to Ms. Vale, "I am going to ignore what you just said."

Ms. Vale's responds to the ignoring by interrupting Kevin again (in Line 114) by asking Kevin what Kelly's warrant was. Kevin responds to the question by answering it but gives a response that is not exactly what Kelly had said. It is what Kevin interpreted Kelly's argument to be. Ms. Vale pushes Kevin to make an inference about Kelly's warranting, which Kevin does in Line 117. It is questionable whether Kevin's representation of Kelly's warranting is accurate; that being said, accuracy may not matter because how Kevin represents Kelly's warranting goes unchallenged and is validated by Ms. Vale (Line 118).

In the interpretation of the brief bit of classroom conversation analyzed above, an interesting issue manifests in Line 113. Despite Ms. Vale's direction and explanation and despite many lessons and classroom conversations on listening to others and responding to what others have said with respect and sense of mutual exploration, Kevin appears oriented to simply stating his position. The questions this raised for the Team are two-fold: How prevalent is the kind of response Kevin made (an ignoring of his teacher's efforts to engage students in a different kind of conversation)?; and How might teachers overcome this kind of ignoring and help students engage in the kind of dialogue that would engage them in more sophisticated arguments that embrace complexity, tension, and contradiction?

From Discourse Analysis to Intervention–Research Cycle 2

Based on their analysis, interpretation, and discussion of the discourse analysis research in Cycle 1, the Team started planning for the kinds of writing assignments to give to the students. They wanted something that would be of high interest, have proximity to students' lives and concerns, and include ease of locating tensions around a specific issue. Ms. Vale suggested "decision making" as a big theme of their writing because how to make decisions is an important and interesting issue for students. Mr. Moon agreed with using this theme and explained that students could easily make connections between the topic and their daily lives and should easily find some tensions to write about as well.

The Team then considered what literary texts or other texts to have students read and to which they would respond. The Team decided to select written texts that speak to each other and provide multiple perspectives on the theme of decision making. The first choice was John Krakauer's (1997) *Into the Wild*.

However, the teachers did not want to begin with a long literary work such as *Into the Wild*. They wanted to start with a shorter piece and move up to a longer one. Mr. Moon suggested that a short excerpt (five sentences) from Steve Jobs's (2005) university commencement speech would be a good start because it is short and closely related to students' interests. After that, the teachers would use the poem "The Unknown Citizen" by W. H. Auden (1940) as it was a bit longer than Steve Jobs's commencement speech. For the text following this poem, Mr. Moon suggested an excerpt of five pages from the book *Moral Courage* by Rushworth Kidder (2006), which could provide a good example of how that author used multiple pieces of evidence to support his ideas about moral courage. In this way, the Team selected the four readings for the second intervention–research cycle based on what they had learned from the first cycle of this research study and that included discourse analysis of key classroom conversations that helped to inform their decision making in this second cycle of the study.

The team continued these cycles of formative and design research and discourse analysis for three cycles, taking them into the eighth month of the academic year.

Final Comments on Microethnographic Discourse Analysis

Microethnographic discourse analysis requires researchers to examine what is happening in classrooms and other educational settings at multiple levels by bringing together ethnographic research and discourse analysis. Here, we have embedded microethnographic discourse analysis within a formative and design research framework in which researchers and teachers collaborate to address complex and difficult issues in teaching and learning. Microethnographic discourse analysis frames what happens in classrooms and other educational settings as cultural and languaging processes. As such, it frames what happens in classrooms in ways that are different from the dominant research and practice frameworks focused on individuals and their psychological states. Microethnographic discourse analysis frames what happens in classrooms and other educational settings as people acting and reacting to each other through languaging, and it provides researchers and teachers with a way to "see" that acting and reacting. Embedded in formative and design research, microethnographic discourse analysis provides a research-based way for teachers, in collaboration with researchers, to address complex pedagogical situations while also contributing to the educational research-base.

Suggested Further Reading

Bloome, D., Carter, S., Christian, B., Otto, S., & and Shuart-Faris, N. (2005). *Discourse analysis of classroom language and literacy events: A microethnographic approach*. New York, NY: Routledge.

Reinking, D., & Bradley, B. (2008). *Formative and design experiments: Approaches to language and literacy research*. New York, NY: Teachers College Press.

Rex, L. A., & Schiller, L. (2010). *Using discourse analysis to improve classroom interaction*. New York, NY: Routledge.

References

Agar, M. (2013). *The lively science: Remodeling human social research*. Minneapolis, MN: Hillcrest Publishing Group.

Agha, A. (2007). *Language and social relations*. New York, NY: Cambridge University Press.

Auden, W. H. (1940). The unknown citizen. Retrieved from https://poets.org/poem/unknown-citizen

Bakhtin, M. (1981). *The dialogic imagination.* (Trans. V. Lapiunov and K. Brostrom). Austin: University of Texas Press. (Original work published 1935).

Barnes, D. R., Britton, J. N., & Rosen, H. (1971). *Language, the learner and the school.* London, England: Penguin Books.

Beach, R., & Bloome, D. (Eds.). (2019). *Languaging relations for transforming the literacy and language arts classroom.* New York, NY: Routledge.

Becker, A. (1988). Language in particular: A lecture. In D. Tannen (Ed.), *Linguistics in context* (pp. 17–35). Norwood, NJ: Ablex.

Becker, A. L. (1991). Language and languaging. *Language & Communication, 11*(1), 33–35.

Bloome, D., Brown, A., Kim, M., & Tang, R. (2019). Languaging personhood in classroom conversation. In R. Beach & D. Bloome (Eds.), *Languaging relations across social worlds* (pp. 235–254). New York, NY: Routledge.

Bloome, D., Carter, S., Christian, B., Otto, S., & Shuart-Faris, N. (2005). *Discourse analysis of classroom language and literacy events: A microethnographic approach.* New York, NY: Routledge.

Bloome, D., Carter, S., Christian, B., Madrid, S., Otto, S., Shuart-Faris, N., & Smith, M. with contributions by S. Goldman & D. Macbeth. (2008). *On discourse analysis: Approaches to language and literacy research.* New York, NY: Teachers College Press.

Boyd, M., Mykula, V., & Choi, Y. (2019). Responsive and responsible teacher telling: An across time examination of classroom talk during whole group writing workshop minilessons. *Research Papers in Education.* 1-29. Retrieved from https://doi.org/10.1080/02671522.2019.1601761

Brown, A. L. (1992). Design experiments: Theoretical and methodological challenges in creating complex interventions in classroom settings. *The Journal of the Learning Sciences,* 2, 141–178.

Carter, S. P. (2007). "Reading all that White crazy stuff": Black young women unpacking Whiteness in a high school British literature classroom. *The Journal of Classroom Interaction, 41/42*(2/1), 42–54.

Castanheira, M. L., Crawford, T., Dixon, C. N., & Green, J. L. (2000). Interactional ethnography: An approach to studying the social construction of literate practices. *Linguistics and Education, 11,* 353–400.

Castanheira, M. L., Green, J., Dixon, C., & Yeager, B. (2007). (Re)Formulating identities in the face of fluid modernity: An interactional ethnographic approach. *International Journal of Educational Research, 46*(3–4), 172–189.

Cazden, C. (1988). *Classroom discourse.* Portsmouth, NH: Heinemann.

Clifford, J., & Marcus, G. (eds.) (1986). *Writing culture: The poetics and politics of ethnography.* Berkeley: University of California Press.

Copland, F., Shaw, S., & Snell, J. (Eds.). (2016). *Linguistic ethnography: Interdisciplinary explorations.* New York, NY: Springer.

Duranti, A. (Ed.) (2009). *Linguistic anthropology: A reader.* Malden, MA: Wiley-Blackwell.

Erickson, F. (2004). *Talk and social theory.* Malden, MA: Polity Press.

Gadamer, H. (1976). *Philosophical hermeneutics* (D. E. Linge, Trans. & Ed.). Berkeley: University of California Press.

García, O., Flores, N., & Spotti, M. (Eds.). (2017). *The Oxford handbook of language and society.* London, England: Oxford University Press.

Green, J. L. (1983). Exploring classroom discourse: Linguistic perspectives on teaching-learning processes. *Educational Psychologist, 18*, 180–199.

Green, J. L., & Castanheira, M. L. (2019). Revisiting the relationship between ethnography, discourse and education. *Caletroscópio, 7*, 10–55.

Gumperz, J. J. (1982). *Discourse strategies: Studies in interactional sociolinguistics*. Cambridge, England: Cambridge University Press.

Gumperz, J. J., & Berenz, N. (1993). Transcribing conversational exchanges. In J. A. Edwards & M. D. Lampert (Eds.), *Transcription and coding in discourse research* (pp. 91–122). New York, NY: Psychology Press.

Habermas, J. (1984). *The theory of communicative action: Reason and the rationalization of society*. London, England: Heinemann.

Habermas, J. (1987). *The theory of communicative action: Lifeworld and system, a critique of functionalist reason*. London, England: Heinemann.

Heath, S. B., & Street, B. V. (2008). *On ethnography: Approaches to language and literacy research. Language & literacy (NCRLL)*. New York, NY: Teachers College Press.

Hikida, M., & Lee, J. (2018). Positioning readers in one-on-one conferences. *Literacy Research: Theory, Method, and Practice, 67*(1), 180–194.

Hong, H. (2018). Exploring the role of intertextuality in promoting young ELL children's poetry writing and learning: A discourse analytic approach. *Classroom Discourse, 9*, 166–182.

Hymes, D. (2013). *Foundations in sociolinguistics: An ethnographic approach*. New York, NY: Routledge.

Jobs, S. (2005, June 14). You've got to find what you love. *Stanford News*. Retrieved from https://news.stanford.edu/2005/06/14/jobs-061505/

Jørgensen, J. N. (2004). Languaging and languagers. In C. Dabelsteen & J. N. Jørgensen (Eds.), *Languaging and language practices* (pp. 5–23). Copenhagen, Denmark: University of Copenhagen.

Kidder, R. (2006). *Moral courage*. New York, NY: HarperCollins.

Krakauer, J. (1997). *Into the wild*. New York, NY: Anchor Books.

Lave, J. (1996). Teaching, as learning, in practice. *Mind, Culture, and Activity, 3*, 149–164.

Lee-Johnson, Y. L. (2017). "That is not very American": A microethnographic discourse analysis of a Chinese ESL learner's appropriation of cultural values at an art exhibition. *TESOL Journal, 8*, 716–739.

Markee, N. (2015). *The handbook of classroom discourse and interaction*. Hoboken, NJ: John Wiley & Sons.

Newell, G., Bloome, D., & Hirvela, A., with Lin, T.-J., VanDerHeide, J., Wynhoff Olsen, A., Buescher, E., Goff, B., Kim, M., Ryu, S., & Weyand, L. (2015). *Teaching and learning argumentative writing in high school English language arts classrooms*. New York, NY: Routledge.

Reinking, D., & Bradley, B. (2008). *On formative and design experiments*. New York, NY: Teachers College Press.

Rorty, R. (Ed.) (1992). *The linguistic turn: Essays in philosophical method*. Chicago, IL: University of Chicago Press.

Rowe, L. W. (2019). Constructing language ideologies in a multilingual, second-grade classroom: A case study of two emergent bilingual students' language-use during eBook composing. *Linguistics and Education, 52*, 1–12.

Rymes, B. (2015). *Classroom discourse analysis: A tool for critical reflection*. New York, NY: Routledge.

Ryu, S. (2016). *Teaching and learning of sophisticated argumentative writing based on dialogic views of rationality in high school language arts classrooms: A formative and design experiment* (Unpublished Doctoral dissertation). The Ohio State University, Columbus.

Saville-Troike, M. (2008). *The ethnography of communication: An introduction*. Hoboken, NJ: John Wiley & Sons.

Seymour, M. (2018). Complexity, contradiction, and carnival: Microethnographic research on student disruption in a high school English language arts classroom. *Acta Paedagogica Vilnensia, 40*, 70–93.

Spindler, G. D. (Ed.). (1987). *Education and cultural process: Anthropological approaches*. Prospect Heights, IL: Waveland Press.

Tannen, D. (2007). *Talking voices: Repetition, dialogue, and imagery in conversational discourse*. Cambridge, MA: Cambridge University Press.

Volosinov, V. (1973). *Marxism and the philosophy of language*. (L. Matejka & I. Titunik, Trans.). Cambridge, MA: Harvard University Press. (Original work published 1929).

CHAPTER 3

Conversation Analysis and the Study of Social Interaction

Aaron Chia Yuan Hung

I STUMBLED INTO Conversation Analysis and its related field of Ethnomethodology quite by accident. In the early 2000s, many educators were excited about video games, and as a graduate student and gamer, I was keen on investigating their potential as educational tools. The learning principles described in Gee (2003) made sense to me because I experienced them myself, but these assertions were yet to be studied empirically. Moreover, I was curious about what gamers (who aren't scholars) had to say, and I became interested in studying how other gamers talk about games and how they taught one another how to play. This led me to wonder: Given that video games involve simulations of natural laws and/or arbitrary rules, how do gamers come to define the boundaries of the game? What resources do they draw on to distinguish between what is or isn't part of the game? These questions brought me to Ethnomethodology and then Conversation Analysis as a tool with which to conduct ethnomethodological investigations.

To be clear, Ethnomethodology and Conversation Analysis are not the same; conducting ethnomethodological research without using Conversation Analysis and vice versa is possible. This chapter is about Conversation Analysis, I promise, but assuming you are new to Conversation Analysis, I start with a bit of its origin story because it helps inform claims about Conversation Analysis as a field in general. Conversation Analysis was not just a new method—it was a new way of thinking about methodology itself, and knowing its origins helped me better understand whether it was the right analytic tool to use. Furthermore, the questions I had about games were similar to the ones that Harvey Sacks and Harold Garfinkel, who developed Conversation Analysis and Ethnomethodology, respectively, had when they were looking for new ways to study social interaction. They were challenging the established methods of sociology by asking questions others had not considered or did not feel were worth asking, questions such as "How do we (researchers) know people are doing what we think they are doing and for the reasons we think they are doing it?" "Why do we need a theoretical framework to study a phenomenon?" and "Why can't we just approach the phenomenon the way the people do?" Conversation Analysis and Ethnomethodology researchers kept their focus on how people make sense of the world, and that was exactly how I wanted to approach my research.

Topics of Study

To understand the topics commonly studied using Conversation Analysis, starting with the premises that Conversation Analysis and Ethnomethodology share about the social world helps.

The Social World Is Orderly

People treat the world as orderly and find ways to account for this orderliness. Here, "order" refers to the patterns, rules, and norms that we follow and anticipate others will follow as well. For example, everyday conversation would be impossible without a shared understanding of what words and utterances mean and how we ensure conversations progress smoothly.

Orderliness Is the Result of Mutually Co-Constructed Achievements

It's not enough that we expect order on our own; we also have to share a similar sense of order with the people we interact with. Ethnomethodology/Conversation Analysis literature often describes orderly accounts as "achievements" or "accomplishments" because this orderliness is a joint effort. Even something as mundane as ending a conversation requires all participants to signal to one another that there are no new topics and that the conversation is coming to a close. Consequently, Conversation Analysis avoids using unobservable constructs such as motivation, attitudes, and values to explain social phenomena and focuses only on what can be observed and demonstrated in the data.

Context Is Fluid

Ethnomethodology/Conversation Analysis literature tends to be cautious about describing context. A conversation between a doctor and a patient doesn't necessarily imply a medical context; it is more fluid and dependent on how the talk is designed by the participants from moment to moment. As such, the relevant context can be observed in how people talk and what they talk about and can change over the course of the interaction.

Orderliness Can *Only* Be Discovered Through Close Analysis of Actual Phenomena

If everyday interaction is orderly, then this orderliness can *only* be discovered through close study of actual phenomena. This is in contrast to approaches that depend on abstract theories, statistical analysis, controlled experiments, or imagined scenarios, all of which are seen to obscure how order is produced. Approaches such as interviews are also inadequate because, although people follow rules of interaction, they cannot always fully and accurately account for them afterward. Conversation Analysis aims to analyze some phenomenon *as it happens in real time*.

One of the seminal studies in Conversation Analysis, and a must-read for anyone interested in this approach, is Sacks, Schegloff, and Jefferson's (1974) "A Simplest Systematics for the Organization of Turn-Taking for Conversation," in which they outline the basic organizing principles of everyday conversation, such as what constitutes a *turn* in conversation and how a turn is passed from one speaker to the next. In lieu of summarizing their findings, here are key implications I consider most important for our discussion. First, everyday conversation is the most basic form of social interaction; all other kinds of interactions differ in what rules of basic conversations are constrained or suspended. For example, although turns and topics are not predetermined in everyday conversation, they often are in institutional settings, such as courtrooms or debates. Institutional talk is also sometimes managed by an authorized figure, such as a teacher or a judge, instead of locally managed among speakers.

Second, conversations are self-correcting systems. If a "glitch" occurs, it self-adjusts through the collaborative effort of all participants involved. A common occurrence is when two people speak at once. In everyday conversation, the turn will be renegotiated so that only one person assumes the *right* to speak. Here, *right* is considered in its moral sense; a speaker can speak because he or she has been granted the right to do so by the other parties, and any violation of this right is treated as a troublesome aberration—an interruption or speaking out of turn.

Third, and relatedly, *trouble*, during which an expected behavior does not occur or is modified, can provide opportunities for observing tacit rules of interaction because it reveals some expectation that has been violated and some action to repair it. In fact, *repair* is a common topic in Conversation Analysis (Mondada, 2014; Schegloff, 2013; Schegloff, Jefferson, & Sacks, 1977) and is not limited to conversation alone. For example, Suchman (2002) analyzed how people reading instructions from a photocopier sometimes used rules of basic conversation when interpreting instructions, which could lead to communication breakdowns. She observed that trouble is often created by information gaps between the users and the photocopier, such as when users tried to make sense of instructions in a locally-situated way but misunderstood them because the engineers who wrote them were writing them for a generic user and setting.

Finally, as noted before, there is orderliness in all interactions, and the task of Conversation Analysis is to find that order through close inspection. Even though participants, topics, and texts of interaction can be endlessly variable, we still need a shared set of rules to get our intended meanings across. These rules may be altered but not fundamentally changed or discarded without negotiation and mutual agreement.

Heritage (1997) categorizes Conversation Analysis research into two overlapping strands. One examines the organization of talk itself. This strand focuses on how people manage turns, offer (Drew, 1984) and decline invitations (Sidnell, 2010), express agreement and disagreement (Pomerantz, 1984), ask questions (Sacks et al., 1974), tell jokes (Sacks, 1974), tell stories (Sacks, 1995), make assessments (Goodwin & Goodwin, 1992), and so on. The other strand examines talk in institutional settings such as workplaces, classrooms, courtrooms, and so on and often focuses on how the values, goals, and structures of the institution are invoked or represented in talk. Although these two strands are not mutually exclusive, knowing about them both might help in deciding what aspect of talk you want to emphasize.

Collecting Data

Conversation Analysis can be used in a wide range of contexts, and different contexts entail different data collection procedures. Here, I offer some advice that should apply to most contexts and address what constitutes Conversation Analysis data, what technical issues to consider, and how to transcribe data.

Naturally-Occurring Data

Naturally-occurring data refers to data from activities that would take place even without the researcher present, in other words, data that are not prompted by the researcher's interventions or questions. Early Conversation Analysis researchers used any data they had access to; such as audio recordings of phone conversations and group therapy sessions (Sacks, 1995). These studies paid little to no attention to the context, topics, or participants and focused on analyzing a particular feature, such as complaints, greetings, and turn-taking, across a range of conversations. Later studies that involved specific participants (e.g., children, students), settings (e.g., playgrounds, classrooms, workplaces), or activities (e.g., using photocopiers, playing games) required collecting data for longer periods with the same people and/or in the same setting instead of isolated, "freestanding" conversations.

The preference for naturally-occurring data typically rules out research designs and methods such as controlled experiments, surveys, and interviews, but there are exceptions. Although Conversation Analysis would not use these methods as *means for collecting data,* these methods can be investigated as *topics* themselves. For example, some Conversation Analysis research looked at how participants make sense of survey interviews (ten Have, 2007) and how interviewees respond to or evade questions in news interviews (Clayman & Heritage, 2002). You can also create setups to make capturing the phenomenon you are interested in easier if the setup does not compromise the phenomenon itself. Suchman's (2002) research, mentioned earlier, involved having two people use a photocopier together to complete an assigned task. This setup might not be strictly "naturally occurring," but it does not undermine the fact that people learning how to use a photocopier by reading its instructions is a naturally occurring phenomenon in the real world. Pairing people merely makes their actions more readily observable because they have to talk to each other. Similarly, in one of my studies, I asked a group to play a video game they had not played before so that I could observe how they made sense of the game (Hung, 2011). If the interactions you are interested in require such a setup, then ask yourself: Is this setup similar to what people can reasonably be expected to encounter outside of a research context? If the answer is yes, then you should be fine.

Technical Matters

The Internet has made it easier to access public, naturalistic data, such as news interviews, political debates, speeches, congressional testimonies, court hearings, livestreams, and so on. However, if the interactions you are interested in involve particular kinds of participants, settings, and/or activities, you will likely have to collect that data yourself. You can get a good-quality audio recording with a relatively simple setup, using a phone application or a digital audio recorder. Any additional equipment, such as microphones, that can further improve the quality of the recording would be ideal. For a more expanded technical discussion, I recommend Mondada's (2013) chapter. Here I focus on two technical issues I encountered regarding video recording and multiple recorders that might be of interest.

Video Recording

The ubiquitous presence of video recording applications on smartphones makes it relatively easy to include video as part of your data. Video might be desirable, even necessary, if knowing what visual information participants are attending to is important. However, there are logistical issues to keep in mind. First, video recordings take up more digital storage space than do audio recordings, especially if you are recording high-quality video, which is recommended. To capture naturalistic data, you will need to keep the recorder on throughout the interaction, even when people are not talking, instead of turning it off and on. This can lead to large file sizes, especially if you also want to keep a backup somewhere (also recommended). Although digital storage devices are steadily decreasing in price, it is still a factor to keep in mind. There is also the issue of how much the recording device can hold before recordings need to be offloaded. If you are recording with your smartphone, a high-quality video will quickly fill up your storage capacity. If you are recording onto external storage such as secure digital (SD) cards, then be sure to have enough SD cards to capture the activity you want and to remember to swap them out when necessary. I suggest finding out how much space 1 minute of high-quality video would take up on your recording device and use that as a planning guide for storage needed. Second, video recordings might lead to poorer quality audio if it means your recorder has to be positioned farther away from the participants. If video is crucial, then consider using an external microphone or adding a second device to capture the audio, although the latter has issues as well.

Multiple recorders. If possible, I recommend keeping audio and video on the same device. There is screen-capturing software for computers and consoles that keep the audio and video in the same file. However, if the setting or activity you are interested in is physically spread out, for example, in a classroom or workspace, then multiple devices might be necessary. Audio and video recordings don't capture real life exactly; they sample it closely enough that the recording appears to resemble real life. However, if you have two or more recording devices—say, one recording a classroom teacher and another recording a student group—and want to synchronize them later, you might encounter audio synchronization drift; this is when two or more audio/video tracks gradually fall out of sync with one another, even though they have been properly synchronized in the beginning. Although this can be adjusted with software, it can be tedious, especially if you have to correct it alone and/or have a lot of data.

Transcribing. The goal of transcripts is to transform audio data into textual data to make it easier to analyze and present on a page. Conversation Analysis studies usually use Gail Jefferson's (2004) transcription format, which captures not only what is spoken, but some aspects of how it is spoken. Conversation Analysis studies vary in the level of detail the transcripts contain. Here, I can only offer the unhelpful advice of being as detailed as you think is necessary and being consistent. The Jefferson transcription conventions typically used include the following:

[ ]	Overlapping talk, with bracket marking the point of overlap
:	Lengthened syllable, indicated by number of colons
-	Cut off utterance
?	Rising intonation or question
ALL CAPS	Stressed tone
=	No interval between end of prior sentence and beginning of next
.hh	Audible breathing intake

hh	Audible breathing out
( )	Uncertainty over verbatim transcription
(( ))	Nonlinguistic feature
(0.0s)	Number of seconds of silence in tenths of a second

I strongly encourage you to do your own transcribing because this is when you become intimately familiar with your data and can develop insights into what is happening. You should expect this process to take a lot of time, especially if you are new to transcribing. When I started, it took me a week to transcribe just a few minutes of audio because I was working with Chinese speakers and needed to add a gloss and translation. Given the level of work required, you should be selective in what you transcribe, especially if you have a lot of data. When transcribing, I recommend using a fixed-width (or monospaced) font such as Courier because it is easier to align features such as overlapping speech. Some word processors also let you turn on line numbers, which makes it easier to reference if you want to make note of interesting features. You can also get audio editing software such as Audacity, which is free for PC and Macs, to improve the quality of your audio. The ability to see audio waveforms also makes the transcribing process easier.

Doing Analysis

There is no single right way to start doing Conversation Analysis as it depends on the kind of data you collected and the features you are interested in. Following are possible avenues of inquiry with some guided questions to get you started, using some sample data of my own for illustration. My sample data comes from recordings of a group of teenage boys in Xbox Live (XBL) party chats (the group chat room on the Xbox 360 console). I met this group during an earlier research study. When they found out I was also interested in video games, they invited me to join their group chats, which they went on after school. There are public and private group chats on XBL; the ones they were on were private and invite-only, so I would wait for them to invite me. I used a game capture device from Elgato to record my screen, the system audio (i.e., sounds from a game), and the chat audio as three separate files. I should note that although these conversations occurred on Xbox 360, they weren't always to do with playing games; in fact, most of the time, they were just talking about a wide range of topics: school, family, dating, gossip, politics, social issues, sports, television shows, movies, and so on.

General

- What do you notice?
- How does the talk compare to everyday conversation?

- What is the context created by the participants through their interactions?

A good way to start Conversation Analysis is through "unmotivated looking" (ten Have, 2007), during which you go through the data with an open mind and without prior assumptions, and note any interesting features or incidents that occurred. If the interaction differs from basic, face-to-face conversation, then compare the features and rules of interaction to those of basic conversation. In my case, I was new to both the group and to party chats on XBL, so I was unsure what the interactions would look like; using Conversation Analysis as a starting point helped ground me in the participants' points of view. For example, just referring to this group as "players" who are "playing video games" when they are on XBL might be tempting, but Conversation Analysis's caution regarding context as fluid, ongoing, and co-constructed moment by moment allowed me to see that they were not always *players*; they were also *classmates, friends, teammates, fans, citizens*, and so on. Even these categories need to be used carefully and only when they are made relevant by the participants. I also became interested in what context they were creating for themselves. Because all conversations follow some kind of rules, some of which are unique to the institutional settings, roles, and/or technologies, you should examine these interactional norms and rules and uncover what they tell you about context and roles (i.e., Who are they speaking as?).

Turn-Taking

- Are turns locally managed or pre-allocated?
- Who gets to speak?
- How long are the turns?
- What is the recipient design?

After acquiring some general observations about the interaction, the next step I recommend is to look at turn-taking. The XBL group chats tend to resemble basic conversation, in which turns are locally managed, anyone can speak, and turn lengths tend to be short. However, I noticed a technological constraint that made these chats different from basic conversation. Although basic conversation prefers only one speaker at a time, schisms can occur in larger groups, during which a conversation splits into two or more parallel conversations (Sacks et al., 1974). This is possible because we can use resources such as gaze, posture, and proximity to focus attention on one conversation over the other. This never happened in their group chats because these resources weren't available.

Before I get into the analysis, let me pause here to describe the steps I took to arrive at the following transcript. As noted before, the purpose of "unmotivated looking" is to acquire a general impression of the talk. This step also allows you to prioritize what to transcribe because transcribing every second of talk is not feasible or necessary unless it is germane to what you are most interested in, especially given the level of detail necessary for Conversation Analysis. For Excerpt 1, I was interested in how participants entered chat rooms, particularly whether they greet the room (and, if so, how), how they make sense of the ongoing conversation, how they join in the conversation, and so on. As such, I looked at all the instances when a new participant joined the party chat, jotted down the dates and timestamps, and then completed a rough transcription (i.e., one that doesn't yet capture the full details of a Conversation Analysis transcript). Then I looked across all the instances to see if there were patterns and how they compared to what other Conversation Analysis studies have observed about opening sequences (cf. Hung, 2017a, 2017b). After that, I identified instances that would allow me to unpack different facets of the phenomenon, for example, by showing the circumstances under which a norm is followed, modified, or violated. These were the ones I would prioritize for a full Conversation Analysis transcription. Now, let's return to the analysis.

Turn management in XBL parties share features of basic conversation. Speakers use *recipient design* to make clear who the intended recipient of the utterance is. This can usually be done without referencing the recipient by name, such as using just enough information for the intended recipient to hear as relevant. For example, in the following excerpt, the party consists of Mitch, Casey, Grant (all pseudonyms), and myself playing Call of Duty: Black Ops 2, when Perry enters:

Excerpt 1

```
1   ((notification that Perry has joined the party))
2   Mitch:   O:::H! (one hit one hit)
3   Casey:   Da:mmit! right when I get it (to::)
4   Grant:   O::h Dra::gunov
5   (2.0)
6   Casey:   ( )
7   Mitch:   Oh can I ple:ase hit it? I have a spe:ctre sti:ll
8            please please   [please please please]
9   Grant:                   [ye::  a::  h        ]
10           [( ) go ahead ( )    ]
11  Perry:   [( ) I'm so ( ) pissed]
12           (1.0)
13  Grant:   Wh::y?
14  Perry:   That was a terrible way to end it
```

15 Grant: Oh! With Hershel getting bit in the leg? Yeah I
16 kno::w ri::ght?

Perry's first turn, "I'm so pissed" (Line 11), is vague and doesn't address anyone in particular. It *sounds* like a complaint, but if that is the case, what or who he is complaining about is not clear (cf. Schegloff, 2005). The vagueness of the utterance is designed like a pre-sequence to invite someone else to ask him to elaborate, but the utterance does not specify a recipient yet. This means anyone can ask for clarification or, alternatively, the entire group can ignore it. After a brief pause (Line 12), Grant responds (Line 13) with "Why?" This turn does not specify the intended recipient, nor does it need to, because it is heard relevantly as a response to Perry's prior utterance. Perry responds with "That was a terrible way to end it" (Line 14), another vague utterance. What does *that* and *it* refer to? But it contained all the information Grant needed to know he was the intended recipient: *It* referred to *The Walking Dead*, and *that* referred to the episode Perry had just watched. Grant, being a fan of the show and had been getting the others to watch it, understands who Perry is addressing and responds accordingly (Lines 15–16). Grant asked me to watch *The Walking Dead* as well, which ended up being helpful for understanding many aspects of their talk, especially as it relates to references to culture or sports that I might not have been familiar with. As a side note, Garfinkel (2002) wrote about the importance of analysts having "unique adequacy," which refers to the ability to make sense of the phenomenon from the participants' point of view. This is crucial in highly technical environments, where participants may use specialized language or tools that an outsider may not understand. In my case, I had to take time to learn not just the passing references to cultural topics but also the language associated with specific game genres (e.g., weapon, scenario types, game settings) as well as slang and interactional norms of the group.

Although recipient design is often sufficient, the lack of visual cues sometimes makes mentioning the intended recipient by name necessary. For example, consider the following two excerpts:

Excerpt 2

1 ((notification that Perry has joined the party))
2 PERRY: why hello:: there why are you guys watching the::
3 fuckin- debate?
4 JENSEN: I'M not (2.9) watchin' ESPN- I'm a ma::n
5 (42.0)
6 PERRY: GRANT!
7 (7.0)
8 GRANT: what's up?

In this excerpt, the party consists of Jensen, Grant, and myself before Perry joins. Perry greets the room (Line 2) but doesn't wait for a response before proceeding to ask why "you guys" are watching the debate (referring to the 2012 presidential debates between Obama and Romney). Every user has a gamer profile that reveals what application you have open, even if they are not in your party. In some cases, such as YouTube, it even reveals the title of the video you are looking at. Perry can only have obtained the information about the debate from looking at the profiles. However, Jensen is the one who responds (Line 4) to acknowledge he is not watching the debate. Perry does not follow up with Jensen, indicating he wasn't interested in pursuing this line of inquiry. Instead, this is followed by a silence of 42 seconds, which normally wouldn't happen in everyday conversation because there is a tendency to avoid even short gaps in talk (Sacks et al., 1974). Both Grant and I are the potentially relevant recipients for Perry's question. I don't answer because I normally assume that questions are not meant for me (which turns out to be true in this case) unless I am addressed by name. After the 42-second gap, Perry addresses Grant by name (Line 6) to make it clear the question was directed at him.

In Excerpt 3, Mitch notices that he received a text message from Grant and asks him about it:

Excerpt 3

((notification that Perry has joined the party))
MITCH: -sent me a (text) saying "what the fu::ck?"
(1.0)
PERRY: Why hello::: there
(1.8)
MITCH: Hi Perry
PERRY: My ga- my chat is turned down really lo::w
MITCH: Gra:::nt why didja just se::nt me::: "what the fuck?"
(1.5)
GRANT: I texted you a he::lla lo::ng time ago: because you
wouldn't join the pa::rty:: hh
MITCH: yeah it was f:- oh that was eight minutes ago
PERRY: then [he probably] sent me that just no:::w
GRANT: [wha::::t?]
PERRY: that I join the party
GRANT: what have YOU:: been up to:::?
((several minutes skipped when Perry talks about a funny
conversation he had last night and they joke around a bit))
GRANT: a:::y Perry what were YOU do::in'?

Here there are two instances when a speaker asks a question with an intended but unnamed recipient (Lines 2 and 16) and then follows up when they don't receive a response by addressing the recipient by name (Lines 8 and 19). In Line 2, it is clear that Grant is the intended recipient because he is the one who sent the text message. Mitch responds to Perry's greeting and then repeats his question (Line 8) as a self-initiated repair (Sacks et al., 1974; Schegloff et al., 1977) to his previous utterance to clarify the intended recipient. Grant's question in Line 16 ("what have YOU:: been up to:::") also doesn't have a named recipient, although his stress on *you* suggests that he does have an intended recipient in mind. He is momentarily sidetracked when Perry starts telling a funny story that takes up a few minutes. After that, Grant returns to the question (Line 19), this time mentioning Perry by name.

So I can formulate some preliminary rules based on these observations (and others that occurred but not excerpted here). First, it appears that there is a preference in this group for following rules of basic conversation and for turns to be recipient-designed without necessarily having the recipient named, unless the recipient design fails. Second, the choice *not* to make mentioning the recipient by name the norm is also interesting, given that naming is more efficient. Halbe's (2012) research on audio conference calls in business meetings shows that recipients are often mentioned by name because there are no visual cues to indicate the intended recipient. In that context, naming seems to be common practice. Not only are recipients mentioned by name more often when compared to basic conversation, but speakers sometimes also self-identify at the start of their turn. Comparing my data with Halbe's, I speculate that the absence of visual cues is not enough to explain whether naming is used. A business call has a specific purpose, schedule, and agenda, so the work of turn-taking and recipient selection is made more efficient by the practice of naming and self-identifying. In the XBL chats, there was no specific purpose or set agenda, and the participants seemed to prefer basic conversation rules over more efficient but formal rules to overcome this issue. This may suggest they were co-constructing a more casual context through their preference for basic conversational norms.

Structural Organization

- Is there a structural organization?
- What phases constitute the structural organization?

A structural organization is common in formal talk and often consists of phases that build toward an ultimate purpose or resolution. This organization requires that participants cooperate to transition from one phase to the next until the goals are reached. For example, Heritage (1997) describes a teacher's call to parents as consisting of four phases:

(1) opening (relevant identities are established to indicate the institutional nature of the conversation), (2) problem initiation (teacher gets into the purpose of the call), (3) disposal (teacher discusses the problem in relation to the bureaucracy of the school and what the parent has to do), and (4) closing (coordinated exit). He showed that both teacher and parent move through these phases to work toward the goal of resolving the issue the teacher was calling about. Business meetings also have phases in their structural organizations, such as the ones participants go through as they transition into and out of the meeting itself. Given what I mentioned about party chats being informal, it is not surprising that the chats don't appear to have a clear structural organization (unless, as other talk in my data show, these chats were tied to a specific shared activity, such as a game).

Sequence Organization

- What sequences do you notice?
- How do sequences compare to similar sequences in other kinds of interactions?

Some common sequences in everyday conversation include greetings, questions, invitations, stories, jokes, and so on that propel the interaction forward. Sequences can involve optional pre-expansion sequences that lead up to the sequence itself (e.g., asking "What are you doing this weekend?" prior to an invitation sequence) and post-expansions that react to a prior sequence. A good place to start is with adjacency pairs. These are sequences that involve two parts, referred to as the first-pair part (FPP) and second-pair part (SPP), with each part uttered by a different speaker (Sacks et al., 1974). When the FPP (e.g., greeting, question, invitation) is uttered, the SPP (e.g., greeting in return, answer, acceptance/declination) is anticipated, usually in the next turn or soon after. Furthermore, Conversation Analysis considers the technology as part of the sequence, most notably in Schegloff's (1968) treatment of the phone's ringing as the FPP of a summoning–answer sequence, which is completed when the answerer picks up the phone and responds. As such, looking at the conversation, as well as the technologies that facilitate the interaction, is important. The private group chats I observed were invitation-only, so the sequence that all participants encounter at some point involves the chat invitation. The invitation has to be sent by the party host to the recipient, who can choose to join the party or ignore the invitation (Hung, 2017b). Because participants can see who is online, this creates the problem of whether an unanswered invitation is interpreted as a missed invitation or an intentional snub. I can make some preliminary observations based on what actions are seen as grounds for complaints and require further accounting, and use that to make further inferences about the sequence organization. Let's start with the complaints:

Excerpt 4

((notification that Mitch has joined party chat))
(7.0)
GRANT: loo::k who:: deci:::ded to jo:::::::in
(6.0)
Mitch?
(9.0)
MITCH: ((noise sounding like headphones being put on))
hello::?
(1.5)
GRANT: su:::p?
MITCH: sorry I didn't uh jo::in earlier I was-
(1.8)
GRANT: wha::::t?
(1.5)
MITCH: a::::h sorry I didn't join earlier I was getting some
food and watching The Walking De::ad
GRANT: hehehe::: [you're in love with that] sho::w
MITCH: [I finished it toda:::y]

Excerpt 4 reveals some wonderfully messy aspects of everyday conversation that can be unpacked with Conversation Analysis. Complaints can reveal information about speakers and context when we examine what is made "complainable" and how people orient to them (Schegloff, 2005). But before we get started, *is* Grant's utterance in Line 3 a complaint? Normally we can find out by seeing whether the intended recipient (Mitch) heard it as a complaint; if so, we would expect him to respond accordingly, such as apologizing, denying its complainability, asking for clarification, and so on. I, as a part of the conversation but not its intended recipient, certainly heard it as a complaint, and Grant also seems to expect a response when he does an availability check with Mitch (Line 5) after a 6.0-second gap. The noise on Mitch's end suggests that he did not have his headphones on prior to Line 7, and the upward intonation to his "Hello" in Line 8 (also an availability check instead of a greeting) suggests he was not available earlier (Hung, 2017a) and therefore did not hear Grant's utterance. After that, he does a preemptive apology (Lines 11, 15–16) and accounts for why he did not join sooner (i.e., when Grant's invitation was first sent), the reason being that he was watching *The Walking Dead*.

Now let's consider the party chat invitation itself. From the point of view of the sender, this sequence runs as follows: (1) A notification flashes up to indicate a friend is online; (2) an invitation is sent; (3) the recipient joins the party (invitation accepted) or nothing happens (uncertainty of whether invitation is declined or missed). The fact that party invitations only flash for a few seconds on the screen also adds to the uncertainty because someone who misses the invitation might not know that they have been invited. Grant is usually online before others, so he tends to be the one who hosts the chat parties. He seems to prefer recipients to accept the invitations soon after they are sent; if that doesn't happen, he sometimes follows up through other channels, such as texting (as seen in Excerpt 3 earlier). Both Grant's complaint and Mitch's apology show a mutual orientation to the complainability of missing or being late in responding to Grant's invitations. Because whoever arrives online first in the evening would usually start the party chat and become the host, Grant was not always the host. However, I have never heard any of the others complain about invitations. Now I have to be careful here because I cannot make any valid assumptions in this case about the absence of complaints. However, I can observe that Grant *does* complain and Mitch *does* treat party invitations as "complainable." As such, analyzing the sequence organization sheds light on their relationships and the context they co-construct together.

Turn Design

- What roles are implied through recipient design?
- What lexical choices are used?
- What are preferred or dispreferred responses (preference organization)?
- How do recipients respond?

Recipient design not only is part of turn-taking management but also has implications for what identities and relationships are implied. In the excerpts presented so far, the participants address one another using their first names. This in itself not revelatory, but compare that to how they address me:

Excerpt 5

Mr. Hung: Hi::?
(59.0)
Perry: Hey Mister Hu::ng what's u:::p?
Mr. Hung: Hey there

5 Perry: Bout time you get o::n
6 Mr. Hung: Ye::ah I was [upda:ting
7 Mitch: [Hey Mister Hu:::ng
8 Mr. Hung: Hey Mitch=

and more playfully:

Excerpt 6

1 Grant: Sup? Aa::ron?
2 Mr. Hung: Hi:::
3 Grant: See? I called you Aaron not Mister Hung
4 Mitch: I (always) call you Mister Hung

Contrary to what Grant says in Excerpt 6, this was the only time he addressed me as "Aaron." At the very least, this difference in recipient design signifies that with me, they have more distance and formality than with one another. Recipient design also involves how the recipient orients to an utterance. For example, in Excerpt 7, Perry joins the party and asks Grant what he is doing:

Excerpt 7

1 ((notification that Perry has joined the party))
2 (4.0)
3 PERRY: Grant?
4 (0.9)
5 GRANT: Perry?
6 PERRY: whatthefuck you:: watchin'?
7 GRANT: hu::h?
8 (0.9)
9 PERRY: whatthefuck you:: watchin'?
10 GRANT: whatdya mean what the fuck am I watching?
11 PERRY: you're watching a last stand easter egg? o::n World
12 at War?
13 GRANT: yeah

Without context, Perry's lexical choice may seem aggressive. However, Perry designed it not to be heard that way by (1) ensuring that it is clear it is intended for Grant (Line 3) to avoid misunderstanding and (2) using an intonation that communicates humor with "whatthefuck" (Lines 6, 9) spoken in a rapid, unserious tone. Likewise, Grant does not orient to Perry's question in a negative way, merely asking for clarification and reusing Perry's wording. In fact, the group often talked to and addressed one another in ways that may appear aggressive out of context but are not usually perceived that way. Like recipient design, lexical choice also signals what relationships or membership categories are signified.

Trouble and Repair

- When does trouble (e.g., miscommunication, mishearing) occur?
- How is trouble noticed and made relevant?
- How is the repair done?

In addition to studying sources of trouble to discover underlying practices, you can also look at trouble that emerges as the result of the technology-mediated environment. Let's go back to invitations again. On XBL, accepting an invitation automatically brings you into the chat room; in other words, there is no way to accept the invitation and join later. This creates the potential problem of accepting the invitation but not being ready to talk. For example, the headset's volume could be turned down (Perry in Excerpt 2, Line 7), or the headset could be unplugged, or the person might have stepped away (Mitch in Excerpt 4, Lines 7–8) or muted the channel. These potential sources of trouble mean that sometimes opening sequences start with an availability check. I had noticed that the person who joins the party tends to be the one who greets the room (Hung, 2017a). Initially I had thought this is because the person who just joined is most likely to be unready, but it appears to be a bit more complicated than that. Unless the host is the only other person in the party, the person joining expects to hear others in mid-conversation. If the person is met with silence, then he or she might wonder if some technical issue has occurred, if everyone is engaging in another activity, and so on. Here is just one example:

Excerpt 8

1 ((notification that Casey has joined the party))
2 (3.0)
3 MITCH: .hhh
4 (17.5)
5 CASEY: is any::one the:::::::::re?
6 (1.4)
7 GRANT: oh my god Mitch look! where'd they all go::? like

8 they're just he::lla
9 CASEY: ( )- get any candy:: thou:gh?
10 GRANT: [( )
11 MITCH: [I can't eat it

Mitch, Perry, Grant, and I were not only all in the chat but also playing *Call of Duty: Black Ops.* Casey happened to enter during a lull in the conversation and didn't hear anyone talking; because he wasn't in the game, he would only have heard silence. After a while, he checks to see if anyone is around (Line 5). He doesn't immediately become part of the group yet because Grant's next utterance addresses Mitch, but once Casey has established that someone is around, he starts to talk (Line 9) and is ratified as a participant when Mitch responds (Line 11).

Critiques of Conversation Analysis

As with any social scientific approach, Conversation Analysis has its share of criticism. One that I often encounter relates broadly to questions about sample size and generalizability. Thus, I recommend that you should plan on collecting as much data as possible. Schegloff (1979) looked at 500 instances of telephone openings. The data presented here come from roughly 75 hours of group chat. Quantity is not important for statistical reasons but, rather, for the chance to understand a phenomenon more broadly. Heritage (1988) likens the work of Conversation Analysis researchers to that of naturalists, for whom the goal is to collect as many specimens of a naturally occurring phenomenon as we can. At the same time, each specimen is itself an example of the phenomenon in question, just as one butterfly is itself an example of its species. In that sense, you can think of all Conversation Analysis research as being part of the same enterprise: to collect as many samples as we can from different contexts, analyzing them closely, and using a shared transcription system to make it easier to make comparisons.

Another concern I've heard raised is, What about other factors, such as demographics and power, that might impact talk? Strictly speaking, Conversation Analysis does not invite speculation about variables that are not observably and relevantly invoked in the talk. This position can be traced back to its roots in resisting the use of abstract constructs to explain social action. Nonetheless, some have applied Conversation Analysis to critical approaches, such as feminist studies, while others have argued against it, believing it goes against the principles of Conversation Analysis (ten Have, 2007). My preference has been to use caution. Unless a factor is demonstrated to be relevant in the context of the interaction, I avoid using it to explain the phenomenon. For example, I have been asked to relate the use of "profanity" to the fact that the participants are male. This insight may be warranted, but I wouldn't make that connection using Conversation Analysis unless I can show its relevance *to the participants.*

To be clear, Conversation Analysis is not silent on issues such as power; Schegloff (1997) sees Conversation Analysis as compatible with critical approaches but argues it is better to start with a technical analysis to maintain focus on what is relevant to the participants and not just what is relevant to the analyst. Grant asking others to account for not accepting his invitation is power. The way they categorize one another through their talk is power. The acceptance or denial of these categories is power (Hung, 2019) and so on. Demographics and power are important in Conversation Analysis, but we cannot start with presumptions about their influence; we have to start with the participants.

Conclusion

I have continued to use Conversation Analysis for several reasons. I appreciate its emphasis on the participants' perspectives and naturally occurring data. As someone who has been interested in studying youth, Conversation Analysis has allowed me to present their voices and worldviews in more authentic ways. For example, in a recent article, I wrote about how their political identities evolved as they chatted in Xbox Live parties (Hung, 2019). Some of them declared they were not interested in politics, yet they still had views about politics when others brought it up. By using Conversation Analysis, I was able to show that these identities were not static constructs but forms of self-presentation that developed from moment to moment, conversation to conversation. Another reason I like using Conversation Analysis is that, although the work of transcription is labor-intensive, it forces me to pay close attention to the interaction and to continually ask myself, "What's going on here? Why was this said? What does this mean in this context?" Here, transcription isn't just the thing I have to do to get to analysis; it is also part of the analysis. The focus on the participants' perspectives also means that I am less inclined to inject my worldviews, which is important, especially if I am studying a group whose views or norms might not align with mine. As noted in the prior section, some might consider this a flaw of Conversation Analysis; I consider this built-in resistance to preformulated social theories an asset.

Suggested Further Reading

Mondada, L. (2013). The conversation analytic approach to data collection. In J. Sidnell & T. Stivers (Eds.), *The handbook of conversation analysis* (pp. 32–56). Malden, MA: Blackwell Publishing.

Sacks, H., Schegloff, E. A., & Jefferson, G. (1974). A simplest systematics for the organization of turn-taking for conversation. *Language, 50*, 696–735.

ten Have, P. (2007). *Doing conversation analysis: A practical guide* (2nd ed.). London, England: Sage Publications.

References

Clayman, S., & Heritage, J. (2002). *The news interview: Journalists and public figures on the air.* New York, NY: Cambridge University Press.

Drew, P. (1984). Speakers' reportings in invitation sequences. In J. M. Atkinson & J. Heritage (Eds.), *Structures of social action: Studies in conversation analysis* (pp. 129–51). Cambridge, England: Cambridge University Press.

Garfinkel, H. (2002). *Ethnomethodology's program: Working out Durkheim's aphorism.* Lanham, MD: Rowman & Littlefield.

Gee, J. P. (2003). *What video games have to teach us about learning and literacy.* New York, NY: Palgrave Macmillan.

Goodwin, C., & Goodwin, M. H. (1992). Assessments and the construction of context. In A. Duranti & C. Goodwin (Eds.), *Rethinking context* (pp. 147–189). Cambridge, England: Cambridge University Press.

Halbe, D. (2012). "Who's there?": Differences in the features of telephone and face-to-face conferences. *Journal of Business Communication, 49*(1), 48–73. https://doi.org/10.1177/0021943611425238

Heritage, J. (1988). Explanations as accounts: A conversation analytic perspective. In C. Antaki (Ed.), *Analysing everyday explanation: A casebook of methods* (pp. 127–144). London, England: Sage Publications.

Heritage, J. (1997). Conversation analysis and institutional talk: Analysing data. In D. Silverman (Ed.), *Qualitative research: theory, method and practice* (pp. 161–182). London, England: Sage Publications.

Hung, A. C. Y. (2011). *The work of play: Meaning-making in videogames.* New York, NY: Peter Lang.

Hung, A. C. Y. (2017a). Conversation analysis, transcription, and local productions of order. In M. Knobel & C. Lankshear (Eds.), *Researching new literacies: Design, theory and data in sociocultural investigation* (pp. 37–58). New York, NY: Peter Lang.

Hung, A. C. Y. (2017b). Hanging out on Xbox Live: How teens enter and open conversations in party chats. *Language@Internet, 14*. Retrieved from https://www.languageatinternet.org/articles/2017/hung

Hung, A. C. Y. (2019). Political socialization on Xbox Live: A sociocultural linguistic approach to adolescent identity. *Journal of Youth Studies*, 1–17. Advanced online publication. https://doi.org/10.1080/13676261.2019.1636009

Jefferson, G. (2004). Glossary of transcript symbols with an introduction. In G. H. Lerner (Ed.), *Conversation analysis: Studies from the first generation* (pp. 13–31). Amsterdam, the Netherlands: John Benjamins.

Mondada, L. (2013). The conversation analytic approach to data collection. In J. Sidnell & T. Stivers (Eds.), *The handbook of conversation analysis* (pp. 32–56). Malden, MA: Blackwell.

Mondada, L. (2014). The local constitution of multimodal resources for social interaction. *Journal of Pragmatics, 65*, 137–156. https://doi.org/10.1016/j.pragma.2014.04.004

Pomerantz, A. (1984). Agreeing and disagreeing with assessments: Some features of preferred/dispreferred turn shapes. In J. M. Atkinson & J. Heritage (Eds.), *Structures of social action* (pp. 57–101). Cambridge, England: Cambridge University Press.

Sacks, H. (1974). An analysis of the course of a joke's telling in conversation. In R. Bauman & J. Sherzer (Eds.), *Explorations in the ethnography of speaking* (pp. 337–353). Cambridge, England: Cambridge University Press.

Sacks, H. (1995). *Lectures on conversation.* Oxford, England: Blackwell.

Sacks, H., Schegloff, E. A., & Jefferson, G. (1974). A simplest systematics for the organization of turn-taking for conversation. *Language, 50,* 696–735.

Schegloff, E. A. (1968). Sequencing in conversational openings. *American Anthropologist, 70,* 1075–1095.

Schegloff, E. A. (1979). Identification and recognition in telephone conversation openings. In G. Psathis (Ed.), *Everyday language: Studies in ethnomethodology* (pp. 23–78). New York, NY: Erlbaum.

Schegloff, E. A. (1997). Whose text? Whose context? *Discourse and Society, 8,* 165–187. https://doi.org/10.1177/0957926597008002002

Schegloff, E. A. (2005). On complainability. *Social Problems, 52,* 449–476. https://doi.org/10.1525/sp.2005.52.4.449

Schegloff, E. A. (2013). Ten operations in self-initiated, same-turn repair. In M. Hayashi, G. Raymond, & J. Sidnell (Eds.), *Conversational repair and human understanding* (pp. 41–70). Cambridge, England: Cambridge University Press.

Schegloff, E. A., Jefferson, G., & Sacks, H. (1977). The preference for self-correction in the organization of repair in conversation. *Language, 53,* 361–381.

Sidnell, J. (2010). *Conversation analysis: An introduction.* Malden, MA: Wiley-Blackwell.

Suchman, L. A. (2002). *Human-machine reconfigurations: plans and situated actions* (2nd ed.). Cambridge, England: Cambridge University Press.

ten Have, P. (2007). *Doing conversation analysis: A practical guide* (2nd ed.). London, England: Sage Publications.

CHAPTER 4

Using Mediated Discourse Analysis to Investigate Literacy Practices

Ryan Rish

If you are interested in conducting New Literacy Studies research, you may already be familiar with the two central theoretical constructs used in this line of inquiry: literacy events (Heath, 1983) and literacy practices (Street, 1995). Instead of being defined as an autonomous set of skills, literacy is defined as multiple, situated social practices that vary from one social arrangement to another (e.g., families, schools, workplaces) and are ideologically framed by the social and cultural contexts in which they are enacted. Literacy events are defined as observable situations in which reading, writing, or related semiotic systems play a nontrivial role in the actions taken by people. New Literacy Studies researchers identify literacy practices by observing multiple, comparable literacy events and making inductions about how people enact, adopt, adapt, resist, and so on literacy practices extant within particular social arrangements (Bloome, Carter, Christian, Otto, & Shuart-Faris, 2005). However, what is not easily understood and often varies among New Literacy Studies researchers is what counts as a literacy event and how inductions are made to identify literacy practices (Barton, 2009), on what scale literacy practices are understood and conceptualized (Baynham & Prinsloo, 2009), and what role tools and materials (e.g., mobile phones, pencils) play within the literacy practice (Coiro, Knobel, Lankshear, & Leu, 2008). Mediated discourse analysis provides a useful methodology for working through these issues inherent in New Literacy Studies research. The term *mediated discourse analysis* is both used to describe a micro- and macro-level methodology and used to refer to a specific microethnographic research method (Norris & Jones, 2005). As I lead you through the design of a study in this chapter, I refer to the overarching methodology as MDA and the specific research method as mediated discourse analysis. As I do so, I point to examples from my study of collaborative writing using MDA.

Planning a Study With MDA

When planning an investigation of literacy practices with MDA as a methodology, you want to identify a social context in which you expect literacy practices to be enacted, and you will be able to observe and eventually interview participants over an extended time. As with other methodologies employed within literacy studies (e.g., ethnography, microethnography, discourse analysis), MDA is most effective when you can collect data across multiple, observable literacy events on a particular time scale. Depending on the social context in which you are planning your study, the time scale may or may not be predetermined by the context. For example, if you are planning a study within an institutional context, such as a school, the time scale may be preestablished by when the participants are available (e.g., school calendar) and when they will be engaged in particular activities that you plan to observe (e.g., school curriculum). However, if you are planning a study within a more informal social context (e.g., a household), you may need to negotiate with participants the time scale for the study, considering that the times they are engaged in the particular activities that you would like to observe may vary.

As much as possible, you want to plan a study that involves observing the same participants across time. This can be particularly challenging in contexts such as schools with high rates of absenteeism or with students frequently being pulled out of the classroom for special activities, such as testing, tutoring, or extracurricular activities. This also can be particularly challenging in contexts where the activity you would like to observe is not based on regular attendance, such as a makerspace in a public library. Therefore, you want to carefully consider the extent to which you will be able to observe comparable literacy events involving a degree of regularity of participants. Not planning for this at the onset can lead to frustration later during data analysis when you are attempting to look across comparable literacy events to make inductions about the literacy practices of particular people in your study.

When I was planning my MDA study of collaborative writing in a high school elective English class, I first spent some time in the class the previous school year to get an idea of the social context of the class and the general roles of the participants (Rish & Caton, 2011). Although the class in which I eventually would conduct the full study varied in enrollment and curriculum compared to the pilot study class, I was able to understand generally what to expect in terms of participant attendance in class and the availability of participants outside the class for group and individual interviews.

Beginning a Study With MDA

The MDA methodology is most useful to literacy studies because it both allows for detailed examinations of literacy events and for broader considerations of what literacy practices are being negotiated within those literacy events. New Literacy Studies researchers examine the interrelationships among the following three levels of analysis: (1) individual activities, understandings, and identities, (2) social events and the interactions they involve, and (3) broader social and institutional structures (Maybin, 2000). Throughout a study that employs MDA, you are reciprocally working on these three levels, identified within MDA as (a) mediated action, (b) sites of engagement, and (c) a nexus of practice. With these three levels of analysis in mind, you will want to follow a careful process of selecting which participants and activities are the focus of your study. Scollon (2001a) outlines a process of data collection and reduction for MDA that is not meant to be sequential or procedural but, rather, helps guide the focus of your study and the related data collection and analysis from the onset.

Participant and Mediational Means Survey

The first part of the iterative research process is a survey of participants and the mediational means they are using to identify your research site and focus on particular people engaged in particular social actions. Scollon (2001a) employs the term *survey* loosely to include questionnaires, interviews, and focus groups to be used to begin to understand the relevant participants and the means through which they are taking actions related to what you are interested in investigating. These surveys may also involve taking initial sets of field notes and writing analytic memos about who is taking actions, with whom, and with what tools.

For example, when I first began visiting the elective class in which I conducted my full study of collaborative writing, my field notes focused on who was in attendance in the class, with whom they were interacting, what actions they were taking related to collaborative planning and writing, and what tools, or mediational means, they were using to accomplish those actions. My early analytic memos were mostly speculative about the participants and how they seemed to be engaged in the planning and writing tasks established by the teacher. Knowing that I would eventually have to focus on a select number of students, I speculated on which participants may be most appropriate for a more focused investigation.

Scene Survey

The second part of the iterative process is a scene survey, which is meant to "narrow down the scope of the research to a few highly salient places or scenes, in which the actions we are interested in are taking place" (Scollon, 2001a, p. 156). At this point, you are moving from a broad consideration of all participants and the range of social actions they are taking to identify particular "scenes" that are representative of the social practices you are interested in investigating. Because you cannot follow all possible participants throughout their entire day, the scene survey helps you determine when, where, and with whom you are likely to observe actions relevant to the focus of your study.

For my purposes, a scene survey helped me to determine that the time devoted to collaborative planning and writing within the elective class was only one among many possible scenes, wherein students were discussing ideas and sharing their thoughts and plans for the collaborative writing project. Other significant scenes included individual use of computers in the library or in the back of classrooms during participants' study halls, hallway conversations, and asynchronous online communication through the project wiki and other social media platforms. Although I was limited to conducting participant observations during the scenes that unfolded within the elective class, I was able to gather artifacts from and ask participants about the other relevant scenes I had identified. Not to have acknowledged the significance of scenes other than those I was observing would have led to a much more limited understanding of how the participants were accomplishing collaborative writing.

Event/Action Survey

The third part of the iterative process is an event/action survey designed to identify specific social actions taking place within the scenes that are relevant to the focus of the study. This survey is an ethnographic continuation of the scene surveys, as this next process involves considering what the main actions unfolding within the identified scenes are. At this point, you are still broadly considering all the actions that are related to the scenes. You have to be careful about ruling out particular actions as irrelevant to your study, because they may be tangentially or even closely related to what you are considering for the focus of your study.

For example, three of the participants in my study engaged in horseplay and mock fighting when assembled to work on the collaborative writing project. This horseplay involved acting out fighting moves from popular video games and animated television shows, accompanied by a significant amount of teasing and making fun of each other. When I first conducted my event/action surveys of the relevant scenes, I dismissed this horseplay as unrelated or even detracting from the collaborative writing project. Later, when I was further along in my data collection and analysis process, I realized that this horseplay was often generative of ideas for the collaborative writing project and played an important role in maintaining the participants' social relationship with one another (see Goff & Rish, 2019). Therefore, returning to the event/action survey to reevaluate the significance of the actions related to horseplay within the identified scenes was significant to the findings of my study.

Focal Groups

The fourth part of this iterative process is the identification of participants within the scope of the identified scenes and events/actions. Because the analytic focus of MDA is eventually narrowed to mediated action of select participants, the selection of particular focal participants is both a practical necessity and a method for verifying the salience of the identified scenes and events/actions (Scollon, 2001a). Interviewing selected participants and/or focus groups early in the data collection process allows for opportunities to determine the relationship of the identified scenes with other possible scenes that may not be accessible to you as the researcher. You also may be able to determine the extent to which the events/actions are central to the scenes you have identified.

For example, early conversations with selected focal groups in my study of collaborative writing helped me understand the scenes that I had identified for the scene survey were an incomplete inventory of all the scenes in which the collaborative writing project was a focus for my participants. Two of my participants played networked video games together outside of school. This video game play involved casual and game-specific conversations using a headset. The two participants shared with me that although the focal action of that scene was the video game they were playing, they also used the time together online to discuss the collaborative writing project. In particular, some of the elements of the video game they were playing were providing source material for their collaborative writing project. Another participant shared with me that the computer in her home was devoted to running her father's business, and she and her siblings could only use the computer during predetermined times devoted to homework. As a result of these constraints on her computer use at home, the writing she produced outside of school for her project involved a significant, although inconsistent and unpredictable, scene for collaborative writing.

Learning the relationship among possible scenes where the identified events/actions are salient is a significant element in contextualizing what you are able to observe as a researcher. Through interviews and casual conversations with your participants, you may learn the extent to which the scenes you are able to observe are central or peripheral to the mediated actions and related social practices you are interested in investigating. You may also begin to learn about the relationship among social practices across contexts. For example, for my participants who played video games together, the social practices of playing networked video games and working on the collaborative writing project were linked in commensurate ways within that particular scene. Alternatively, for my participant who worked on the project inconsistently at home, the social practices of computer use in the home were not always linked in commensurate ways with the collaborative writing project within that particular scene. In fact, her father questioned her at one point if the collaborative writing project was actually homework or not, as other siblings also needed time on the home computer.

Mediated Action

The last part of the iterative process of planning your data collection is a focus on mediated actions within your identified events. Mediated action is the focal unit of analysis when using MDA. Mediated action is defined by Wertsch (1998) as the irreducible tension between mediational means and the agent of the action. The purpose of defining mediated action as a tension is to avoid oversimplifying social action as determined by the mediational means (the cultural tools being used) or wholly explainable by the action of the agent. Mediated action often involves many different goals that may be in conflict with one another, and the mediated action may or may not "map neatly onto the goals with which the mediational means are typically associated" (Wertsch, 1998, p. 34). Additionally, mediated actions do not unfold in isolation but, rather, within broader social structures, such as cultural models, literacy practices, discourses, and so on. MDA acknowledges that mediational means carry with them social structures and ideologies based on historical patterns of their use (Jones & Norris, 2005). Alternatively, these social structures do not exist without concrete, material action (Scollon, 2001b). Therefore, a seemingly narrow focus on mediated action within selected events is related to a broader consideration of what social practices are being enacted through those social actions.

For the purposes of my study of collaborative writing, I conceptualized the act of writing as a socially mediated action that involves an array of sociohistorically provided resources, or mediational means (Prior, 2006). Writing as mediated action not only involves the actions of inscribing words on paper or typing words on a screen but also involves dialogic processes of invention (Bakhtin, 1981) as my participants used such mediational means to shape their collaborative writing as literacy practices associated with recreational and school-based writing, genres and conventions related to fantasy and science fiction, and in-person and online conversations with one another about the project. Along these lines, the relevant mediational means not only included the material tools (e.g., hand-drawn maps, an online wiki) but also included literacy practices related to the participants' histories as writers. These literacy practices were related to each other in complex ways, shaping how and why the collaborative writing projects were accomplished.

Data Collection

As previously stated, multiple sources of data are collected across the iterative processes of identifying relevant participants and mediational means, scenes, events and actions, focal participants, and mediated actions. These multiple sources of data are categorized into four types: participant histories and generalizations, participant observation, individual participant experiences, and member checks. These four sources of data are used with the specific methods of mediated discourse analysis and nexus analysis and are important for comparison and triangulation as you attempt to understand the relationships among the mediated actions you observe and the social practices they constitute in part (Scollon & Scollon, 2004). (For a clear and useful diagrammatic representation of data filters and the overall data filtering process that informed my approach, see Scollon, 2001a, p. 153.)

Participant Histories and Generalizations

When attempting to understand how the mediated actions of your participants are located and understood within larger social practices, you will want to understand what the participants consider to be normative of selected scenes and events. This will provide you with some insight into the participants' histories with the literacy practices you are interested in investigating as they are situated in the particular contexts in which you are observing. However, you may note that what people describe as normative for a particular scene can be at odds with the mediated actions you observe them taking or the mediated actions they report taking. This can give you insight into what participants perceive as the expected social and literacy practices compared to the ones they are enacting or reporting to have enacted historically.

For example, participants in my study could readily name school-sanctioned literacy practices that have framed their in-school writing experiences. The writing prompt is typically provided by the teacher, and the teacher is typically the only reader of their writing even though they are meant to be writing for a larger, imagined audience. The writing is meant to be produced in a procedural series of steps in the writing process and shared with peers within a designated revision window of time. Even though students could readily name the expected literacy practices associated with their history with in-school writing, they were also quick to point out how their individual literacy practices differed from what was expected. They reported completing steps of the writing process out of order (e.g., completing the prewriting activity after the final draft was completed). These histories and generalizations helped me understand how students were negotiating the literacy practices associated with the collaborative writing project in relation to the literacy practices that they typically associated with school and the ones they reported enacting historically (Goff & Rish, 2019; Rish, 2015).

Participant Observation

In addition to learning the histories of your participants and the generalizations they make about the scenes you are interested in investigating, you will also want to conduct participant observations of (and video record, if possible) the mediated actions taken within your focal events. Oftentimes, the actions people take are at odds with their reported personal histories and/or the generalizations they make about what is normative within particular scenes. There are any number of reasons why this may occur, as mediated actions may be simultaneously associated with multiple social practices that may conflict with one another. Conflicts among what is observed and reported may also be a result of participants negotiating among different social practices in any given event (Rish, 2017). Taking note of these conflicts can be very productive for understanding the context and conditions in which participants are agentively making choices to take particular mediated actions over others.

In the case of collaborative writing in which multiple participants were negotiating the expected literacy practices related to the project, participants were often enacting literacy practices that were both at odds with what is normative within school and their personal histories with writing. In many cases, this conflict between the mediated actions they were taking and their histories and generalizations was a result of negotiating among what was expected of them and how their group members wanted to go about accomplishing the collaborative writing related to the project.

Individual Participant Experiences

Conducting individual interviews about what you are observing, therefore, is an essential source of data for understanding how and why individual participants are taking the mediated actions that you are observing. This can help you understand conflicts among what you have come to understand as normative within particular scenes and the histories of individual participants. Social and literacy practices are under continuous negotiation through each enactment, and the experience of individuals can help you understand the extent to which participants are adopting, adapting, resisting, rejecting, and so on the social and literacy practices that you are coming to understand as relevant to the mediated actions you are observing.

Within my study of collaborative writing, one of the collaborative writing groups was made up of three students who enacted literacy practices related to the project in ways that were at times complementary and at other times incongruent (Rish, 2015). This led to some negotiation among them, which for some of them resulted in the enactment of literacy practices that ran contrary to their histories and generalizations. After speaking with them individually, I was able to get a sense of who was making adjustments to their literacy practices for the sake of the project and who was enacting literacy practices consistent with their personal histories. However, the negotiations did not always play out in predictable ways; therefore, speaking to the participants individually became an important part of the process of understanding the complex and oftentimes unpredictable ways mediated actions were associated with particular literacy practices and not others.

Member Checks

To resolve conflicts among the first three types of data, member checks are necessary to learn how participants account for your emergent analyses of the meaning of the observed mediated actions and the social and literacy practices with which they are associated. Early in your data collection process, you may find that your initial inductions do not capture the complexity completely or are not representative of the participants' experiences. Conducting member checks early and often is a way to ensure your emergent analyses are keeping in line with the experiences of your participants and a way to account for conflicts among data sources as they arise.

In my research, I have found that my early inductions about the meaning of an observed mediated action in relation to participants' generalizations and histories are either incomplete or not at all representative of their experiences. These moments of getting it wrong early in the research process lead to more informed decision making when reducing a potentially large data corpus down to particular focal scenes and events. As researchers, we can move too quickly to make associations among mediated actions and social practices and gloss over much of the complexity when attempting to understand our participants. Regular member checks help us to pause and take stock of what we are beginning to understand and to confirm with participants to see if our data triangulation is resulting in representative inductions.

Data Analysis

Throughout the data collection and data filtering process, you have already begun to analyze your data through the comparison of the four sources of data: participant histories and generalizations, participant observation, individual interviews, and member checks. Keeping an ongoing record of your data collection and filtering process can be accomplished through the writing of analytic memos, in which you are considering the meaning of mediated actions you are observing, the social and literacy practices with which the actions may be associated, and instances of congruence or conflict among your triangulated data sources. Additional methods may be employed throughout the data collection and data filtering process on two different levels. On the macro level, a collection of methods under the umbrella term *nexus analysis* can be used to understand the relationships among social practices. On the micro level, there are some specific ways mediated discourse analysis can be used to understand the meaning and significance of mediated actions taken within identified events and how those mediated actions aggregate over time to constitute social and literacy practices.

Nexus Analysis: Relationships Among Social Practices

Nexus analysis involves three overarching activities. The first activity involves the researcher engaging in the mediated actions affiliated with the social issue of interest. By beginning the data collection and filtering process previously described, you are already involved with engaging the relevant actions and social practices. The second activity involves the researcher "navigating and mapping the cycles of discourse, of people, and of mediational means which are at the heart of the significant actions being studied" (Scollon & Scollon, 2004, p. 152). The third activity involves revealing how changes at the level of mediated action can effect broader changes at the level of social practices within the nexus of analysis (Wohlwend, 2014).

Engaging the nexus. Engaging the nexus begins from the onset of the study as you engage in the iterative processes of data collection and filtration. Your initial participant and mediational means survey can be additionally guided by the following five activities: establishing the social issue you are investigating, identifying the crucial actors, observing the interaction order, determining the significant cycles of discourse, and establishing a zone of identification (Scollon & Scollon, 2014).

Establishing the social issue of your investigation sounds fairly straightforward; however, this is an important initial step that will guide your future decision making. You may find that the social issue you identify becomes more nuanced, but you ultimately want to have an initial focus to guide all other decision making related to designing and conducting your investigation. In my study, the social issue of the investigation was how adolescents accomplish collaborative writing.

Identifying the primary actors in the mediated action will begin to narrow your investigation. Who these potential participants *are* matters not only in terms of their multiple, intersectional identities in relation to the social issue you are investigating but also in terms of their personal histories with the mediated actions you are investigating. You want to know what their social roles are in relation to the mediated actions you observe and what history led up to them taking the mediated actions in the ways and purposes in which they do. In my study, I identified participants who were and were not working well together to produce collaborative writing. I wanted to know why some of the students enacted mediated actions related to collaborative writing while others did not.

Another significant activity during the participant and mediational means survey is to consider the interaction order among the participants. Interaction orders are social arrangements that people use to form relationships and take action in social interactions (Goffman, 1983). People act differently depending on the social arrangement (e.g., alone, group, crowd, cue) and the social occasion. Therefore, you want to consider what interaction orders are related to the mediated actions you are focusing on for your investigations. In some cases, the interaction orders can help you determine your selection of primary actors, as the mediated actions you are interested in may involve a select group of participants. In my study, students self-selected collaborative writing groups; the arrangement of these groups, as well as pairings within the groups, constituted the interaction orders which made the mediated actions related to collaborative writing possible.

A useful activity for scene selection is the identification of significant cycles of discourse related to the focal mediated actions. Discourses may be overt or covert, spoken or written, and central or peripheral to the mediated actions you are considering. The best way to define what Scollon and Scollon (2014) mean by cycles of discourse is through an example. In my study of collaborative writing, multiple cycles of discourse were associated with how and why the participants took the mediated actions they did related to collaborative writing. Discourses related to fantasy and science fiction were cycling through mediated actions in terms of tropes and genre conventions that the participants considered cliché or too derivative in their collaborative writing. Other cycles of discourse were at work related to grades, establishing and maintaining friendships and romantic relationships, and processes of writing as enacted in school and in the personal lives of the participants. Identifying when and where relevant cycles of discourse are at work to mediate the action the participants are taking can help you identify relevant scenes to investigate.

These four activities are important for recognizing a significant nexus of practice. The fifth and last activity involved with engaging the nexus of practice is to locate yourself within a zone of identification with the participants. Scollon and Scollon (2014) recommend that you should not resist becoming part of the nexus of practice that you are investigating because your research activity will unavoidably shape the mediated actions participants take and change the nexus of practice in some ways. Therefore, you want to consider your own role as your research activities merge with your participation activities within the nexus of practice. The zone of identification is how you will account for your changing role within the nexus of practice. In my study, my role shifted among roles that included an observer, an occasional co-teacher, a popular culture resource for students, and a sounding board for students celebrating and complaining about different aspects of the collaborative writing project. I was a full-fledged participant in the nexus of practice I was attempting to understand and ultimately shift toward the goal of students completing their collaborative writing projects.

Navigating the nexus. After the activities related to identification when engaging the nexus of practice are completed, the next part of nexus analysis is to

> map the cycles of people, places, discourses, objects, and concepts which circulated through this micro-semiotic ecosystem looking for anticipations and emanations, links and transformations, their inherent timescales, and to place a circumference of relevance around the nexus of practice. (Scollon & Scollon, 2004, pp. 159–160)

In short, the goal of navigating the nexus is to understand what all is involved that led up to the observed, focal mediation actions, as well as what the actions give further impetus to in the future. I discuss particular cycles that may be relevant to your investigation in brief and encourage you to consult Scollon and Scollon's (2014) field guide for greater detail. I also discuss the cycles relevant to my investigation and my processes for mapping them.

Participant histories are important for understanding how they came to be part of the mediated action and have the capability to carry it out. At the beginning of my study, I conducted student profile interviews in which I asked participants about their histories with writing and their interests related to fantasy and science fiction. These histories provided a guide for mapping how their previous experiences and interests shaped the mediated actions they took throughout the collaborative writing project. Through ongoing member checks, I came to understand that these histories informed but did not determine the mediated actions they took.

Understanding how objects (or cultural tools) are used as mediational means can help you determine the historical role the objects play. In my study, the teacher introduced an online wiki as the primary organizing tool for students to both produce their collaborative writing on wiki pages and plan their projects using the discussion boards associated with each wiki page. Understanding how, when, and under what conditions this object (the wiki) was used across the project helped me understand the mediated actions students were taking during my observations and the *frozen actions* (Norris, 2004) that became embedded in the wiki as student and teacher posts of writing and images. Due to differences in access to a computer and the online wiki among the participants, other objects were also significant to the mediated actions, such as personal journals, hand-drawn maps, and illustrations, among others. Mapping the significance of objects involved observations, interviews, images of artifacts the students produced by hand, and a content analysis of the timestamped online wiki.

Understanding how concepts (also cultural tools) shape mediated action can help you understand how participants are drawing on available resources, such as language, forms of knowledge, and social codes for behavior, across the course of your investigation. For my purposes, I primarily relied on a content analysis of the participants' writing and observation of their collaborative writing and planning to identify genre conventions and story elements related to fantasy and science fiction. Mapping these concepts helped me understand how story elements were considered proprietary among participants and required consent and oversight of their use. This mapping helped me to understand the literacy practice of maintaining storyline continuity within collaborative writing projects (Goff & Rish, 2019).

Time-scale identification and mapping can help you understand when and why participants take mediated actions related to what you are interested in investigating. Multiple time scales were at work within my investigation. The school semester time scale determined the length of the elective class and informed the teacher's planning of the collaborative writing project. The time scale of the school day determined when the class met for the collaborative writing events that I observed. Students' individual schedules served as a time scale for when they could meet together in person and online. Also, the asynchronous functionality of the online wiki imposed micro time scales related to who could work on a wiki page when.

Not exhausting the list of possible types of mapping that Scollon and Scollon (2004) identify in their field guide, another significant activity used to navigate the nexus of practice is conducting mediated discourse analysis of selected events to consider how these semiotic cycles and processes are at work on the micro level. In a separate section later, I discuss mediated discourse analysis in detail.

Changing the nexus. By conducting the activities associated with engaging and navigating the nexus of practice, you have in some way changed the nexus you are attempting to understand from an ethnographic perspective and that you may be attempting to change from a critical perspective. What is not possible is that no change occurred as a result of your identification and mapping processes and practices. The discourses related to mapping and analyzing data resemiotize the mediated actions you are attempting to understand and become mediational means that unavoidably inform the historical body, interaction order, and discourses in place that make up the nexus of practice. In my study, my actions as a researcher served to encourage and draw attention and awareness to practices and processes related to collaborative writing. These interactions with the students and the teacher within the collaborative writing project mediated, in part, the actions they took and how they negotiated literacy practices related to collaborative writing. A cycle of nexus analysis concludes with a consideration of how your actions of analysis are "altering trajectories for yourself and others in the nexus of practice and that in itself is producing social change" (Scollon & Scollon, 2004, p. 178).

Mediated Discourse Analysis: Relationships Among Actions

Mediated discourse analysis as a microethnographic method considers how action and discourse are mutually constitutive, focusing "upon the concrete, real-time social action to see these social actions as fundamentally discursive" (Scollon, 2001b, pp. 8–9). Mediated discourse analysis strives to privilege neither discourse nor social action but, rather, to consider discourse as one of many available tools with which people take action. To accomplish this, mediated action is given analytic primacy as the unit of analysis (Wertsch, 1994). This focus primarily on mediated action is what differentiates mediated discourse analysis from other forms of discourse analysis.

Site of engagement. Mediated action unfolds within what mediated discourse analysts refer to as a site of engagement. Scollon (2001b) defines a site of engagement as a "real-time window that is opened through an intersection of social practices and mediational means (cultural tools) that make that action the focal point of attention of the relevant participants" (p. 4). Site of engagement is conceptualized with the consideration that social actions do not unfold within objective moments or locations but, rather, are "the results of orientation toward time and space that participants bring to interaction" (Jones, 2005, p. 141). In any given event that you identify in your research, multiple sites of engagement may overlap, simultaneously occur, or conflict with one another.

Site of engagement is a useful theoretical construct to account for complexities related to the enactment of literacy practices as mediated action. Literacy events were initially defined by their patterned predictability (e.g., Heath, 1983), and the construct of sites of engagement provides a way of investigating literacy events by their "momentary occurrence with multiple, alternative, or virtual possibilities, as always more than can be perceived, replete with potentialities" (Burnett & Merchant, 2018, p. 8). Defining literacy events as composed of multiple, possible sites of engagement allows for a consideration of how the event may be composed of multiple levels or layers of social interaction (Bloome & Bailey, 1992; Bloome et al., 2005), how social actions may be simultaneously oriented toward multiple activities (Engeström, 1987; Leont'ev, 1978), and how multiple space-times are implicated within and across literacy events (Leander & McKim, 2003).

When you are conducting mediated discourse analysis, you are investigating how the social action you are considering is mediated by a person's historical body, the interaction order among the participants, and the discourses-in-place. This has been rendered visually in a clear and helpful way as a site of engagement by Scollon and Scollon (2004, p. 20).

Mediated discourse analysis allows for a consideration of how social practices aggregate over time within individuals as habitus (Bourdieu, 1977) or alternatively as a historical body (Nishida, 1958). For Bourdieu, habitus is developed in relation to a field, which researchers in literacy studies (e.g., Albright & Luke, 2008) have used to conceptualize different social and cultural domains (e.g., home, school, community). Scollon (2001b) extends Bourdieu's term of *field* to consider how an individual's habitus is developed within and across multiple overlapping nexus of practice that may or may not map onto bounded social domains or social groups. By considering your participants' histories and observed actions across events, you can gain a sense of how their habitus as an aggregate of social practices over time shapes the mediated actions they take in coordination with others. An illustrative example from my study is Erika, who had a history of writing fan fiction within an online community. She had aggregated over time the literacy practice of only providing feedback once she had read someone's writing. Erika brought this literacy practice along to her collaborative writing project group, which caused tensions with Zina, who wanted immediate feedback on her writing ideas. Erika's habitus mediated in part the social actions she took within her collaborative writing group (Rish, 2015).

Mediated discourse analysis employs Goffman's (1983) construct of *interaction order* to conceptualize social arrangements that people use as mediational means to take social action with one another. People use interaction orders as shared conventions for displaying, giving, and getting attention (Jones, 2005). By considering the interaction order and what it represents to the mediated action, you can distinguish between people who are merely co-present and people who constitute what Goffman (1983) refers to as a "with" or a "small group of two or more people who are socially together, who have special rights to each other's attention and who also have special rights to ignore and be ignored by others in their vicinity" (Scollon & Scollon, 2004, p. 22). In my study of collaborative writing, the groups working on the project together constituted one interaction order, but others overlapped groups or were contained within one group. For example, one collaborative writing group divided into two factions that shaped not only the contents of the writing (two groups of people at war with each other) but also split the group along lines of preexisting friendships and romantic interests. These complex, overlapping interaction orders mediated the social actions that participants took in relation to the project.

The physical environment has the potential to mediate social actions and channel attention based on the configuration of the place, the available cultural tools, and people's social and cultural histories with similar places. The concept of discourse-in-place is used by mediated discourse analysts to consider the "social meaning of the material placement of signs and discourses and of our actions in the material world" (Scollon & Scollon, 2004, p. 2). Places rarely serve single purposes; therefore, when taking social action people selectively foreground aspects of the place and available mediational means and background others (Scollon & Scollon, 2004). An example of this is a multipurpose room in an elementary school. At lunchtime, the room is arranged for students to eat lunch, and the daily menu posted on the wall becomes relevant to the actions taken within the room at that time. However, later in the day, the room is arranged for gym class, and the menu is no longer a relevant discourse-in-place. Through mediated discourse analysis, you can consider which discourses-in-place are mediating the actions taken there, resolving tensions between the local and the global (Brandt & Clinton, 2002). For example, in my study, the students worked on their projects in their classroom, the library, and a computer lab. Each built environment was designed for specific social interactions, and students had a history in each environment that shaped their social actions.

A fourth construct that you will find helpful when conducting mediated discourse analysis is attention structure. Jones (2005) argues that people construct sites of engagement through "fairly durable patterns of orientation towards different spaces and timescales" (p. 151), which he refers to as attention structures. Furthermore, Jones argues that these attention structures are partially "built into" the mediational means and physical surroundings (discourses-in-place), social practices and norms of interaction (interaction order), and the histories of individuals (habitus). People draw on attention structures as mediational means to bring particular cultural tools into focus to take social action. This is related to Lankshear and Knobel's (2002) consideration of how the distribution and management of attention occur within an attention economy. They argue that attention is not an individual, cognitive attribute but, rather, a social commodity that is granted, withheld, or sought in social interaction. Furthermore, they consider what attention structures are required to organize and maintain attention within and across different attention economies.

Attention structures are a very useful heuristic for determining when a site of engagement opens and closes or shifts in some way and for marking the boundaries of where a literacy event begins and where it ends. A consideration of how people draw on their attention structures to take social action mediated by the interaction order, the discourses-in-place, and their individual habitus provides you with a way to select literacy events for mediated discourse analysis and a way to parse the lines or segments of your transcription scheme.

Mediated discourse analysis transcription scheme. There is no standardized transcription scheme used by mediated discourse analysts. However, there are some important considerations to make when adapting this method for your study. Because mediated discourse analysis gives analytic primacy to mediated action, the first or second column of the transcript is typically reserved for a description and analysis of the social action taken and the relevant mediational means. The purpose of placing mediated action within one of the leftmost columns is to privilege (Ochs, 1999) social action as the first consideration in the analysis and the second is the role of discourse as mediational means in that action. In the following, I review three mediated discourse analysis transcription schemes from different studies.

In Wohlwend's (2007) study of literacy play in a kindergarten classroom, mediated discourse analysis is used to identify how the children's social practices were transformed through social actions that involved talk, body position, gesture, and manipulation of books and toys, all of which shaped the meaning of objects, texts, and children's identities. Wohlwend's (2007) mediated discourse transcription scheme of a selected play event includes the following columns for analysis: action/context, talk at each turn, classroom identity, play identity, effect on meaning, effect on participation. The transcript is parsed with lines by the turns the children were taking within the play event (see Wohlwend, 2007, p. 383). The first column used for analysis includes not only the mediated actions that the children took but also descriptions of the cultural tools. The second analytic column includes the spoken discourse of the children, which mediates their actions in part. The next two columns are reserved for analysis of the different identities the children are enacting within the social actions. The last two columns include analysis of the effects of the social actions on the shifts in meaning and participation. Across mediated discourse analysis of selected play events such as this one, Wohlwend makes inductions about the different discourses at work and their social consequences for the children engaged in this literacy play.

In Wargo and Clayton's (2018) investigation of secondary students' video production as a form of civic engagement, they employ mediated discourse analysis to "make visible the creative tensions surrounding youths' individual, group, and cultural identities" (p. 6). Their mediated discourse transcription scheme employs the following columns for analysis: mediated action, transcribed talk, site of engagement, and social positioning. The transcript is parsed with rows marked by shifts in the site of engagement and mediated action (see Figure 4.1).

Video Time	Mediated Action	Transcribed Talk	Sites of Engagement	Social Positioning
12:05	Wargo sits across from Monica and Justyna, who sit in front of computer-editing stations	**Wargo:** So, tell me a little bit about your project. Just sort of like the topic, the questions when you first started?	Monica takes up Wargo's proposed face-to-face interaction and looks at audio recorder. Justyna shifts her attention away from the group.	Wargo is across from Monica and Justyna. Monica and Justyna share the position as listener and sharing group members.
12:11	Monica turns to look at Justyna and then to Wargo.	**Monica:** OK, our topic is gun violence. Our main question was, how do we show that it's affecting young Black people's lives and like with Justyna (looks at Justyna), she	Justyna removes herself from interaction order. Monica sustains face-to-face interview interaction.	Monica maintains her position as listener. Justyna resists.

Figure 4.1. Mediated discourse analysis transcript from Wargo and Clayton (2018)

Source: Wargo, J. M., & Clayton, K. (2018). From PSAs to reel communities: Exploring the sounds and silences of urban youth mobilizing digital media production. *Learning, Media and Technology,* 43(4), 1–16, p. 12. Reprinted by permission of the publisher (Taylor & Francis Ltd, http://www.tandfonline.com).

In keeping with the conventions of mediated discourse analysis, Wargo and Clayton (2018) reserve the first analytic column for mediated action. The second column includes the talk that mediates, in part, the social action in the first column. The third column considers how the site of engagement is unfolding in relation to the social actions taken and shifts in attention structure and interaction order. The fourth column considers the social positioning unfolding among the participants. Wargo and Clayton's (2018) use of mediated discourse analysis allowed them to partially understand how the participants were making sense of their video production in relation to broader discourses related to civic engagement.

In my study of collaborative writing, I used mediated discourse analysis to consider selected literacy events that were illustrative of the participants' social interactions with one another and literacy practices they enacted in relation to the ones the teacher was attempting to support (see Figure 4.2). In keeping with mediated discourse analysis conventions, my first column of analysis is reserved for mediated action, including shifts in proxemics and gaze, as well as cultural tools. The third column is a transcription of the spoken discourse during the social action. The fourth column includes details related to the multiple sites of engagement, marked primarily by shifts in interaction order and attention structure. Changes in the sites of engagement also marked the parsing of the rows in the transcript. The last column is reserved for social positioning, which helped me to understand shifts in the participants' identities within and across events. See Rish (2015) for findings related to this transcript.

Video Time	Mediated Action	Transcribed Talk	Sites of Engagement	Social Positioning
26:05	Erika looks back at Zina. Nico looks away from the group.	**Zina:** And now, um, they can travel and stuff, but like the ancient Senoves is what keeps, um, Speir afloat because they do like an infinite dance sort of deal under it which keeps Speir afloat. But then the down dirt Senoves, they're, they are free of that, um,	Erika again takes up Zina's proposed face-to-face interaction order. Nico shifts his attention away from the group.	Erika and Zina resume their positioning as listener and sharing group member, respectively.
	Nico turns to look at Zina and Erika. Zina is facing Erika and Nico. Erika briefly looks at her screen at Nico's wiki page, "Thesis history."	**Zina:** Sort of like link or whatever. **Erika:** Mm Hmm. **Zina:** Like they are not bound to forever dance. **Erika:** Yeah. **Zina:** So they, they can't travel, or go down and travel on Thesis, and when they travel they are like shadows, which I used that whole idea for these guys.	Erika and Zina maintain their interaction order; Erika shifts her attention momentarily to her screen. Nico shares the site of engagement briefly.	Erika and Zina maintain their positioning as listener and sharing group member, respectively. Though, Erika's attention is divided.

Figure 4.2. Mediated discourse analysis transcript

This transcription scheme allowed me to understand how the mediated actions taken by the participants shaped the negotiation among literacy practices at work, including the literacy practices each participant brought along to the project, as well as the literacy practices they enacted as a result of their negotiation through the collaborative writing process. I also was able to consider how identity as social positioning developed across events and shaped the social actions that were taken. Ultimately, understanding social actions on the micro level provided necessary detail for understanding how literacy practices were related to one another on the macro level to form a particular nexus of practice. Knowing how and why the collaborative writing was produced in the way it was helped reveal the complexities involved when students are asked to negotiate literacy practices that are new to them.

Your Future MDA Study

Hopefully this overview of MDA methodology and the two methods of nexus analysis and mediated discourse analysis will provide you with some guidelines for designing your study. The processes and procedures outlined in this chapter represent a selection of the range of concepts and activities detailed by the researchers who developed MDA (Norris & Jones, 2005; Scollon & Scollon, 2004). I argue that this selection provides a useful methodology for conducting New Literacy Studies research (see also Stornaiuolo, Smith, & Phillips, 2016). The reconceptualization of a literacy event as multiple sites of engagement opens many possibilities for analysis and addresses many concerns New Literacy Studies scholars have held about the original construct of literacy event as defined by patterned predictability. The reconceptualization of relationships among literacy practices as a nexus of practice helps mobilize the construct of literacy practice as situated within particular contexts to a consideration of how literacy practices are negotiated and enacted within and across sites of engagement that are not necessarily bound by social domains and group membership. This chapter provides a guide for designing your own MDA study; however, you should feel encouraged to use this chapter as an overview to orient you to the more in-depth descriptions and field guides that you should carefully consider. See the following list of suggested further reading.

Suggested Further Reading

Norris, S. (2004). *Analyzing multimodal interaction: A methodological framework*. London, England: Routledge.

Norris, S., & Jones, R. H. (Eds.). (2005). *Discourse in action: Introducing mediated discourse analysis*. London, England: Routledge.

Scollon, R. (2001a). Action and text: Towards an integrated understanding of the place of text in social (inter)action, mediated discourse analysis and the problem of social action. In R. Wodak & M. Meyer (Eds.), *Methods of critical discourse analysis* (pp. 139–183). Los Angeles, CA: Sage Publications.

Scollon, R. (2001b). *Mediated discourse: The nexus of practice*. New York, NY: Routledge.

Scollon, R., & Scollon, S. (2004). *Nexus analysis: Discourse and the emerging Internet*. New York, NY: Routledge.

References

Albright, J., & Luke, A. (Eds.). (2008). *Pierre Bourdieu and literacy education*. London, England: Routledge.

Bakhtin, M. M. (1981). *The dialogic imagination* (C. Emerson, & M. Holquist, Trans.). Austin: University of Texas Press.

Barton, D. (2009). Understanding textual practices in a changing world. In M. Baynham & M. Prinsloo (Eds.), *The future of literacy studies* (pp. 38–53). New York, NY: Palgrave Macmillan.

Baynham, M., & Prinsloo, M. (2009). Introduction: The future of literacy studies. In M. Baynham & M. Prinsloo (Eds.), *The future of literacy studies* (pp. 1–20). New York, NY: Palgrave Macmillan.

Bloome, D., & Bailey, F. (1992). Studying language and literacy through events, particularity, and intertextuality. In R. Beach, J. L. Green, M. L. Kamil, & T. Shanahan (Eds.), *Multidisciplinary perspectives on literacy research* (pp. 181–210). Urbana, IL: NCTE.

Bloome, D., Carter, S. P., Christian, B. M., Otto, S., & Shuart-Faris, N. (2005). *Discourse analysis and the study of classroom language and literacy events: A microethnographic perspective*. Mahwah, NJ: Erlbaum.

Bourdieu, P. (1977). *Outline of a theory of practice*. London, England: Cambridge University Press.

Brandt, D., & Clinton, K. (2002). Limits of the local: Expanding perspectives on literacy as a social practice. *Journal of Literacy Research, 34*, 337–356.

Burnett, C., & Merchant, G. (2018). Literacy-as-event: Accounting for relationality in literacy research. *Discourse: Studies in the Cultural Politics of Education*. https://doi.org/10.1080/01596306.2018.1460318

Coiro, J., Knobel, M., Lankshear, C., & Leu, D. J. (2008). Central issues in new literacies and new literacies research. In J. Corio, M. Knobel, C. Lankshear, & D. J. Leu (Eds.), *Handbook of research on new literacies* (pp. 1–22). New York, NY: Routledge.

Engeström, Y. (1987). *Learning by expanding: An activity-theoretical approach to developmental research*. Helsinki, Sweden: Orienta-Konsultit.

Goff, B., & Rish, R. (2019). What's brought along and brought about: Negotiating writing practices in two high school classrooms. *Learning, Culture, and Social Interaction*. https://doi.org/10.1016/j.lcsi.2019.02.016

Goffman, E. (1983). The interaction order: American Sociological Association, 1982 presidential address. *American Sociological Review, 48*, 1–17.

Heath, S. B. (1983). *Ways with words*. New York, NY: Cambridge University Press.

Jones, R. H. (2005). Sites of engagement as sites of attention: Time, space and culture in electronic discourse. In S. Norris & R. H. Jones (Eds.), *Discourse in action: Introducing mediated discourse analysis* (pp. 141–154). London, England: Routledge.

Jones, R. H., & Norris, S. (2005). Introducing mediational means/cultural tools. In S. Norris & R. H. Jones (Eds.), *Discourse in action: Introducing mediated discourse analysis* (pp. 49–51). London, England: Routledge.

Lankshear, C., & Knobel, M. (2002). Do we have your attention? New literacies, digital technologies, and the education of adolescents. In D. Alvermann (Ed.), *Adolescents and literacies in a digital world* (pp. 19–39). New York, NY: Peter Lang.

Leander, K. M., & McKim, K. K. (2003). Tracing the everyday 'sitings' of adolescents on the Internet: A strategic adaptation of ethnography across online and offline spaces. *Education, Communication & Information, 3*, 211–240.

Leont'ev, A. N. (1978). *Activity, consciousness, and personality* (M. J. Hall, Trans.). Englewood Cliffs, NJ: Prentice Hall.

Maybin, J. (2000). The New Literacy Studies: Context, intertextuality and discourse. In D. Barton, M. Hamilton, & R. Ivanič (Eds.), *Situated literacies: Reading and writing in context* (pp. 197–209). New York, NY: Routledge.

Nishida, K. (1958). *Intelligibility and the philosophy of nothingness*. Tokyo, Japan: Maruzen.

Norris, S. (2004). *Analyzing multimodal interaction: A methodological framework*. London, England: Routledge.

Norris, S., & Jones, R. H. (Eds.). (2005). *Discourse in action: Introducing mediated discourse analysis*. London, England: Routledge.

Ochs, E. (1999). Transcription as theory. In A. Jaworski & N. Coupland (Eds.), *The discourse reader* (pp. 166–178). London, England: Routledge.

Prior, P. (2006). A sociocultural theory of writing. In C. A. MacArthur, S. Graham, & J. Fitzgerald (Eds.), *Handbook of writing research* (pp. 54–66). New York, NY: Guilford Press.

Rish, R. M. (2015). Researching writing events: Using mediated discourse analysis to explore how students write together. *Literacy, 49*(1), 12–19.

Rish, R. M. (2017). Mediated discourse analysis. In K. Peppler (Ed.), *The SAGE encyclopedia of out-of-school learning* (pp. 476–479). Thousand Oaks, CA: Sage Publications.

Rish, R. M., & Caton, J. (2011). Building worlds together with collaborative writing: Creative, social, and pedagogic challenges. *English Journal, 100*(5), 21–28.

Scollon, R. (2001a). Action and text: Towards an integrated understanding of the place of text in social (inter)action, mediated discourse analysis and the problem of social action. In R. Wodak & M. Meyer (Eds.), *Methods of critical discourse analysis* (pp. 139–183). Los Angeles, CA: Sage Publications.

Scollon, R. (2001b). *Mediated discourse: The nexus of practice*. New York, NY: Routledge.

Scollon, R., & Scollon, S. (2004). *Nexus analysis: Discourse and the emerging Internet*. New York, NY: Routledge.

Stornaiuolo, A., Smith, A., & Phillips, N.C. (2016). Developing a transliteracies framework for a connected world. *Journal of Literacy Research, 49*(1), 68–91.

Street, B. (1995). *Social literacies: Critical approaches to literacy in development, ethnography, and education*. London, England: Longman.

Wargo, J. M., & Clayton, K. (2018). From PSAs to reel communities: Exploring the sounds and silences of urban youth mobilizing digital media production. *Learning, Media and Technology, 43*(4), 1–16.

Wertsch, J. V. (1994). The primacy of mediated action in sociocultural studies. *Mind, Culture, and Activity, 1*, 202–208.

Wertsch, J. V. (1998). *Mind as action*. London, England: Oxford University Press.

Wohlwend, K. E. (2007). Reading to play and playing to read: A mediated discourse analysis of early literacy apprenticeship. In D. W. Rowe (Ed.), *56th yearbook of the National Reading Conference* (pp. 377–393). Chicago, IL: National Reading Conference.

Wohlwend, K. E. (2014). Mediated discourse analysis: Tracking discourse in action. In P. Albers, T. Holbrook, & A. S. Flint (Eds.), *New methods in literacy research* (pp. 56–69). New York, NY: Routledge.

CHAPTER 5

Exploring Multimodal Literacy in Language Teaching and Learning

Ingrid K. Jakobsen and Elise Seip Tønnessen

IN THIS CHAPTER, we present the research method we used to investigate multimodal literacy in an English-language classroom in a Norwegian lower secondary school. The analytic approach we present combines multimodal analysis with a design-oriented view on learning as a social meaning-making process. The analysis is applied in a small-scale qualitative study of multimodality and literacy in an English as a foreign language (EFL) classroom in Norway. In what follows, we present how we dealt with observations, interviews, and learning materials from work with the novel *The Absolutely True Diary of a Part-Time Indian* (Alexie, 2007) in a Year 10 classroom. In particular, this chapter aims to demonstrate the process from data to multimodal analysis and go behind the scenes of writing it up. Multimodality serves the double role as an object of study *and* an analytical approach.

Ingrid visited this classroom as part of her PhD research, and Elise, as one of her supervisors, followed her empirical work closely and took part in analyzing the material and in co-writing the journal article this chapter builds on. Hence, when Ingrid writes "I," she refers to her experiences in the classroom. Otherwise, we present ourselves as "we," referring to numerous discussions in our joint efforts to make sense of the processes observed and documented. The finished article, "A Design-Oriented Analysis of Multimodality in English as a Foreign Language" (Jakobsen & Tønnessen, 2018), was published in *Designs for Learning*, a Scandinavian open-access journal.

We start by tracing how the research idea began. An interest in images in texts used in English literature teaching led Ingrid to the seminal book *Reading Images* by Kress and van Leeuwen (2006). In this thorough introduction to multimodality, Kress and van Leeuwen point out that "most texts now involve a complex interplay of written text, images and other graphic or sound elements, designed as coherent . . . entities" (p. 17). They are quite uncompromising in their characterization of the consequences of overlooking multimodality as part of literacy:

> But the skill of producing multimodal texts of this kind, however central its role in contemporary society, is not taught in schools. To put this point harshly, in terms of this essential new communication ability, this new "visual literacy," institutional education, under the pressure of often reactionary political demands, produces illiterates. (Kress & van Leeuwen, 2006, p. 17)

This same year, in 2006, a new national curriculum in Norway introduced multimodality as a main area of focus in the subject Norwegian (as first language/mother tongue). The curriculum referred to an expanded notion of text where writing, sound, and images work together in making meaning and gave a series of examples, including comics, advertising, web pages, and film (Norwegian Directorate for Education and Training, 2006). More generally, this curriculum has been coined a "literacy reform" (Berge, 2005), since basic skills such as reading, writing, and numeracy were highlighted across the curriculum. Hence, literacy and multimodality were regarded in this curriculum development as important characteristics that were connected explicitly for the mother tongue subject Norwegian but only implicitly in other subjects.

In *Reading Images*, Kress and van Leeuwen (2006) present a metalanguage for exploring multimodal communication that also has inspired systematic exploration of other modes beyond images. This opened up my (Ingrid's) thinking about personal experiences as a student and, later, as a teacher. I felt that the English subject area was evidently multimodal in spite of the high status of written language in schools. I decided I wanted to know more about multimodality, and rumors that curriculum revisions in 2013 would bring multimodal texts into the English language subject—as mentioned earlier, already present in the Norwegian language subject—further motivated and spurred on my research project. After first contemplating a research design based on interventions, I decided that I could not attempt to change a practice that, in fact, was little researched from a multimodal point of view. I chose to begin, therefore, by asking, "What role does multimodality play in the English language subject area?" The Norwegian language subject curriculum employed a translated and slightly modified version of the expression "multimodal texts," and to maintain a wide scope, I decided to focus on multimodal literacy. Literacy is basic to education, "enabling individuals to achieve their goals, to develop their knowledge and potential, and to participate fully in their community and wider society" (UNESCO, 2004, p. 13). It not only involves texts but also includes the context in a way that not all approaches to textual analysis encompass to the same extent.

Multimodal Literacy

Our approach to literacy is inspired by perspectives commonly known as New Literacy Studies, resting on a basic understanding that literacy is a social practice (Barton & Hamilton, 2000; Street, n.d.). This entails that our relations to texts—what they mean, how they can be used, and why one should bother about texts in the first place—are shaped and developed by the settings in which we live and learn. Another, and related, inspiration comes from The New London Group, an international group of scholars who met in New London (New Hampshire), in 1994, and produced a manifesto on the need for what they called "a pedagogy of multiliteracies" (New London Group, 1996, p. 60). The group's main argument was related to a changing context for literacy: In an increasingly globalized world, the normal state of affairs is multilingual and multicultural. At the same time, digital technologies change the way we communicate and the kind of texts we "read" and produce. One major change is through making modes other than writing, such as images and sound, available on the same technological platform. In this context, there is a need for a more diverse understanding of communication and meaning making. This is the rationale for introducing the plural term *multiliteracies* (New London Group, 1996, p. 64).

In search for a perspective that would be open to change and sensitive to practice, the New London Group introduced the term *design* in their metalanguage about literacy. One of the members, Gunther Kress, argues for design as a forward-looking concept in his book, *Literacy in the New Media Age*:

> Design does not ask "what was done before, how, for whom, with what?" Design asks, "what is needed now, in this one situation, with this configuration of purposes, aims, audience, *and with these resources*, and given *my* interests in this situation?" (Kress, 2003, p. 49, emphasis in original)

The New London Group sees design as a process where any literacy event makes use of *available design*. Examples may be not only semiotic resources such as the words and images we find in *The Absolutely True Diary of a Part-Time Indian* (Alexie, 2007) or technological resources made available on the computers all the students in the classroom we studied had access to but also conventions around the use of resources in a specific context. In the process of *designing* new meaning, the meaning-maker makes use of available design and transforms it for his or her purpose within a certain context. This results in the *redesigned*, a new meaning that more or less radically changes the patterns of meaning in use. In the next instance, the redesigned forms part of the available design for future acts of meaning making. This ensures a dynamic view of literacy and how it constantly changes in a social context that itself is also always changing (New London Group, 1996).

This rather abstract metalanguage has been taken into the classroom in Staffan Selander and Gunther Kress's (2010) book, *Designs for Learning: A Multimodal Perspective* (our translation; a short account in English can be found in Kress & Selander, 2012). Here they distinguish between the teacher's design *for* learning and the students' design *in* learning. Design *for* learning on one (cultural) level includes plans and curricula, the practical organization of schools, textbooks and learning materials, and systems of evaluation and assessment. These norms, conventions, and preconditions frame the next level, which we are interested in: The activity in the classroom, which is designed in the teacher's lesson plan. Her choice of the literary text, of how to present it and her design of learning activities and tasks for the students, is all part of her design *for* learning. She is not, however, the only one to influence what is going on in the classroom. The students are offered what the teacher makes available in the classroom, but they make their own choices as to what they take in and how they answer the tasks given (or avoid answering them). In their act of design *in* learning, they transform the resources made available to them into knowledge they find interesting and relevant and, eventually, take away as new knowledge. We found this notion of design *for* and *in* learning interesting since it created a space for seeing the activities in the classroom from the perspective of the teacher and the learners, respectively. Selander and Kress (2010) include a third element that they call *signs of learning*. This is connected to assessment and involves what is valued and recognized as knowledge and learning in a particular context (Kress & Selander, 2012). What the teacher emphasizes in her assessment will at all times influence how and what the students choose to produce for assessment, and assessment affects both design *for* learning and design *in* learning.

Multimodal Studies of English in a Classroom Context

An often-referred-to classroom study is *English in Urban Classrooms: A Multimodal Perspective on Teaching and Learning* (Kress et al., 2005), conducted in the United Kingdom. In spite of the differences one must be aware of between English taught as a first language and English as a second or foreign language, there is plenty of inspiration to find in this study in terms of method as well as findings. The book reports from a large research project in which three English classrooms are analyzed from a range of different multimodal perspectives, such as classroom layout, displays on walls, voice, time, texts, and gaze and position in interaction, to name a few. In addition, the context, social aspects, and policy documents are taken into account in the analysis and discussion. The units of analysis vary from large teaching units to just a few seconds of classroom interaction in lessons. Among the findings is that English in school is in transition "from being a subject that deals with values-as-meaning, into one in which meanings are becoming curricularized as knowledge" (Kress et al., 2005, p. 166). In terms of policy and education, this is a very interesting finding that deals with the overall question of what the English school subject (whether as a foreign language or not) is, can be, and ought to be. Another important aspect of the study is to show what a multimodal approach is able to accomplish. Findings from the studies in the book show that a multimodal perspective can uncover aspects that research on spoken or written language alone would not have done, such as how teachers adapt to the (perceived) ability of students without them stating this explicitly or how classroom wall displays shape learning, to give two examples.

Another important and inspiring publication is Jewitt's book (2006) *Technology, Literacy and Learning: A Multimodal Approach*. Jewitt poses important questions about how digital technology shapes education. Multimodal data collection, transcription, and analyses are at the heart of this study, and video observation is one of the methods used and discussed. Jewitt looks at pedagogy as design, and one of the aspects she examines is the use of CD-ROMs in English classes. She finds that digital technology does have an impact on pedagogic practices for both teachers and students and concludes that seeing both as designers of meaning can open things up for further pedagogic development.

Ethnographic Exploration: How It Looks in Practice

To find out more about the role of multimodality in EFL teaching in Norway, we decided to use an ethnographic approach and make observations of classroom practice. One reason behind this choice was the fact that we were looking at a phenomenon that is not explicitly embedded in the curriculum (Norwegian Directorate for Education and Training, 2013). We hypothesized that the lack of a common language and understanding of multimodal texts and multimodal literacy might render other research approaches, such as surveys or interviews, without attention to context difficult. After a pilot study (i.e., observation and interviews in a local school), Ingrid proceeded to collect data in two different schools. She observed two Year 10 classrooms (students at 15 to 16 years of age), which is the final year of obligatory education in Norway. We chose the second of these two classrooms as a case study for analysis in our published article, as it constituted a longer but still clearly delimited period of reading a novel in full. We elaborate on data collection in the next section.

Aiming to better understand the role of multimodality in the literacy practice of English in Norway, looking at lessons that were authentic, everyday lessons was important. The sampling of this school was purposeful in the sense that it was based on Ingrid's previous knowledge of the school and the teacher as being open to research but otherwise representative of the "common" that can be found in many places in Norway. The researcher stressed that the teacher was not to make any modifications or adapt anything for the researcher but to continue with teaching as planned. The novel the teacher had chosen is in itself multimodal and contains so many drawings that it comes close to the genre of graphic novel. The unit plan extended over seven hour-long lessons including an introductory lecture by the teacher, silent individual reading, and activities such as writing a reading log and constructing and playing a Kahoot quiz about the novel. At the end of this unit, the students handed in a written product and took part in an oral conversation for assessment. This range of possible data well suited our multimodal analytic approach, which may be applied on different scales, from a large-scale view on the modes of communication in classroom interaction over time to zooming in at one particular text, such as a student assignment produced within this larger context. Indeed, for a satisfying empirical approach, I wanted to make sure my data covered both large and small-scale perspectives.

For the collection or construction of data, I decided to use observation, interviews, and artifact collection. First, a simple observation form guided my attention during my presence in the classroom, complemented with head-mounted cameras and one fixed camera that captured the whole classroom. There were two head-mounted cameras, and one boy and one girl were picked randomly among volunteers in the class to wear them during each lesson. Texts used and produced were also collected. All the students and their parents had given informed consent to participate, and the study was registered and approved by the relevant authorities. After the observation period, the students were interviewed, two at a time. As a prompt, the students were shown a still picture of the most prominent activity captured on film while they were wearing head cameras and were asked to describe and comment on the scene and what was taking place. We chose to audio record the interviews, rather than capture them on video, to make the situation more informal and to make the power-balance differential and affective filter as low as possible. Finally, when the observation period was finished, the teacher was also interviewed. She was given the interview questions beforehand to help her prepare, and the interview was conducted in Norwegian—again with the aim of leveling out a possible imbalance of power between this teacher and the researcher. As with the students, this interview was audio recorded.

Transcription and Handling Data

After observing the classroom through a period of 4 weeks, we ended up with a variety of data, as you often do in qualitative research. The data may seem overwhelming, especially when the approach is open (in new fields in which you may not know precisely what you are looking for). We applied an ethnographic approach to study one case in depth, which meant that we tried to gather as much information as possible about what was going on in the classroom during the period the class was reading *The Absolutely True Diary of a Part-Time Indian* (Alexie, 2007). A crucial moment in qualitative research is when you are moving from collecting/constructing data into analyzing that data. Now it is time to turn back to the research questions and theoretical framework you started with. In some cases, it is also time to adjust the research question(s) because you now know more about what sorts of questions your material may be able to answer.

Transcription is not neutral, and the analysis inevitably starts with the way researchers handle their data material. We had an overall aim of examining what role multimodality plays in the English subject, and working toward more specific research questions, we started by mapping out our data. All our observation forms were coded in several cycles, first, looking at modes in play, then at the interplay between modes, and finally, by considering whether the observations could be characterized as prereading, while-reading, or postreading learning activities.

Planning to code the video recordings in a similar fashion as the observation forms, we watched all the recordings. Initially projected to be a central part of the data, it turned out the video material would rather serve as backing. Several episodes of interest could have been subjected to detailed multimodal analysis. We could have decided to take a close look at fragments of interaction in the classroom. Prompted by what we had seen from the observation forms, however, we decided to take a bird's-eye view on the video material, using it to support and expand the observation notes. The intention when entering the classroom was to learn more about the literacy practices they were engaging in, and by not going into depth on instances of interaction and keeping a larger perspective, we could say more about the design *for* and *in* learning (cf. Selander & Kress, 2010).

Next, the interviews were transcribed. Translation from Norwegian to English worked as a way of defamiliarizing the researcher from the context, as well as having the effect of making the researcher "taste" each word more carefully in the process. This was not an issue in the article but is worth keeping in mind for people who write and publish in a second language. The interviews were not coded. Rather, statements that could shed more light on the observations were highlighted. So were statements that "stood out." Generally, the interviews were important in how they allowed access to the thinking behind the spoken and written products of the students.

All the teaching material was collected, including the written assignments of students who consented to share their essays for research purposes. When we looked at these, we decided to go into depth and apply multimodal analysis to these essays. For one, the essays showed signs of learning that were more accessible than those from the video recordings. Moreover, we observed that some of the students had decided to use images, a mode not required by the teacher but one that the medium of the computer made available to them and that they chose to use. This incongruity kindled our interest. As with the observation forms, we approached the texts by tracing modes and interplay between modes. We looked at choice of image, positioning of image and writing in terms of layout, and the meaning communications of the multimodal ensembles.

After we had organized the observations, we could connect our interview material to the events we were particularly interested in studying. We had interviewed the teacher about her design of the whole unit, and we had interviewed some of the students. Moreover, we had the students' explanations in their essays. This provided additional understanding of how the teacher and students, respectively, might have motivated their activities and literacy practices. For us, identifying tensions between the teacher's design *for* learning and the students' design *in* learning would be of interest to a discussion of the role multimodality plays in the language classroom.

Choosing the Analytical Focus

As mentioned earlier, we established early on that our theoretical framework was New Literacy Studies and that we wanted to view what we experienced in the classroom from a multimodal design-oriented perspective. The New Literacy Studies framework entails an understanding of literacy as a social practice, where the context in which you engage with texts, and the purpose for doing so, are fundamental for understanding what is going on. The design-oriented perspective made us aware that different agents were acting in this classroom and that the teacher and her students may have been driven by different interests and have had different understandings of what is going on.

In examining the data material and mapping it out as described earlier, it quickly emerged that multimodal practices played an integral role in this English classroom and that these practices were not the same from the teacher's and the students' points of view. This led to the following research questions: In what way does multimodality come into play, first, in the teacher's design for learning including her choice of learning materials and second, in the students' design in learning?

The teacher's design *for* learning could be studied from her lesson plans and supplemented by our observations of how it was executed in the classroom, as well as from her motivations and reflections expressed in her interview responses. We found the tasks she gave to her students particularly interesting from a design-oriented perspective because these could be studied in a direct connection to how the students actually responded to the tasks. Observing what the students *did* in response to the learning content presented and the tasks given by the teacher gave us a chance to study the students' design *in* learning. Because we wanted to study the multimodal literacy practices in this EFL classroom, we needed to take into account both what the teacher had meant to happen and what the students actually did.

Practices are not directly observable. Practices are patterns of behavior, habits, and ways of doing things that are established over time through repeated experiences with reading and writing, or making meaning from semiotic resources, as one would say within a multimodal framework. What *can* be observed are events in the classroom. We therefore found the terms *literacy practice* and *literacy event* (Barton & Hamilton, 2000) from New Literacy Studies useful as we approached our data analysis.

Analysis entails simplification to get a clear view of patterns in the material. To make sure this does not happen in a random way, we needed to find ways to organize and systematize our data. We decided to map out the literacy events we had observed in the classroom. As a working definition, we decided to call any activity that involved interactions with text (understood multimodally) a literacy event. Because events unfold in time, we anticipated that it could be useful to look into a time sequence that included pre- and postwork as well as the actual time spent with the text in question. In the classroom we observed, we encountered several texts. First and foremost was the literary text, *The Absolutely True Diary of a Part-Time Indian* (Alexie, 2007), which was present during all 4 weeks of observation. In addition to this novel, there were other texts produced by the teacher as well as by the students. The teacher's unit plan expressed her designs *for* learning. It related to overarching documents such as the national curriculum with its aims and outcomes for the teaching of English on an institutional level. It also related to the novel and expressed the teacher's understanding of what it could afford for the teaching of English in her classroom. The students received the unit plan along with a copy of the novel, giving them an opportunity to prepare for working with the novel. Hence, the novel and the unit plan were texts on an overarching level, relevant all through the period we observed.

On a more detailed level, we found texts and activities limited to single lessons. The teacher's initial presentation of the novel and its author was densely multimodal, including meaning-making resources such as images, video, and written text in a digital presentation, which supplemented her oral discourse/lecture. An important text in her design for learning was the task she formulated for the students' written essays. These essays were one of the main textual contributions from the students' side, in which they could voice their responses to the novel. In addition, there was the oral conversation, or literature circle, about the novel, where the teacher and the students met in dialogue. The students also engaged in two other literacy events during their reading of the novel: They kept a written reading log, and they designed questions and answers for a Kahoot quiz they played in class.

Accordingly, based on the texts we had observed in the classroom, we could organize our observations into a series of literacy events, including agents and activities, as follows:

- Planning the sequence of lessons in a unit plan (teacher)
- Reading the novel (teacher and students)
- Presenting the novel and the author (production by teacher, reception by students)
- Writing a reading log (students individually)
- Designing questions and answers about the novel for a Kahoot quiz (students individually, assembled by the teacher)
- Playing Kahoot quiz (students collectively)

- Designing tasks for the students' written assignments (teacher)
- Writing the assignments (students individually)
- Oral conversation about the novel (teacher and students collectively)

During this sorting out of the material, it became clear that delineating a literacy event is not always straightforward. One question is where one event ends and the next one starts because events may overlap in different ways. We found that pre- and post-work with the text often linked to other literacy events. In fact, we found that literacy events often piggybacked on each other in a coherent didactic design, where one event may prepare for the next, as the preparation of questions and answers prepared for the common experience of playing Kahoot. In other cases, literacy events go on over time, intertwined with other events, as in the case of reading the novel and writing a log. Another challenge was that texts can appear in events on different levels. In our case, the most prominent example was the novel, *The Absolutely True Diary of a Part-Time Indian* (Alexie, 2007), which was the object of study all through the sequence we studied. Thus, it was, in some sense, part of all the other events. To try to obtain an overview of events and levels, we constructed a model. It started with overlapping circles showing the different learning activities. Initially we used it as a thinking tool to outline the kinds of literacy events we had observed. Next, we found that using cogwheels allowed for a better representation of what we saw. The model shows, visually, how the events were connected and therefore dependent on each other (see Figure 5.1).

To face the challenge of levels we turned to theory again. Qualitative research (in contrast to quantitative research) is informed by theory all the way through. The theoretical framework is not just where you start when you design your project; it also guides your observations, your categorizations, your analysis, and your discussion. Jay Lemke, who has worked extensively with language in didactic contexts, has presented the notion of *time scales* as a tool to analyze different levels of activity and how they are connected. He starts one article with the intriguing question, "How do *moments* add up to *lives*?" (Lemke 2000, p. 273). In complex systems, the fundamental unit of analysis is a process, he claims, and in studies of people's meaning-making activities, these processes must be understood as part of a larger eco-social system (Lemke, 2000, p. 275). His example is from a science classroom, and his advice is to analyze scale hierarchies in groups of three levels at once (Lemke, 2000, p. 276). In a subsequent interview, Lemke explains that

> the model is essentially a "sandwich" with three levels in which you put whatever level you are interested in in the middle, and then you look at least one level above it, meaning longer than it, and one level below, meaning shorter than it. The meanings that you make or the actions and activities you do that typically take place at the level in focus, are themselves organizations out of smaller activities and actions or units of words or sentences below, and they are subject to the constraints and affordances of the longer

term activities that are going on at the time. (Lemke, in Andersen, Boeriis, Maagerø, & Tønnessen, 2015, p. 124)

This model helped us stay true to the understanding that literacy events must always be understood in a greater context, and it helped us distinguish the processes (literacy events) we had observed as different levels of activity.

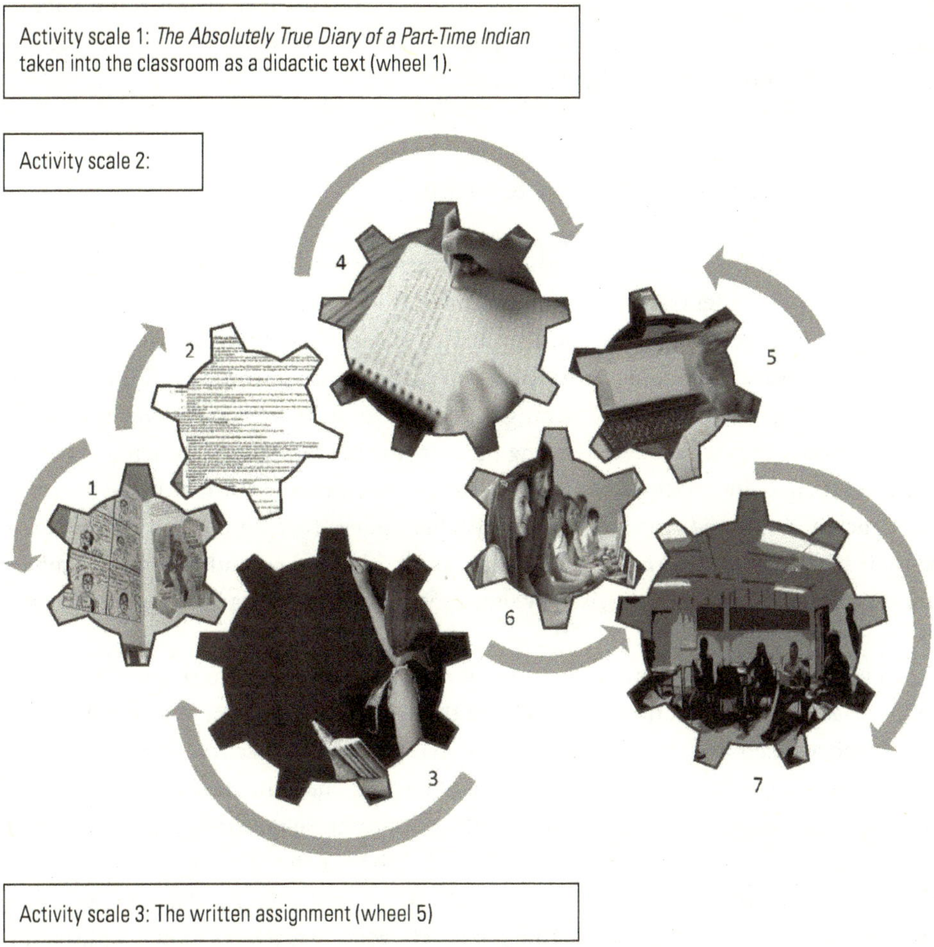

Figure 5.1: Cogwheel model of the sequence of literacy events

Source: From Jakobsen and Tønnessen (2018, p. 45).

Note: In Activity Scale 2, the numbers represent the following: (1) the novel, (2) the lesson plan and assignment, (3) the teacher's lecture, (4) the student logs, (5) creating the written assignment, (6) the interaction when the teacher helps the students with their written assignments, and (7) the conversation in a circle.

The weakness of the model we ended up with is that it is not straightforward; it must be studied to be understood. The strength of the model is (hopefully) that it quickly conveys the idea that past learning is affected by new learning, that is, it emphasizes the dynamic character of learning that never ends. Moreover, the model contains the idea that students in their design *in* learning will turn the wheels in their own personal manner; they will respond according to their interest. By bringing in time scales, we felt the model became even more precise, although the playfulness of the design was toned down. In the end, as our model developed, we decided to use it as an illustration of our thinking in the article we published (see Jakobsen & Tønnessen, 2018). We now turn to the part of the process of writing up our study.

Making Sense of the Analytic Results

The main findings in our study were that the teacher used varied multimodal designs to stimulate her students' motivation, understanding, and learning, and we found that she regarded these as valuable teaching tools. We also saw that the basis for assessment were linguistic products: writing and speaking. In other words, we found that the students were given a more limited range of modes for producing texts than the assortment of modes they were offered during the learning process. Many students, however, included images and placed them purposefully in their essays without being asked to. We concluded that the students and the teacher adhere to different cultural patterns in their social semiotic formations (Lemke, 2000). Images and multimodal ensembles are regarded differently in the literacy practices in designs *for* learning and in designs *in* learning.

In writing up the study we structured our analysis according to the model we had made, that is, in three sections to match the three time scales. First, we needed to present the novel itself and the affordances it carried for English teaching in a multimodal setting. Second, we analyzed the sequence of lessons and how they could be seen as representing the literacy practices of the EFL classroom seen from the perspective of the teacher and students, respectively. Third, for the shortest time scale, we selected the written assignment for more detailed analysis. One reason for this latter choice was that this activity represented a meeting point between the teacher's design *for* learning and the students' design *in* learning. Another was our previous knowledge of the school culture we were studying. We knew from previous research (e.g., Løvland, 2006, 2011) that Norwegian school culture tends to value written language in the sense that written texts are seen as particularly apt for conveying knowledge in both textbooks and student work. Within this cultural view of the world, teachers give their grades based on written work, and sometimes also on oral presentations, when the subject content is language learning. All the other things that are going on in the classroom—speaking, singing, drawing, gesturing, dramatizing and moving around, and so on—may be encouraged as supporting activities, but they are rarely considered part of the basis for assessment (Løvland, 2006). In this study, we wanted to find out how the multimodal ensemble functioned in the language classroom, and we anticipated that the teacher and the students might have different takes on that matter. This was why we decided to focus on the activity where the teacher's textual practice met the students' practices.

Multimodal Analysis of Students' Essays

We included copies of four selected student essays in the published article to show the layout and positioning of images. We reproduced them as blurred facsimiles to protect privacy. Three essays were on the topic of image and included the images they discussed. In addition, we chose to include a student essay (written by Julie) that was not about images but nonetheless used images to communicate multimodally. Our analysis of Julie's text can serve as an illustration of how a multimodal perspective on texts can give insights that go beyond what a text-focused analysis or evaluation shows. We interpret Julie's multimodal text as displaying an acute understanding of the novel, as well as complex communicative skills, despite some language slips. By highlighting the communicative competence that a multimodal approach to an essay can reveal, we wanted to exemplify what a multimodal approach to EFL can do.

In our article, the main focus was on the time scale of multimodal literacy practices in the classroom. In this chapter, we go more into depth in our analysis of Julie's understanding of the novel and her communicative skills.

In her introduction to multimodal analysis, Carey Jewitt (2014) refers to the linguist, M. A. K. Halliday, who saw language as realizing three metafunctions or types of meaning: *ideational* meaning representing our experiences in and of the world, *interpersonal* meaning about social relations between text and reader and within the text, and *textual* meaning, which organizes the text into a coherent whole (Jewitt, 2014, p. 25). In a multimodal text, the meaning comes forth as an interplay between the semiotic resources involved. In a school context, the most common combination is verbal language and images, which we find in textbooks, in the novel our students read, and in many of the students' written work. Both modes offer affordances for communicating meaning, and the way they are combined in the layout may extend and elaborate the meanings made by each mode (van Leeuwen, 2005, p. 230).

In Julie's book report (see Figure 5.2) images and words are combined to coherent *textual* meaning in a page design where the images are anchored or specified (van Leeuwen, 2005, p. 30; see also Barthes, 1977) by titles and captions. The book cover is inserted between the two text lines of the title, both representing the novel and introducing to the reader what the text is about. The drawing taken from the book accompanies Julie's cliffhanger question: "Will they ever be friends again? Or will Rowdy hate Arnold forever?" Finally, the image of the author is specified with the caption: "The book is written by Sherman Alexie." In this manner, Julie's written text is surrounded by elements expected in a book report: an introduction of the book and a reference to the author. We observe how her multimodal composition realizes the *textual* metafunction by creating coherence through such resources as *size* and *color* highlighting the title and book cover (both in matching green) as the visually most salient elements and connecting verbal and visual meaning through proximity.

Making the book itself prominent through layout allows Julie to proceed directly to what she finds most central in the novel on page 2, where she presents main plot points and central characters in her verbal text. Initially, she presents Arnold as the main character and guides the reader through plot points that she finds interesting. This is first summed up as "a lot of pain" and "some ups too" before more details are given: a potential love affair, friendship, deaths in Arnold's family, his father's problems with alcohol, bullying, health problems, and artistic aspirations. Central characters are mentioned: Arnold, Penelope, Arnold's best friend Rowdy, and Arnold's father. In a few sentences, Julie shows that she understands the two most prominent *ideational* dimensions of narrative fiction: events and characters (Chatman, 1978, p. 26). She also shows some sense

Figure 5.2: Modified pages of Julie's essay text

Note: This figure illustrates the placement of image and writing in Julie's layout. The original images are modified to prevent copyright infringement. Furthermore, Julie's text is blurred to the point of illegibility in accordance with the terms for consent to research.

of dramaturgy, leading her summary up to the central plot point where Arnold and Rowdy fall out and leaving the reader to wonder about how the conflict may be resolved. This dramaturgic peak is made even stronger because the situation is represented both verbally and visually, highlighted as a separate meaning cluster in the layout.

The *interpersonal* metafunction concerns the relations created both within the text and between text and reader. The relationships that Julie presents are of a kind that will be familiar to young readers: family, best friend, (potential) girlfriend, and schoolmates. This creates a relation of recognition for the reader. Julie's choice of images strengthens the interpersonal message. Both the image of Rowdy and the image of the author show an individual who looks directly at the viewer, calling for involvement.

Seeing Julie's book report as the result of a design process in the classroom makes asking what available design she has included and how she has recontextualized it in her redesign to create a new text interesting. She has combined the available design from the novel and that of the teacher's introductory lecture about Sherman Alexie with her own words in a text that responds to the task set by the teacher (i.e., to write a book report). Seeing genres as available design, Julie may know book reviews from other contexts. In the classroom, it is mainly an analytical genre expressed verbally, but it also resembles book reviews that Julie may know from newspapers, magazines, or web pages. The convention of presenting the book through an image of the cover may come from these kinds of contexts. So may the structure of the verbal text, which emphasizes presenting the plot without revealing the resolution of the conflict. This combination of available designs from contexts in and out of school may explain why Julie's text functions as an appetizer rather than an analysis with a conclusion.

As we have seen, a multimodal analysis of Julie's text in context may reveal her cultural repertoires of resources for literacy practices and how they may differ from cultural patterns expected in a school context. The teacher may focus on verbal language in her assessment of the written work, but a multimodal analysis that takes the whole range of meaning-making resources into consideration will reveal a broader picture of the potentials and shortcomings of Julie's literacy practices in the reception as well as the production of texts.

Ending up with an analysis of a fairly traditional writing task may seem a quite narrow outcome from the very rich material we generated across 4 weeks of observation. We could have made other choices, as discussed later. However, we find that an important point in our case study became to view this activity in light of the other levels of analysis: the choice of text and the design of lesson plans. In our context of teaching EFL, we also realized that the modes of written and spoken language were vital, in spite of our interest in multimodal communication. This understanding was rooted in curriculum documents at yet another level of context. At this point, we started getting a bigger picture of a complex interwoven structure of literacy events taking place within a school context ultimately governed and controlled by political documents.

The teacher, who follows curriculum guidelines, is a creative and highly skilled professional. Consequently, in our writing up for the article, it was important to clarify that our conclusion—namely, there is a multimodal potential, so to speak, that is not taken advantage of in this EFL classroom—is not a criticism of the teacher. Instead, our conclusion leads to a criticism of the policy documents that operate on the larger time scale and that emphasize written and spoken language as the significant signs of learning outcomes.

Concluding Reflections

What else could we have done with all the data our explorations generated? We could have focused on other literacy events, such as the teacher's introductory presentation or the students' oral activities, documented in detail with video cameras attached to the students' heads. The head-worn cameras show what the students looked at or in the direction of, and this gives a unique perspective on the interaction in the classroom with texts and with people. Another interesting perspective could be on the Kahoot quiz and how technological resources made the students collective designers of this learning activity. Alternatively, we could have chosen a more clear-cut perspective, viewing the classroom practices from either the teacher's or the students' vantage points. The students' perspective could, for instance, focus on their reception of the novel and how the images may have influenced their interpretation and supported their linguistic understanding. Indeed, the rich and varied data resulting from an empirical approach, all contributing to the understanding of multimodal communication in the EFL classroom, can be seen from several perspectives. On one hand, this requires critical reflections on the findings written out, compared to what might have appeared from a different perspective. On the other hand, it may be seen as part of the never-ending story of research, where every finding leads to new questions to explore.

Our findings contribute, on a general level, to the intersecting fields of literacy studies, multimodal studies, and educational studies. What we observed is similar to the conclusions of other studies both in Norway and internationally, in which teaching and learning activities include several modes in interaction, but the learning outcome is measured by written and spoken production. There is very little research on multimodality and EFL in Norway, and our article addresses this gap. We ended the article by calling for a change that would recognize multimodality in the curriculum. In this manner, we aimed to contribute to the level of policy development and, thereby, to changes in practices. Whether or not it is a response to our call, the latest curriculum revision (Norwegian Directorate for Education and Training, 2019), to be initiated from 2020, does bring in multimodal texts in English, and this time for production purposes, as well as for reading and learning.

Suggested Further Reading

Bezemer, J., & Kress, G. (2009). Visualizing English: A social semiotic history of a school subject. *Visual Communication, 8*(3), 247–262. https://doi.org/10.1177/1470357209106467

Kress, G. & Bezemer, J. (2016). *Multimodality, learning and communication: A social semiotic frame*. London, England: Routledge.

van Leeuwen, T. (2017). Multimodal literacy. *Viden om Literacy, 21*, 4–13. Retrieved from https://www.videnomlaesning.dk/media/2127/21_theo-van-leeuwen.pdf

References

Alexie, S. (2007). *The absolutely true diary of a part-time Indian*. New York, NY: Little, Brown.

Andersen, T. H., Boeriis, M., Maagerø, E., & Tønnesen, E. S. (Eds.). (2015). *Social semiotics: Key figures, new directions*. London, England: Routledge.

Barthes, R. (1977). Rhetoric of the image. In *Image-Music-Text* (S. Heath, Trans., pp. 32–51). London, England: Fontana Press.

Barton, D., & Hamilton, M. (2000). Literacy practices. In D. Barton, M. Hamilton, & R. Ivanič (Eds.), *Situated literacies: Reading and writing in context* (pp. 7–15). London, England: Routledge.

Berge, K. L. (2005). Skriving som grunnleggende ferdighet og som nasjonal prøve – ideologi og strategier [Writing as a basic skill and as a national test: Ideology and strategies]. In A. J. Aasen & S. Nome (Eds.), *Det Nye Norskfaget* [The New Norwegian subject] (pp. 161–188). Bergen, Norway: Fagbokforlaget.

Chatman, S. (1978). *Story and discourse. Narrative structure in fiction and film*. Ithaca, NY: Cornell University Press.

Jakobsen, I. K., & Tønnessen, E. S. (2018). A Design-oriented analysis of multimodality in English as a foreign language. *Designs for Learning, 10*(1), 40–52. https://doi.org/o.16993/dfl.89

Jewitt, C. (2006). *Technology, literacy and learning: A multimodal approach*. London, England: Routledge.

Jewitt, C. (2014). An introduction to multimodality. In C. Jewitt (Ed.), *The Routledge handbook of multimodal analysis* (2nd ed., pp. 15–30). London, England: Routledge.

Kress, G. (2003). *Literacy in the new media age*. New York: Routledge.

Kress, G., Jewitt, C., Bourne, J., Franks, A., Hardcastle, J., Jones, K., & Reid, E. (2005). *English in urban classrooms: A multimodal perspective on teaching and learning*. London, England: Routledge.

Kress, G. & Selander, S. (2012). Multimodal design, learning and cultures of recognition. *Internet and Higher Education, 15*(4), 265–268. https://doi.org/10.1016/j.iheduc.2011.12.003

Kress, G., & van Leeuwen, T. (2006). *Reading images: The grammar of visual design*. London, England: Routledge.

Lemke, J. L. (2000). Across the scales of time: Artifacts, activities, and meanings in ecosocial systems. *Mind, Culture, and Activity, 7*(4), 273–290. https://doi.org/10.1207/S15327884MCA0704_03

Løvland, A. (2006). *Samansette Elevtekstar: Klasserommet som arena for multimodal tekstskaping* [Multimodal Student Texts: the Classroom as Arena for Multimodal creation of texts]. (Doctoral dissertation). Agder University College, Kristiansand, Norway.

Løvland, A. (2011). *På Jakt etter Svar og Forståing: samansette fagtekstar i skulen* [In search of answers and understanding: Multimodal factual texts in school]. Bergen, Norway: LNU/Fagbokforlaget.

New London Group. (1996). A pedagogy of multiliteracies: Designing social futures. *Harvard Educational Review, 66*(1), 60–92.

Norwegian Directorate for Education and Training. (2006). *National curriculum for knowledge promotion*. Retrieved from http://www.udir.no

Norwegian Directorate for Education and Training. (2013). *National curriculum for knowledge promotion*. Retrieved from http://www.udir.no

Norwegian Directorate for Education and Training. (2019). *National curriculum for knowledge promotion*. Retrieved from http://www.udir.no

Selander, S., & Kress, G. (2010). *Design för lärande: Ett multimodalt perspektiv* [Designs for learning: A multimodal perspective]. Stockholm, Sweden: Norstedts.

Street, B. (n.d.). *Autonomous and ideological models of literacy: Approaches from New Literacy Studies*. Retrieved from http://www.media-anthropology.net/street_newliteracy.pdf

UNESCO. (2004). *The plurality of literacy and the implications of its policies and programs* (UNESCO Education Sector Position Paper). Paris, France. Retrieved from http://unesdoc.unesco.org/images/0013/001362/136246e.pdf

van Leeuwen, T. (2005). *Introducing social semiotics*. London, England: Routledge.

CHAPTER 6

Tracing Opportunities for Learning Across Times, Events, and Configurations of Participants: Interactional Ethnography as a Logic of Inquiry

Maria Lucia Castanheira, Beth V. Yeager, and Judith L. Green

In this chapter, to introduce readers to an Interactional Ethnographic logic-of-inquiry and multiple levels of analyses, we foreground the logic-of-analysis that Maria Lucia Castanheira (2000, first author) developed to collect and analyze records (video, formal and informal conversations of process, field notes, artifacts) from her ethnographic archive constructed during the fieldwork phases of her yearlong microethnographic study in the 1996–1997 school year in Beth Yeager's (second author) bilingual fifth-grade class. The aim of Castanheira's study was to develop theoretical understandings of how Yeager engaged her linguistically, socially, and academically diverse students in constructing an inclusive culture-of-inquiry (Castanheira, 2000; B. Yeager, Castanheira, & Green, 2020; E. Yeager, 2003).

Our goal in this chapter is twofold. First, we seek to make visible what is meant by the conceptual argument that Interactional Ethnography is an epistemology (a way of knowing), not a method (Anderson-Levitt, 2006; Green & Castanheira, 2012; Green, Skukauskaite, & Castanheira, 2013). Our second goal is to unfold progressively (Gutierrez, 1993) different levels of analytic scale that Castanheira constructed to analyze the developing community processes and practices developed by Yeager (who also was teacher-as-ethnographer/ethnographer-as-teacher) with her diverse students on the first morning of the 1996–1997 school year. Through this process of presenting Castanheira's logic-of-analysis/analyses, we seek to make transparent (i.e., make visible), how, and in what ways, Interactional Ethnography, as a logic-of-inquiry, guided Castanheira as she entered Yeager's class and began her analysis of the developing community-of-inquiry.

Through these goals, we unfold how Castanheira (2000) took up the position of *ethnographer-as-learner* (Heath & Street, 2008) with the students on the first day to learn *from the participants* (students, teacher, student teacher, and teacher assistant) what was entailed in *being a student in this class*, as well as who had access to what kinds of learning opportunities from the first moments of the first morning of class. Additionally, by focusing on the first morning of Yeager's class, we introduce readers to what is involved in being an ethnographer-as-learner (Agar, 2004, 2006a; Heath & Street, 2008).

In taking this approach, we seek to create a *telling case study* (Mitchell, 1984; see also Sheridan, Street, & Bloome, 2000, and defined further later) of how Castanheira developed a *reflexive logic of analyses* that supported her in (re)constructing and analyzing how Yeager discursively and interactionally engaged students in developing ways of knowing and of being a student in this particular class as the group developed a *community-of-inquiry* (B. Yeager, Castanheira, & Green, 2020). Furthermore, as we unfold the logic-of-analyses, we also introduce *orienting theories* that guided Castanheira's *analytic processes* in her microethnographic study conducted in Yeager's bilingual class.

Framing What Constitutes a Telling Case Study

A telling case study, as defined by anthropologist Clyde Mitchell (1984) is captured in the following:

> [Telling] case studies are the detailed presentation of ethnographic data relating to some *sequence of events* from which the analyst seeks to make some *theoretical inference*. The events themselves may relate to *any level of social organization:* a whole society, some section of a community, a family or an individual. . . . Each case study is a description of a *specific configuration of events* in which some *distinctive set of actors* have been involved in *some defined situation* at *some particular point of time*. (p. 222, emphasis added)

Mitchell's argument applies to our approach to presenting Castanheira's original study, and our particular focus on her logic-of-analyses, as a *telling case study.* As we show, the key elements identified by Mitchell in the extract also informed, and are reflected in, Castanheira's processes for producing her dissertation (Castanheira, 2000; see also

E. Yeager, 2003, who conducted her ethnographic study 3 years later and drew on the archived ethnographic records from the 1996–1997 class).

In this chapter, therefore, written more than 20 years after Castanheira's (2000) original study, we (re)trace the particular levels of analyses and ways Castanheira analyzed the records that she and Yeager collaboratively collected concerning the developing actions, interactions, and discourse processes that Yeager proposed to students as they entered and developed the first morning of their bilingual fifth-grade class. By (re)constructing Castanheira's logic of analyses, we, therefore, construct a telling case study of multiple levels of analytic scale Castanheira developed to trace the developing *culture-of-inquiry-in-the-making* in this class (Collins & Green, 1991).

Through this approach, we seek to provide readers with a foundation for taking an *if-then* approach to engaging with the Interactional Ethnography logic-of-inquiry, as well as a foundation upon which to engage with Castanheira's logic-of-analyses. That is, as you engage with our (re)presentation of Castanheira's actions, decisions, and theories that we make visible and unfold, consider how, when, and if these might guide your research process.

Theory–Epistemology–Relationships Guiding Castanheira's Logic-of-Analyses

Given that Castanheira's logic-of-analyses was guided by an Interactional Ethnography logic-of-inquiry, we present in the remainder of this chapter theoretical constructs that guided each level of analysis, along with the decisions Castanheira made concerning each level of analysis. However, rather than presenting theoretical constructs in a traditional manner, we have elected to draw on written excerpts from two of Yeager's Grade 6 and 5 classes (1992 and 1995, respectively) in which students became *students-as-ethnographers* and authorities on their communities (B. Yeager, 1999; B. Yeager, Floriani, & Green, 1998; E. Yeager, 2003). The excerpts selected make transparent how particular members of Yeager's classes inscribed—in their end-of-year essays (Green, Yeager, & Castanheira, 2008; B. Yeager et al., 2020)—theoretical perspectives on insider–outsider knowledge of processes, practices, and disciplinary events through which such knowledge was constructed within their classroom across the school year. In doing so, we seek to blur the boundaries between established theories and theories developed by students-as-ethnographers in Yeager's classes to make the research process come to life (as called for in international dialogues; see, e.g., Kumpulainen, Hmelo-Silver, & César, 2009).

Through this approach, we also unfold what is meant by conceptualizing *ethnographer-as-learner* from, and through, communication, actions, and interaction with members of the class *as a developing community-of-inquiry*. Throughout this chapter, therefore, we unfold *theoretical perspectives* that guided each phase of Castanheira's

(2000) analyses on the first morning, and that Yeager (2003), in her subsequent study, extended across the entire day. We also make transparent *graphic approaches*, ways of *mapping* particular levels of social discourse and interactions, to develop local and situated theoretical understandings of developing, social, and communicative processes that shaped what counted as ways of knowing, being, and doing everyday life in Yeager's class in 1996–1997 (cf. Heath, 1982). Through this process, we (re)construct ethnographic processes, theories, and practice relationships that constitute an Interactional Ethnographic epistemological approach to microethnographic studies of lived experiences of students with their teachers and others across times, events, and configurations of actors (cf. Green et al., in press-a; Smith, 1978; Street, 2005).

Theoretical Perspective 1: Insider–Outsider Understandings Inscribed by Two Students

In this section, we identify a series of conceptual perspectives that informed Castanheira's journey to becoming an ethnographer guided by an Interactional Ethnographic logic-of-inquiry. These perspectives include: *ethnographer-as-learner, classes as cultures-in-the-making*, and *insider-outsider understandings* of the developing class that students inscribed in their end of year essays. As we will make visible, these inscriptions by students reflect how they viewed their class as a *culture-in-the-making* in ways that relate to anthropological theories of culture as a verb (e.g., Agar, 2006b; Street, 1993), and discourse theories in education (e.g., Bloome, Carter, Christian, Otto, & Shuart-Faris, 2005; Gee & Green, 1998; Markee, 2015). We include excerpts from students' end of year essays from two different school years to make our case. Each student author raises challenges that outsiders (ethnographers, visitors, and students) encounter when becoming a new member of any school-based community, whether entering on the first day of school or after the beginning of the school year.

The following excerpt from Arturo's (10 years old) end of year essay makes visible what he understood from his position as student-as-ethnographer in the class by the end of the 1994-1995 school year. In this essay, he also framed what outsiders would need to consider and examine in order to develop an understanding, not only of what was happening in the class, but how the language, processes, and practices of the class were constructed in and across times, events, cycles of activity, and configuration of participants.

In his essay, Arturo inscribes an *iterative, recursive*, and *abductive process* of learning (see Agar, 2006a, 2006b) and the role of language(s) that transcends particular moments. Arturo also frames the need to examine how the *language of the class* is constructed, as well as how and when it was used and for what purposes, to reference what actions and practices for learning are central to understanding how insider knowledge was constructed (cf. Beach & Bloome, 2019; Castanheira, 2019). Finally, he also frames *limits to understanding* (Baker & Green, 2007) that become visible when a researcher asks

In our Tower community [an insider name for the "classroom," which is in the tower of the school], *we have our own language as well as the languages we bring from outside (like Spanish and English) which helped us make our own language. So, for example, someone that is not from our classroom community would not understand what insider, outsider, think twice, notetaking/notemaking, literature log and learning log mean. If Ms. Yeager says we are going to "make a sandwich", the people from another class or room would think that we were going to make a sandwich to eat. Of course we aren't, but that is part of our common language.*

To be an insider, which means a person from the class, you also need to know our Bill of Rights and Responsibilities which was made by the members of the Tower community. And if Ms. Yeager said, "Leave your H.R.L. on your desk," people would not understand unless someone from the Tower community told him/her and even if we told him/her that H.R.L. stands for 'Home Reading Log,' they still would not understand what it is and what you write in it. If we told a new student, "It's time for SSL and ESL," he would not understand.

These words are all part of the common Tower community language and if someone new were to come in, we would have to explain how we got them and what they mean. We also would tell them that we got this language by reports, information, investigations, and what we do and learn in our Tower community.

Figure 6.1. Excerpt from Arturo's (10 years old) community essay, Grade 5, 1995

Source: From Green, J., Yeager, B. & Castanheira, (2008). Talking texts into being: On the social construction of everyday life and academic knowledge in the classroom. In N. Mercer & S. Hodgkinson (Eds.) *Exploring talk in classrooms: Inspired by the work of Douglas Barnes* (p. 118). London, England: Sage. Used with permission.

insiders about processes without grounding them in a specific event where the ethnographer wonders what is happening and how it came into being (Agar, 1994). In stating that "we got this language by reports, information, investigations, and what we do and learn in our Tower community," Arturo frames the need to trace *how* particular actions, language, and knowledge were being constructed in and across particular events and configurations of participants.

Alex, a student in 1991–1992, provides further insights into insider–outsider relationships in his end-of-year essay (Green & Dixon, 1993). In this excerpt, Alex raises additional challenges central to understanding a class as a *culture-in-the-making* (Castanheira, Green, Dixon, & Yeager, 2007).

Our community has a lot to do over the year. Sometimes our community gets different during the year. What I mean is like the first day I walked in the door. I was new and nervous just me thinking who am I trying to make friends. I came in the door. Other students explained how to do the Writer's Workshop. I didn't understand the three logs. Other kids and the teacher explained. Now I'm just part of everyone else.

Figure 6.2. Excerpt from Alex's (11 years old) community essay, Grade 6, 1992

Source: Reprinted from Green, J. & Dixon, C. (1993). Introduction. Talking knowledge into being: Discursive and social practices in classrooms. *Linguistics and Education,* 5(3–4), 231–240, p. 235, with permission from Elsevier.

As indicated in this excerpt, Alex raises critical challenges facing outsiders (e.g., a new student), who enter after the class has begun (for related issues facing administrators, see Carney, 1999; Flores, 1999).

Research in other classes in other school settings (e.g., Cordóva & Balcerzak, 2013; Dixon, Green, & Brandts, 2005; Lin, 1993; Rex, 2001), as well as across multiple years in Yeager's class, has provided convergent evidence for Alex's conceptual argument about entering after the class has begun. Interactional Ethnographic research has shown that Alex's argument can also be applied to a student who has been absent for a period of time (cf. Putney, 1997). Additionally, studies across sites have led to further confirmation that a student, who has been pulled out during a particular period of the day for special help, will face a similar challenge (e.g., Brandts, 1999; Green, Brock, Baker, & Harris, in press-b).

Additionally, as Alex makes transparent, when entry for students, researchers, and external actors is not possible on the first day, the person entering has *limits to certainty* about what he/she is hearing, seeing, and thus understanding (see Baker & Green, 2007; Green et al., in press-b). As Alex explains, when entry for ethnographers on first days of school is not possible, ethnographers face a challenge that requires engaging different participants in tracing the roots of present events.

Alex also confirms Arturo's argument concerning the language *of* the class and provides insights into the need for *multiple angles on phenomena* in the classroom. He also points out that not all members have the *same* knowledge. His argument also makes visible the theoretical argument that *words only mean in context* (Castanheira, Street, & Carvahlo, 2015; Duranti & Goodwin, 1992; Manalo, 2020; Mishler, 1979; Wegerif, 2020). His personal understandings converge with theoretical arguments that all moments of discourse and social activity have histories within sustaining social contexts and groups within these contexts (e.g., Bakhtin, 1986; Fairclough, 1992).

Taken together, Arturo (1995) and Alex (1992) provide evidence of the importance of understanding *insider language, actions, and sources of actions* and *knowledge* as well as *how* such knowledge and understandings are constructed by participants in local classes. Arturo and Alex, therefore, challenge *ethnographers-as-learners* to ask the following questions to construct deeper understandings of what *insiders* know that *those external* to the class may not know or understand when entering a class at particular points in its history:

- Who engages with whom
- How
- In what ways
- When and where
- Under what conditions
- For what purposes
- With what material resources (constructed by, and afforded to, participants)
- With what outcomes and consequences for individuals and the collective for future actions and learning

These questions provide a foundation for analyzing what members of a class have constructed as meanings (referential/semiotic system) *for* particular artifacts and actions as well as the material, social, and activity systems that guide the collective and individual members' ways of engaging in this developing *community of inquiry* (cf. Gee & Green, 1998; Putney, Green, Dixon, Durán, & Yeager, 2000). Thus, Arturo and Alex make visible for ethnographers how understanding what is being *said, heard,* and *seen* in a class requires seeking multiple ways of learning about and exploring what the teacher *with* learners together *inscribe, and thus make visible,* about classroom life in their spoken and written communication (Bakhtin, 1986; Baker & Däumer, 2017).

Theoretical Perspective 2: Defining Processes Guiding Ethnographers-as-Learners

In this section, we introduce a set of principles that constitute an *orienting perspective* for researchers as they construct a local and situated *logic-of-inquiry* from the perspective of *ethnographer-as-learner.* These principles are derived from the work of social and linguistic anthropologists (e.g., Agar, 2006a, 2006b; Heath, 1982; Heath & Street, 2008; Street, 1993) and define how we conceptualize processes involved in, and goals for, Interactional Ethnography as an epistemological approach. These principles, therefore, guide Interactional Ethnography researchers as they seek to construct understandings of what members of a sustaining and/or developing social group know that they as outsiders do not know. These principles involve the following:

- Suspending (stepping back from) known categories and personal (prior) understandings about life in classrooms to construct local and situated understandings of *actions* and *referential meanings* of actions being developed and taken up by participants
- Acknowledging differences between what ethnographers know and what actor(s) in the context know and jointly construct
- Constructing new ways of knowing for the ethnographer grounded in local and situated discourses, interactional processes, and practices of everyday life within a social group or configuration of actors in particular events
- Developing ways of (re)presenting based on analytic processes what is known by local actors and what ethnographers learn from analyses at different levels of analytic scale and angles of analyses within and across times, events, and configurations of actors

For different traditions of ethnographic research *of, in,* and *for* education, see Bloome, Beauchemin, Brady, Buescher, Kim, and Schey (2018).

(Re)constructing Castanheira's Analytic Logic-of-Analyses: A Telling Case Study

Castanheira's decision to engage with Yeager in the study of her class as a *culture-of-inquiry-in-the-making* led to the question, *When would it be possible to enter Yeager's class?* Entry on the first day was a negotiated process with Yeager and Green (the latter was Castanheira's dissertation advisor and another ethnographer in Yeager's class). Castanhiera's goal for entering on the first day, as framed previously, was to develop understandings of how Yeager introduced students to processes and practices and the developing *language of the class* (Lin, 1993) as students assigned to this class entered their classroom for the first time.

This decision was grounded in a challenge by Yeager, as teacher-ethnographer, to Castanheira that Castanheira *step back* and *suspend her categories* of *who would count as a special needs* student; Castanheira's research interest was grounded in assumptions drawn from her previous work in Brazil. This challenge led to a reflexive process for *how* Castanheira would need to identify these students through their actions in class, as well as Yeager's discourse and interactions with students across times and events.

This difference between Castanheira's prior knowledge, and what she would construct through her Interactional Ethnographic study in Yeager's class in 1996–1997, led to a 3-week immersion in Yeager's class. This decision also led to a series of reflexive observations, a set of videos, and field notes and other records, as well as dialogues with Yeager to identify potential "tracer," or focal, "units" to study (i.e., students who were pulled out of Yeager's class for special help during the school day). That is, this process involved an iterative, recursive, and abductive reflexive logic-of-analysis that led to the identification of who counted as a "special needs" student at the school level, rather than at Yeager's class level, because Yeager worked with students to develop an inclusive environment that integrated students across languages, academic histories, and opportunities for learning in previous settings in and out of schooling contexts. Although an intensive period was required to identify tracer/focal students, Castanheira did not stop with this period; rather, given her research questions, she continued to explore how Yeager supported these students through a set of inclusive processes and practices across the school year (Castanheira, Green, & Yeager, 2008)

(Re)presenting the Logic-of-Analyses of the Developing Culture-in-the-Making

Figure 6.3 (re)constructs a logic-of-analyses that makes transparent how, and for what reasons, Castanheira undertook multiple levels of analyses and what constituted iterative, recursive, and abductive processes in her study of the first morning of Yeager's bilingual fifth-grade class in 1996–1997. As indicated in Figure 6.3, the logic-of-analyses that she constructed involved *generating data sets* from archived records for particular questions and levels of analyses as well as *identifying emerging analytic questions.* Figure 6.3 also indicates that Castanheira constructed five levels of analysis to address three overarching analytic prompt questions concerning the first morning (as well as the year-long ethnographic study): (1) How are opportunities for learning constructed in this class? (2) How do different participants contribute to this process of construction? and (3) In which ways can this process of construction be (re)presented?

To address these questions, Castanheira constructed multiple data sets for each of what she framed as *telling case studies.* Each of these supported her work in tracing particular actors and/or processes within and across times and events on this first morning to answer the questions framed. This form of (re)presentation of her logic makes visible how, for each telling case she constructed, Castanheira framed what the analysis *was a case of*; that is, she framed the *class of phenomena* in each case and then described the elements of that class of things that she was focusing on (Green et al., in press-a). For each phase, Castanheira developed the following interrelated set of processes:

1.0 Positing Overarching Questions—Framing Telling Case Studies

How are opportunities for learning constructed in this class?
How do different participants contribute to this process of construction'?
In which way can this process of construction be (re)presented'?

2.0 Analyzing the Onset of Community Processes and Practices as a Telling Case

2.1 Posing Question:
What was accomplished through construction of the events identified?
How were students positioned in these events?

2.2 (Re)presenting Data:
Production of more detailed event maps describing participants' actions within event phases (e.g., chains of actions, proposed meanings/referential system, and subevents)

2.3 Analyzing events:
(Re)viewing transcript and event maps for identifying which roles and relationships and demands and expectations were established through the interaction among participants

3.0 Analyzing Transitioning as a Telling Case

3.1 Creating a new set of data representation:
Producing transcript(s) of talk and interactions among participants at different levels of units of analysis (e.g., message units, interaction units, sequence units, and event units)
Production of a Multiple-Level Event Map

3.2 Analyzing Transitioning Telling Case:
Situating transitioning activities from one event to another within the flow of activities developed in the day
Developing microanalysis of participants' actions and talk to identify the nature of their contribution to the construction of the classroom collective text

4.0 Tracing Interactions as a Telling Case:

4.1 Creating a new set of data representation:
Producing transcript representation organized in sequence unit of analysis
Producing representation of results of semantic analysis and predominant discourse themes

5.0 Analyzing Interactional Processes to Construct a Telling Case:

5.1 Situating events analyzed within day and cycle of activity
5.2 Analyzing social significance of what was proposed, recognized, and acknowledged by participants
5.3 Examining how students were positioned by and positioned themselves through talk and actions

Figure 6.3. (Re)Presentation of the process of constructing data sets

- Posing questions to guide a particular level of or angle on analysis
- Constructing local and situated data sets from archived records to address questions posed
- Analyzing data to develop theoretical insights into what was being socially, discursively, and interactionally accomplished

As indicated in Figure 6.3, each set of analyses often raised new questions or a new phenomenon that required further exploration. This iterative, recursive, and abductive process formed a *reflexive process* central to Interactional Ethnographic research that was framed in and by the concept of *stepping back from the known.*

Thus, and as indicated in Figure 6.3, two goals guided Castanheira's (2000) construction of her *logic-in-use* for this phase as well as for her yearlong study. Her first goal was designed to help her develop understandings of *how to construct a theoretically and epistemologically grounded approach for studying how opportunities for learning were jointly constructed by and with the group as a collective* (e.g., Edwards & Mercer, 1987; Mercer & Hodgkinson, 2008). The first goal led to a second goal: to examine

> the epistemological consequences of adopting different *analytic angles* (emphasis added) which are defined from a particular theoretical and methodological approach, to study the joint construction of opportunities for learning in the classroom. (Castanheira, 2000, p. 38)

Thus, for Castanheira, each level of analysis involved constructing a telling case that focused on a particular dimension of students' lived experiences at particular points in time. That is, each *posing question* in Figure 6.3 generates the foundation for the construction of a new telling case analysis, as well as for subsequent exploration of relationships between and among different phases of analyses. As such, these Interactional Ethnography reflexive processes provided a ground on which Castanheira constructed theoretical understandings of what constituted *inclusive discourse, actions, processes, and outcomes*. Figure 6.3, therefore, constitutes a (re)construction of Castanheira's *reflexive logic-of-analyses* undertaken across times, analytic cases, and events across the first morning (and then the entire school year).

Analytic Level 1: (Re)constructing the Morning of Day 1 of Beth Yeager's Class

Figure 6.4 provides a meso level of analysis of the first set of subevents (see the fourth column) that were constructed in the first hour of the school day: entering the Tower and the Welcoming to the Tower (*Tower* is a folk term used throughout the school to refer to the classroom located in the school's tower).

These two subevents—entering the Tower and the Welcoming to the Tower—together constituted an event that Castanheira framed as *The Onset of Community* (see Column 5). By framing this period as the "onset" of community (and not the "beginning"), she captured the ongoing and dynamic processes and practices that Yeager constructed for and with students within this initiating phase of the first morning (see Columns 1 to 3 in Figure 6.4).

Figure 6.4 constitutes a *meso level of mapping* of the developing flow of action that oriented students to ways that count as expected participation when entering the Tower as a student. Figure 6.4, therefore, makes transparent multiple levels of analysis that Castanheira constructed of one event to demonstrate the *part–whole relationships* of

Column 1: Time	Column 2: Actions by Participants in and Across Times and Developing Events	Column 3: Interactional Spaces	Column 4: Subevent	Column 5: Event	Column 6: Analytic Induction of Processes for Creating Opportunities for Community (Participants) to Read and Observe Class as a Developing Text
8:10 8:30 Period prior to the official opening of the school day 20 minutes	- Sts arriving in the classroom - Sts meeting teacher - Sts choosing where to sit - Sts decorating name square - Sts talking to classmates sitting at table group - Sts talking to T, Teacher Aide and Student teacher who are greeting students at their desks	**Teacher - Individual** **Individual-Table Group** **Individual-Individual**	**ENTERING THE TOWER**	**ONSET OF COMMUNITY**	- Seeing and "reading" what other participants are doing - (Re)establishing contact with friends - Meeting new people - Getting acquainted with others - (Re)situating self within large group - Choosing language to interact in - Becoming bilingual community - Getting support from adults - Helping students to learn her (Castanheira's) job as ethnographer as partner - Students becoming ethnographer - Knowing local community ways of leaving - Making decisions about routine aspects within the norms being established for group - Becoming a tower community member - Exploring own knowledge and experience in constructing tower community '96/'97 - Defining uses and exploring multiple spaces
8:55 9:35 40 Minutes	- T Introducing chime as a sign - T Celebrating the languages of the Tower Community: Spanish and English - T Explaining way of using Spanish and English in the classroom - T Introducing adult members to students - T Introducing Ethnography as community practice - T Defining basic routines: drinking water, signing up for lunch, bathroom, recess, break times, etc. - T Exploring students' knowledge about the Tower community and introducing the notion of Tower as community that has its traditions - T Presenting the multiple physical spaces of Tower classroom and discussing possibilities of use	**Teacher-Whole Group**	**WELCOMING TO TOWER**		

Figure 6.4. Mapping onset of community

Source: Adapted from Castanheira (2000, p. 150).

different units of analysis central to constructing warranted—that is, empirically justified—accounts of ways Yeager engaged students in constructing the first event of the morning.

As indicated in the graphic (re)presentation in Figure 6.4, Castanheira constructed an event map (an Interactional Ethnography insider term) that included *time markers* (beginning and ending time and amount of time within the developing event), a *running record* of the *actions taken by the teacher with the students represented as present-continuous verbs/gerunds + objects of actions; interactional spaces constructed* (individual, whole class, teacher–students), *subevents being interactionally constructed* (entering the Tower and Welcoming to the Tower), and *the event as a local and situated construction* (Onset of Community).

As indicated in Column 2 of Figure 6.4, Castanheira inscribed a *running record* of developing actions and objects of the actions. The running record constitutes a form of transcript construction at the *level of actions,* not linguistic or conversation forms of talk, which establishes a way of (re)presenting the developing *sequence of actions.* This formulation is based on English as a subject–verb–object language.

Through this process, Castanheira was able to (re)present not only *actions* but also what actions and physical spaces students were being *oriented to.* Figure 6.4, Column 2, therefore makes transparent how Castanheira constructed *action statements,* including the teacher's *discursive choices* for actions as well as the *nonverbal* actions of students. These actions formed a basis for *progressively disclosing* (Gutierrez, 1994) chains of interrelated activity as they were being developed (i.e., the flow of activity).

In this way, Castanheira constructed a graphic (re)representation of the developing *ebb and flow* of how Yeager *oriented* students to particular ways of being a participant in these subevents. That is, Castanheira (re)constructed and theorized what Yeager proposed to students and how actions were then recognized, acknowledged, and interactionally taken up by members of this class as the subevents were developing (cf. Bloome et al., 2005; Green & Wallat, 1981). In so doing, Castanheira (re)presented how she interpreted what was being proposed and accomplished discursively and interactionally by actors within developing events. In this way, she makes transparent a *set of principles* for (re)presenting actions being proposed to and recognized by children as they engaged in a process of becoming students in this class (see also Green et al., in press-b).

Column 3 was included to show *different configurations* of actors (e.g., teacher, student, others), and *types of configurations of participants* that supported students in being part of this developing class-as-a-culture-in-the-making (e.g., individual, individual-to-individual, whole class, small group). Columns 2 and 3, therefore, when considered together, establish a deeper foundation on which to examine multiple configurations of actors in the class and examine which students were the focus of particular actions.

Column 6, in contrast to Column 2, presents interpretations that Castanheira made as her analysis unfolded to theorize what work was potentially being accomplished in and through discourse, actions, and interactions, as well as the configuration of participants (re)presented in other columns. Thus, Column 6 provides information about how Castanheira *interpreted* and *theorized* and thus made transparent developing actions and discourses of the first event and how Castanheira was making sense of both as an ethnographer. In her study, Castanheira characterizes this process as exploring the opportunities Yeager was developing with students to *interpret the class as a developing text* (Bloome & Egan-Robertson, 1993). This process led her to explore, as indicated in Column 6, opportunities for creating *possibilities for future action* and for framing *what counts as being a student in the Tower at the collective level.* Later, this process also enabled her to (re)examine which students had access to which forms of activity.

This analytic process captures how Castanheira built theoretically on Bloome and Egan-Robertson's (1993) argument about "textualizing the class." It also makes visible how this conceptual argument is critical for members of a class (i.e., being able to read the "text" of the class), as well as ethnographers-as-learners, if both are to understand what counts as social and academic processes and practices as they are being proposed by their teacher and constructed in and across events. Thus, analysis of her graphic (re) construction and analysis of this first morning demonstrates how Castanheira, as an *outsider,* sought to develop *insider* understandings as Yeager engaged with students on this first morning of the 1996–1997 school year.

Analytic Level 2: Transitions as Socially Accomplished

To identify processes involved in transitioning between subevents of this first morning, Castanheira engaged in a series of new levels of analysis, that is, *micro levels* that focused more closely on discursive processes that signaled a transition. Before presenting these analyses (a narrative and a transcript-based analysis), we return to Figure 6.4 to construct a context for Table 6.1 that follows. As indicated in Figure 6.4 presented previously, at 8:10 a.m., Yeager initiated a process of transitioning students, as they arrived at the door of the Tower, from being outsiders to taking up positions as insiders within the class. In this initial subevent, students entered the class and were greeted in English and/or Spanish by Yeager and/or the student teacher. They were then directed to a table to select their Name Square (a folk term) and to choose a table group to join. They were asked to decorate their Name Squares and to interact with tablemates.

Castanheira (2000) framed the challenges in conceptualizing the developing understandings of this subevent and its relationship to subsequent subevents as follows:

> Boundaries between events were not established in a clear-cut fashion but involved a process in which participants gradually re-organized the participation structure for constructing a new social event. This process of engaging in the social construction of a new event can be marked by changes in [the] physical arrangement of the group, changes in the topic of discussion or purpose of activities. (p. 163)

This set of conceptual arguments led Castanheira to identify a set of *rich points* for tracing *when* and *how* Yeager initiated the transition from the morning arrival in the class to a whole group space (Figure 6.4). She observed that Yeager engaged in a process of *negotiating with students* the transition to the whole-group space. Castanheira's growing reflexive awareness of the absence of clear boundaries between classroom subevents led her to return to the video recording of the first subevent to explore further *how* Yeager signaled the transition. This analysis is presented later as a narrative of the actions and patterns of interactions that Yeager (and a student teacher) proposed to students. This process is also presented as a second analysis, a more micro-level analysis (see Table 6.1), of the discourse and interactions of the transition process as it was being negotiated with students. These two levels of analyses, as we show, made visible a two-phase process of transitioning from one class event to another: *foreshadowing the transition and negotiating with students the transition* from small-group activity to the whole class.

The following extract from Castanheira (2000, pp. 162–163) (re)presents the *narrative level* of (re)construction of her findings from (re)viewing the video recording of the onset of the class-as-community and the transition event:

> While students were still working on their Name Squares and talking to classmates sitting at the same table group, the teacher initiated the process of informing one group at a time that she was going to ring a chime bell soon. The teacher approached each table group saying:
>
> > in two minutes I'm going to ring one chime bell that is going to be
> > a sign for you to look at me
>
> The teacher walked around the room, repeating this statement to each table group, while collecting Name Squares from students. This pattern was also undertaken by the Student Teacher on the other side of the room. As Yeager and the student teacher passed by each table, they also informed students that they could "keep working on their Name Squares at another time if they thought they had more to do." (Castanheira, 2000, p. 163)

These levels of analyses make visible the argument that context(s) of talk are discursively and interactionally constructed and help to explain how Yeager, with the student teacher, created a *metadiscourse* that signaled to students that their *local* and *situated work* would be supported. This *metadiscourse* also signaled the role of *foreshadowing* future actions and ways students would need to prepare for *(re)orienting* from a local individual or small-group task to a whole-group activity. This process makes transparent the importance of identifying the role of the teacher's (and the student teacher's and students') *metadiscourse(s)* that orients hearers to particular phenomena, processes, or disciplinary knowledge being constructed in a class as a culture-in-the-making.

Analytic Level 3: Identifying Tracer Units

In (re)visiting this event, Castanheira also noted on the video record that Joseph, one of the students sitting at Table 5, got a book from his backpack and started to read while most of the students continued talking to each other. This observation led her to select Joseph as a *tracer unit* to explore how he and the other students transitioned from the table-group activity to the whole-class orientation.

As indicated in Figure 6.4, at 8:55 a.m., the teacher walked to the front of the room. The sound of the chime filled the room for a few seconds and co-occurred with the sounds and signs of movement by students. The actions of students, therefore, signaled to the teacher that all the students were (re)orienting from their table group and the Name Square activity, with one exception: Joseph.

To capture this process, Castanheira decided to create a *physical map* that displayed what the students were doing in response to Yeager's earlier proposal and to the actual ringing of the chime. Thus, Figure 6.5 is a (re)presentation of the class structure and students by table groups. The arrows indicate *eye gaze* to (re)present to *whom* and to *what* students were orienting.

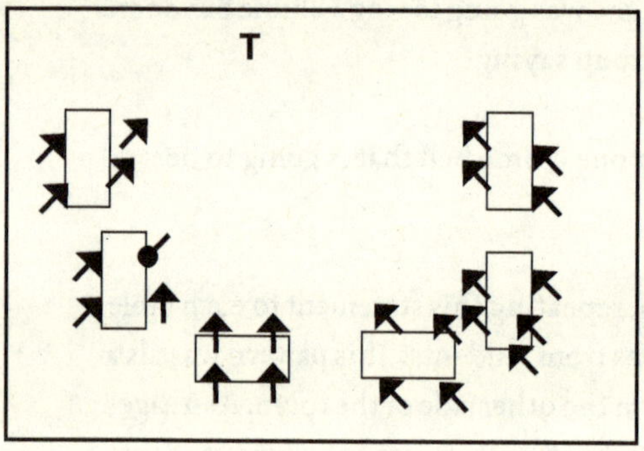

Figure 6.5. Participants' orientation in response to the chime

Source: Drawn from Castanheira (2000).

Figure 6.5 (re)presents a meso level of analysis that shows how Joseph (dot-and-line) was orienting to his book—a self-selected, personal activity—which was appropriate in the entering and table phase of the first morning but not in this developing event (a transition event). However, to understand how Yeager responded to Joseph's and the rest of the class's initial orientation to the chime, Castanheira decided to engage in a micro-level analysis, in which she constructed a transcript of ways in which students, individually and collectively, responded to the chime and how Yeager responded to students' actions.

Castanheira constructed Table 6.1 to analyze the potential consequences of these actions for the *transition* to a whole class process. Table 6.1 (re)constructs Castanheira's transcript and analyses of this text to examine teacher–student patterns of discourse and interaction. Table 6.1 also (re)presents Castanheira's process of theorizing the actions, interactions, and discourse to examine the contributions of each level of analysis for constructing warranted accounts of the class as a developing text as well as a *culture-in-the-making*.

Table 6.1. (Re)Orienting students: Transition to whole group

Transcript lines	Message units	Teacher (BY)		Students' nonverbal acions	BY's discourse choices	Theorizing consequences of discourse and actions
		Verbal discourse	Nonverbal actions			
168	NV MU		T rings chimes	- Students stop what they are doing and look at T - but Joseph is reading a book	Theme: chime as a signal	Establishing a collective signal for constituting whole class interactional space, a process that was signaled in teacher and student teacher discourse and interactions 10 minutes prior to the ringing of the chime (foreshadowing actions)
Chime rings throughout class						
169 170	MU MU 2 MUs tie = AU	Oh That was great		- Students are smiling and orienting to BY - but Joseph is reading a book	T congratulates students for (re)orienting when chime rang	
171 172 173 174	MU MU 2 MUs=AU MU MU 2 MUs=AU	We should try again Hablen bastante Pause Oh That is great	Gestures as states this to model talking T waits for a few seconds and rings chime again/pause	J continues to read his book - Students start pretending to talk to each other. - Students stop pretending to talk and (re) orient to T - All students oriented to BY except for J, still reading	Gives them another try Interwoven use of Spanish and English, not literal translation Confirming action expected	Reading students' actions—students as texts for the teacher Teachers actions (gestures and discourse) are available to students as texts Reaffirming meaning of signal
Pause shows end of one ***Interaction Unit*** (exchanges in turns: T-Sts-T exchanges) at whole-group level but Joseph has not participated at that point						
175 176 177	3 Mus=AU	Joseph That would be a signal For you to look up	Said directly to J in low tone	- J stops reading and puts book away and (re)orients to T	Addressing J to indicate he is not participating in group activity but focusing on own activity	Reorienting J to collective activity to create inclusivity and to ensure he understands what is expected for new activity
Shifts from talking with Joseph back to whole class			pause	All students oriented to common focus on BY	Reformulating rationale for whole group. i.e., on how the whole group transition might interrupt what they are doing previous to when the chime rings Moving between English and Spanish, but not engaging in literal translation, to build on what was said before	Using metadiscourse about practice and process Using two languages to position Spanish and English speakers as interlocutors. Demonstrating the place for using Spanish and English in interwoven manner to build common understanding of developing processes

Transcript lines	Message units	Teacher (BY)		Students' nonverbal acions	BY's discourse choices	Theorizing consequences of discourse and actions
		Verbal discourse	Nonverbal actions			
178	MU	una campana	The following			
179	MU	hay que escuchar	chain of			
			message/action			
180	MU	it may be that you	units is			
181	MU	you know	addressed to			
182	MU	you are in the	the whole class,			
	MU	middle of doing	not to J alone.			
	MU=AU2	something	J therefore			
183	MU		becomes an			
184	MU	o que están	overhearing			
185	MU	trabajando en	member of the			
186	MU	algo y si oigan	T's statement,			
187	MU	esa campana	not the direct			
188	MU=AU3	tendría que mirar	focus of the			
		arriba y escuchar	action units			

Note: MU = message unit, AU = action unit (AUs are tied MUs as identified through contextualization cues—pitch, stress, intonation contour pause/juncture, gesture, eye gaze, etc.).

Castanheira's micro-level analyses in Table 6.1 are based on a set of conventions for (re)presenting discourse, nonverbal interactions, and the developing text through a process of transcription (cf., Bloome et al., 2005; Green & Kelly, 2019; Green & Wallat, 1981). As indicated in Columns 1 to 3, this process is based on the identification of a series of developing units in which the message unit level is the smallest level of (re)presentation (e.g., a bit of meaning) and forms a foundation for tracing the developing text (Fairclough, 1992) of the event as it is being proposed to, recognized by, acknowledged, and interactionally accomplished by members (Bloome et al., 2005; Green & Wallat, 1981). That is, the analytic process begins by identifying a *message unit*, a bit of meaning being proposed, not a sentence. Then, the analyst identifies how one message unit can be an action unit or ties to other message units to create an action unit. Action units tie together to make a turn unit (i.e., a turn for speaking), and turn units tie together to make interaction units (exchanges among speakers).

This micro level of analysis is grounded in an interactional sociolinguistic approach (Gumperz, 1982) and the concept of *contextualization cues* (cf. Gumperz & Herasimchuk, 1972) to identify the boundaries and ties among units: Pitch, stress, intonation contour, pause/juncture, gesture, eye gaze, proxemics (distance and orientation of participants), kinesics (body movement), lexicon (words), and grammar are used to identify message units. In summary, tied message units constitute a larger form of text construction that enables hearers to engage with and/or understand more about the intended actions proposed to them in a class. Other units of analysis also are identified by examining how action units constitute a turn at speaking, and interaction units—that is, exchanges between speakers and hearers—constitute sets of interactions.

Additionally, interaction units tie by topic to make sequence units, and sequence units are tied by phases of activity to (re)present the developing subevents and ultimately the boundaries of the event as a developing text. This approach to transcription reflects Fairclough's (1992) argument that an utterance is a text, a social process, *and* a discourse practice. Utterances therefore shape and are shaped by the developing text as it is being composed.

Returning now to Table 6.1, we trace the levels of units in Columns 1 to 3 and then examine the developing text in relation to nonverbal actions of the teacher and students. Additionally, as indicated in Columns 6 and 7 in Table 6.1, Castanheira included theoretical interpretations at two levels. The first focused on Yeager's discourse choices—which were framed as present continuous verbs/gerunds plus objects/or purposes of the discourse—as she addressed students and engaged them in developing understandings of the social processes and practices necessary for constructing the whole-class space for the next event. In this way, as a second level of analysis, Yeager framed with students that the class, as a text, was a developing one. In Column 7, Castanheira also made visible her theoretical understandings of the actions and chains of activity and what each afforded members of the class.

Table 6.1, therefore, demonstrates multiple levels of analyses Castanheira engaged in to build a basis for making warranted (empirically justified) claims (Heap, 1995) about her growing understanding of how Yeager was constructing the cultural processes and practices of the class with students and others, that is, in constructing the ways that students (and others) would need to know and understand in order to be a member of this class within and across developing events of the class on this first morning as well as on subsequent days (Green & Heras, 2011).

By focusing on how Joseph responded to the chime, Castanheira also made transparent how Yeager shifted between the individual and the collective; a process also visible in Yeager's use of two languages, in which she did not engage in literal translations of statements. Rather, Yeager communicated in English and Spanish using a process of code-switching to signal to the English-speaking, bilingual, and Spanish-dominant students that both languages would be used in this class and needed to be attended to (for a detailed discussion of two languages–one community, see E. Yeager, Green, & Castanheira, 2009).

The construction of Table 6.1, therefore, provides a further example of the logic guiding Castanheira's analyses, which engaged her in examining interactional and discourse processes that framed the meanings and intentions of the developing class texts for students. As indicated in Table 6.1, a critical goal of Castanheira's analytic actions was to explore what was being accomplished on this first morning in each event being constructed and how discourse and interactions positioned students in particular ways.

Analytic Level 5: Tracing Developing Spaces for Learning to Think as a Mathematician

In Figure 6.6, we present one final analysis undertaken by Castanheira for the Watermelon Problem Event, the final event of the first morning. In this figure, we make visible how Castanheira (re)constructed and traced students across the spaces for learning that enabled students to explore at multiple levels (personal, small group, whole class; see headings in Line 1) how to think as mathematicians about the cost of the watermelon that was given to their group.

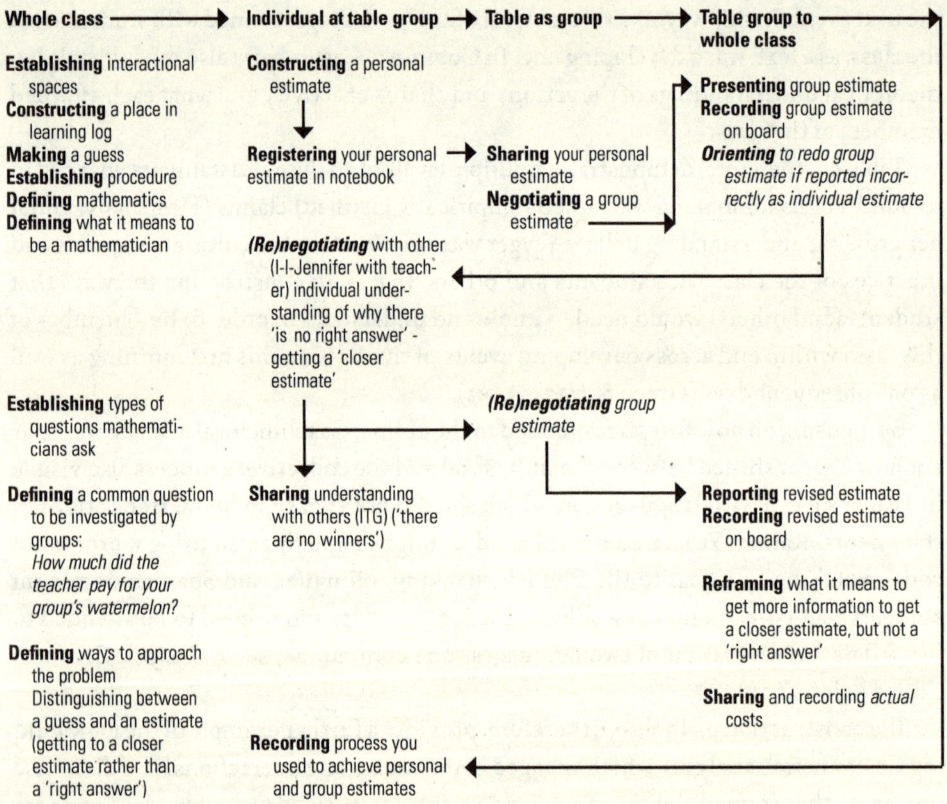

Figure 6.6. Nonlinear unfolding of the Watermelon Problem Event

Source: Reproduced from Yeager, B., Castanheira, M. L., & Green, J. (2020). Extending students' communicative repertoires: A culture of inquiry perspective for reflexive learning. In E. Manalo (Ed.), *Deeper learning, dialogic learning and critical thinking: Research-based strategies for the classroom* (pp. 84–104). London, England: Routledge. Permission granted by publisher.

As indicated in Figure 6.6, this event involved a series of interactional spaces (indicated in the top line in bold) and corresponding opportunities to learn as indicated by actions registered in present-continuous tense. All students were afforded a common opportunity to engage in a range of processes that began with a whole-class introduction and then engaged students in constructing personal estimates of the cost of the watermelon given to their table group. This then led to small-group interactions in two languages (Spanish and English, as needed) to explore how each student constructed their estimate. This phase also included actions that enabled students to collect and contrast, in two languages, information by weighing the table's watermelon and collecting information about cost per pound.

This phase then led to two students (re)presenting their table's work in English and Spanish to the whole class. This public (re)construction provided a basis for comparing, challenging, and learning from the actions of other class members, thereby creating a shared norm that members' knowledge was a text to examine and contrast. Finally, as indicated in Figure 6.6, different routes (indicated by arrows) were created that led not to a single correct answer but, rather, to one that engaged each table group in (re)visiting their initial understandings and to begin to (re)vise and extend their understandings, thinking, and approaches to solving this mathematical problem.

Analytic Level 6: From Micro-/Meso- to Macro-Level Analysis Across the Day

Castanheira's developing multilevel analyses, therefore, provided multiple sources of information that supported her growing understanding of what counted as being a student on the first morning. The analyses also make visible theoretical perspectives guiding the ways Castanheira interpreted how students engaged with and interpreted their watermelon data. This process involved, as indicated in Figure 6.7, different levels of analyses that parallel analyses presented previously (e.g., discourse, interaction, orientation, proxemic analysis, among others).

The final analytic process is grounded in Yeager's (2003) analysis of events on the first day of class, a process that included (re)examining Castanheira's data and analyses of the first morning and extending that analysis by tracing how students engaged in the ongoing construction of events across the day. As an ethnographer in 2003, in her dissertation study, Yeager stepped back from her knowledge as the teacher of this class to construct the following *taxonomy* of what was entailed in *being a student in the Tower.*

To construct this taxonomy, Yeager (2003) was guided by Spradley's (1980/2016) approach to *domain analyses*. Spradley argued that domain analysis entails the construction of categories based on *semantic relationships* (e.g., *x* is a kind of *y*, a step in *y*, a reason for *y*, a way of doing *y*, among others). Figure 6.7 (re)constructs part–whole relationships of Yeager's domain analysis (re)presented as a taxonomy. This taxonomy forms the basis for making visible what Yeager-as-ethnographer constructed as practices that constituted ways of being a student in the Tower class on the first day of the school year.

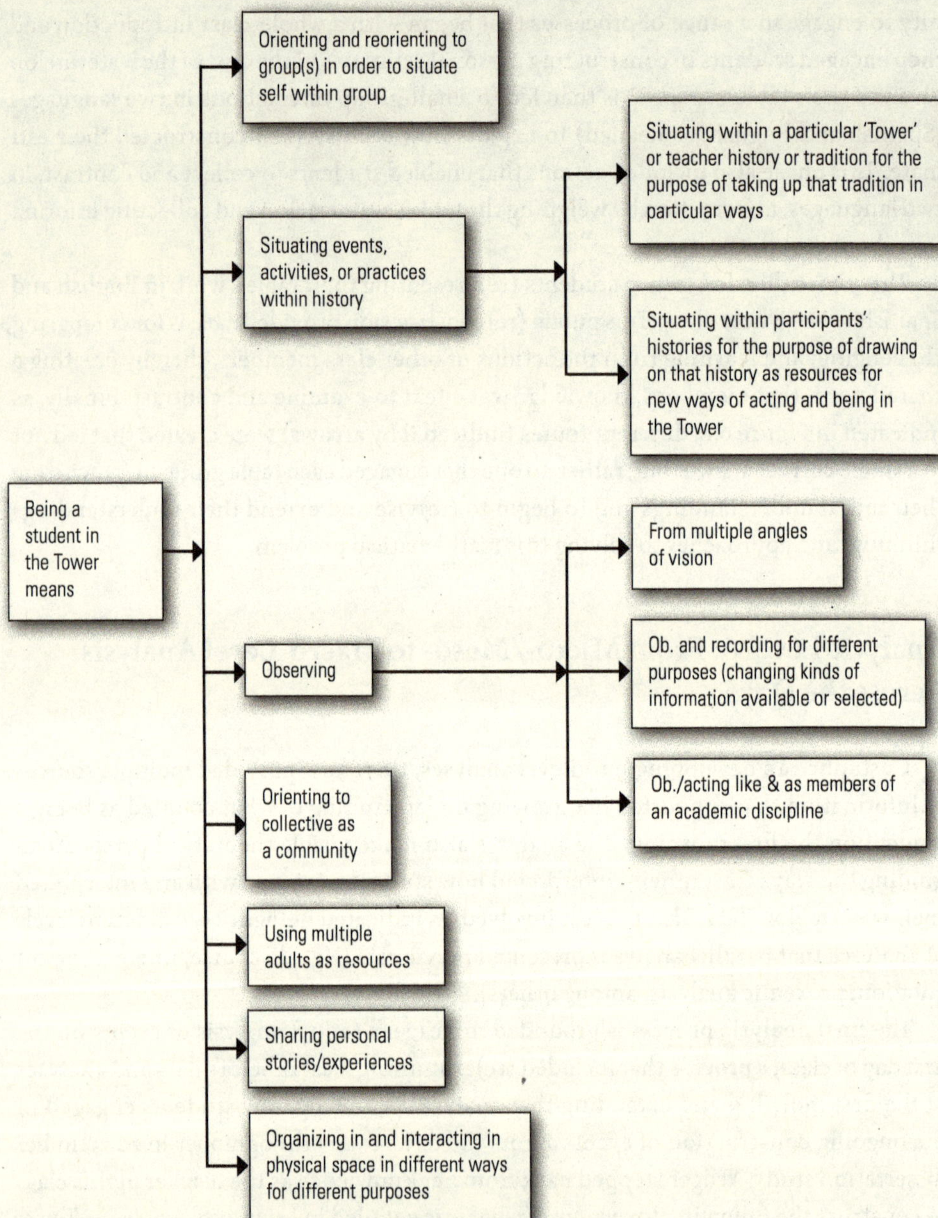

Figure 6.7. A range of potential practices and ways of being a student in the Tower as identified on the first day of class

Source: Adapted from Yeager (2003, p. 299).

Yeager's taxonomy of *Being a Student in the Tower Community* (Figure 6.7), therefore, demonstrates how domain analyses form the foundation for identifying the developing norms and expectations, roles, relationships, and actions that students constructed with Yeager and others across the day. Although not a full (re)presentation of the complex levels of analyses Yeager engaged in, this taxonomy (re)presents the range of practices identified through an Interactional Ethnographic logic-of-inquiry within and across levels of analyses. That is, this taxonomy forms the foundation for examining practices across the entire day and laid a base for tracing how and in what ways these actions were present across the school year, as well as across years (Green & Heras, 2011).

A Closing and an Opening: Final Thoughts for Potential Next Steps

The telling case study of Castanheira's and Yeager's logics-of-analyses made visible how levels of analyses were critical to tracing developing processes and practices being discursively and interactionally constructed in Yeager's class. Collectively, these analyses provide understandings of how these processes and practices created particular positions and potential identities for students and their teacher (and the ethnographer and others) within and across developing events (see also McVee, Brock, & Glazer, 2011). It also made transparent the following areas that an Interactional Ethnography logic-of-inquiry supports the following:

- Understandings of how to conceptualize learning as a developing process
- Understandings of culture as a verb—that is, ways of identifying developing norms and expectations, roles and relationships, and disciplinary or epistemic knowledge (Kelly, 2016)—as discursively and interactionally constructed in and across times, events, and configurations of participants

As framed in this chapter, an Interactional Ethnographic logic-of-inquiry constitutes an epistemological approach that supports analyses of classes as cultures-in-the-making. It further supports analyses of what constitutes *insider knowledge* from the perspective of ethnographers-as-learners who seek to construct more formal theories of classroom life. This latter conceptual argument makes visible potential relationships between scientific (i.e., research-based) knowledge and knowledge of those in whose lifeworld research is being undertaken. This process, therefore, raises the question of whose knowledge counts, in what ways, for what purpose, under what conditions, and in what contexts when we study others as part of academic practice.

The Interactional Ethnographic logic-of-analyses introduced in this chapter also made transparent how each level of analysis provides a basis for constructing particular theoretical insights as an event or activity is being proposed to, recognized, and acknowledged by particular participants (Bloome et al., 2005). Additionally, this logic-of-analyses made transparent ways of building warranted accounts of what counts as ways of learning, being (identities), and doing disciplinary, social, communicative, and cognitive life in the dynamic and developing lifeworld of a class (Heap, 1995; Green et al., in press-a; Kelly, 2016; Kelly & Green, 2019). Finally, the (re)construction of Castanheira's levels of analyses, and inclusion of Yeager's domain analysis, made visible the importance of taking up the position of *ethnographer-as-learner,* whether as an external (outsider) ethnographer entering a class or as a teacher-as-ethnographer engaged in (re) analysis of his or her class.

The question left unanswered for our authorial team is, *How and in what ways will you as readers construct your own local and reflexive logics-of-inquiry and logics-of-analyses in the sites you have selected?* Additionally, we look forward to engaging with readers exploring how Interactional Ethnography can provide a basis for your work.

Suggested Further Reading

Baker, W. D., & Green, J. (2007). Limits to certainty in interpreting video data: Interactional Ethnography and disciplinary knowledge. *Pedagogies: An International Journal,* 2(3), 1–13.

Green, J., Castanheira, M. L., Skukauskaite, A., & Hammond, J. (2015). Developing a multi-faceted research process: An ethnographic perspective for reading across traditions. In N. Markee (Ed.), *Handbook of classroom discourse and interaction* (pp. 26–43). Oxford, England: Wiley-Blackwell.

Santa Barbara Classroom Discourse Group. (1992). Do you see what we see? The referential and intertextual nature of classroom life. *Journal of Classroom Interaction,* 27(2), 29–36.

References

Agar, M. (1994). *Language shock: Understanding the culture of conversation.* New York, NY: William Morrow.

Agar, M. (2004.) We have met the other and we're all nonlinear: Ethnography as a nonlinear dynamic system. *Complexity, 10*(2), 16–24.

Agar, M. (2006a). An ethnography by any other name . . . *Forum Qualitative Sozialforschung/ Forum: Qualitative Social Research,* 7(4). Retrieved from http://www.qualitative-research.net/fqs

Agar, M. (2006b). Culture: Can you take it anywhere? *International Journal of Qualitative Methods,* 5(2), 1–12. Retrieved from http://www.ualberta.ca/~iiqm/backissues/5_2/PDF/agar.pdf

Anderson-Levitt, K. (2006). Ethnography. In J. Green, G. Camilli, & P. Elmore (Eds.), *Handbook of complementary methods in education research* (pp. 157–173). Mahwah, NJ: Earlbaum.

Baker, W. D., & Green, J. (2007). Limits to certainty in interpreting video data: Interactional Ethnography and disciplinary knowledge. *Pedagogies: An International Journal, 2*(3), 1–13.

Baker, W.D. & Däumer, E., (2015): Designing interdisciplinary instruction: exploring disciplinary and conceptual differences as a resource, *Pedagogies: An International Journal, 10*(1), 38-53. DOI: 10.1080/1554480X.2014.999776

Bakhtin, M. M. (1986). The problem of speech genres. In C. Emerson & M. Holmquist (Eds.), *Speech genres and other late essays* (pp. 60–102). Austin: University of Texas Press.

Beach, R., & Bloome, D. (2020). *Languaging relations for transforming the literacy and language arts classroom*. New York, NY: Taylor & Francis.

Bloome, D., Beauchemin, F., Brady, J., Buescher, E., Kim, M.-Y., & Schey, R. (2018). Anthropology of education, anthropology in education, and anthropology for education. In H. Callan (Ed.), *The international encyclopedia of anthropology* (pp. 1–10). Oxford: John Wiley & Sons.

Bloome, D., Carter, S., Christian, B., Otto, S., & Shuart-Faris, N. (2005). *Discourse analysis and the study of classroom language and literacy events: A microethnographic approach*. Mahwah, NJ: Erlbaum.

Bloome, D., & Egan-Robertson, A. (1993). The social construction of intertextuality in classroom reading and writing lessons. *Reading Research Quarterly, 28*, 305–333.

Brandts, L. (1999). Are pullout programs sabotaging classroom community in our elementary schools? *Primary Voices K–6, 7*(3), 9–16.

Carney, J. M. (1999). How classrooms as cultures influence entire schools. *Primary Voices K–6, 7*(3), 53.

Castanheira, M. L. (2000). *Situating learning within collective possibilities: Examining the discursive construction of opportunities for learning in the classroom* (Unpublished doctoral dissertation). University of California, Santa Barbara.

Castanheira, M. L. (2019). Ideologies languaged into being: Examining conversations on schooled and religious literacies as ideologies. In D. Bloome, M. L. Castanheira, C. Leung, & J. Rowsell (Eds.), *Re-theorizing literacy practices* (pp. 50–80). New York, NY: Routledge.

Castanheira, M. L., Green, J., Dixon, C., & Yeager, B. (2007). (Re)Formulating identities in the face of fluid modernity: An Interactional Ethnographic approach. *International Journal of Education Research, 46*, 172–189.

Castanheira, M. L., Green, J. L., & Yeager, E. (2008). Investigating inclusive practices: An interactional ethnographic approach. In K. Kumpulainen & M. César (Eds.), *Investigating classrooms: Methodologies in action* (pp. 235–268). Rotterdam, the Netherlands: Sense Publishers.

Castanheira, M. L., Street, B., & Carvalho, G. T. (2015). Navigating across academic contexts: Campo and Angolan students in a Brazilian university. *Pedagogies: An International Journal, 10*(1), 70–85.

Collins, E., & Green, J. (1991). Learning in classroom settings: Making or breaking a culture. In H. Marshall (Ed.), *Redefining learning: Roots of educational restructuring* (pp. 59–86). Norwood, NJ: Ablex.

Cordóva, R.A., & Balcerzak, P. (2013). Co-constructing cultural landscapes for disciplinary learning in and out of school: The next generation science standards and learning progressions in action. *Cultural Studies of Science Education, 4,* 1223–1242.

Dixon, C., Green, J., & Brandts, L. (2005). Studying the discursive construction of texts in classrooms. In R. Beach, J. Green, M. Kamil, & T. Shanahan (Eds.), *Multidisciplinary perspectives on literacy research* (pp. 349–390). Cresskill, NJ: Hampton Press.

Duranti, A., & Goodwin, C. (1992). Rethinking context: An introduction. In A. Duranti & C. Goodwin (Eds.), *Rethinking context: Language as an interactive phenomenon* (pp. 1–42). Cambridge, MA: Cambridge University Press.

Edwards, D., & Mercer, N. (1987). *Common knowledge.* New York, NY: Methuen.

Fairclough, N. (1992). Intertextuality in critical discourse analysis. *Linguistics and Education, 4,* 269–293.

Flores, S. (1999). Classrooms as cultures from a principal's perspective. *Primary Voices K–6, 7*(3), 54.

Gee, J. P., & Green, J. (1998). Discourse analysis, learning and social practice: A methodological study. *Review of Research in Education, 23,* 119–169.

Green, J., Baker, W. D., Chian, M., Vanderhoof, C., Hooper, L., Kelly, G., Skukauskaite, A., & Kalainoff, M. (in press-a). Studying the overtime construction of knowledge in educational settings: A microethnographic-discourse analysis approach. *Review of Research in Education.*

Green, J., Brock, C., Baker, W. D., & Harris, P. (in press-b). Positioning theory and discourse: Lenses and explanatory theory. In N. Nasir, R. Pea, C. Lee, & M. McKinney de Royston (Eds.), *Handbook on cultural foundations of learning.* Nasir, N., Lee, C., Pea, R., & McKinney de Royston, M. (forthcoming). The Handbook of Culture & Learning. Routledge: New York.

Green, J. L. & Castanheira, M. L. (2012). Exploring classroom life and student learning: An interactional ethnographic approach. In B. Kaur (Ed.), *Understanding teaching and learning: Classroom research revisited.* (pp. 53–65). Rotterdam, the Netherlands: Sense Publishers.

Green, J., & Dixon, C. (1993). Introduction. Talking knowledge into being: Discursive and social practices in classrooms. *Linguistics and Education, 5,* 231–240.

Green, J., & Heras, A. I. (2011). Identities in shifting educational policy contexts: Two languages, one community to English only. In G. Lopez-Bonilla & I. Englander (Eds.), *Discourses and identities in contexts of educational change* (pp. 155–194). New York, NY: Peter Lang.

Green, J., & Kelly, G. J. (2019). Appendix. In G. J. Kelly & J. Green, J. (Eds.). *Theory and methods for sociocultural research in science and engineering education* (pp. 264–270). New York, NY: Routledge.

Green, J., Skukauskaite, A., & Castanheira, M. L., (2013). Studying the discursive construction of learning lives for individuals and the collective. In O. Erstad & J. Sefton-Green (Eds.), *Identity, community, and learning lives in the digital age* (pp. 126–145). Cambridge, England: Cambridge University Press.

Green, J., & Wallat, C. (1981). Mapping instructional conversations: A sociolinguistic ethnography. In J. Green & C. Wallat (Eds.), *Ethnography and language in educational settings* (pp. 161–205). Norwood, NJ: Ablex.

Gumperz, J. J. (1982). *Discourse strategies.* Cambridge, MA: Cambridge University Press.

Gumperz, J. J., & Herasimchuk, E. (1972). Conversational analysis of social meaning. In R. Shuy (Ed.), *Sociolinguistics: Current trends & processes* (pp. 99–134). Washington, DC: Georgetown University Press.

Gutierrez, K. (1993). How talk, context, and script shape contexts for learning: A cross-case comparison of journal sharing. *Linguistics and Education, 5*, 335–365.

Heap, J. L. (1995). The status of claims in "qualitative" educational research. *Curriculum Inquiry, 25*, 271–292.

Heath, S. B. (1982). Ethnography in education: Defining the essentials. In P. Gilmore & A. A. Glatthorn (Eds.), *Children in and out of school: Ethnography and education* (pp. 33–55). Washington, DC: Center for Applied Linguistics.

Heath, S. B., & Street, B. V. (2008). *On ethnography: Approaches to language and literacy research*. New York, NY: Teachers College Press.

Kelly, G. J., (2016). Methodological considerations for the study of epistemic cognition in practice. In J. Greene, W. Sandoval, & I. Braton (Eds.), *The handbook of epistemic cognition* (pp. 393–408). New York, NY: Routledge.

Kelly, G. J., & Green, J. L. (Eds.). (2019). *Theory and methods for sociocultural research in science and engineering education*. New York, NY: Routledge.

Kumpulainen, K., Hmelo-Silver, C. E., & César, M. (2009). *Investigating classroom interaction: Methodologies in action*. Rotterdam, the Netherlands: Sense Publishers.

Lin, L. (1993). Language of and in the classroom: Constructing the patterns of social life. *Linguistics and Education, 5*, 367–409.

Manalo, E. (Ed.) (2020). *Deeper learning, dialogic learning and critical thinking: Research-based strategies for the classroom*. London, England: Routledge.

Markee, N. (Ed.). (2015). *Handbook of classroom discourse and interaction*. Oxford, England: Wiley-Blackwell.

McVee, M. B., Brock, C. H., & Glazier, J. A. (Eds.). (2011). *Sociocultural positioning in literacy: Exploring culture, discourse, narrative, and power in diverse educational contexts*. Cresskill, NJ: Hampton Press.

Mercer, N., & Hodgkinson, S. (Eds). (2008). *Exploring talk in school: Inspired by the work of Douglas Barnes*. London, England: Sage Publications.

Mishler, E. (1979). Meaning in context: Is there any other kind? *Harvard Educational Review* 49(1), 1–19.

Mitchell, C. J. (1984). Typicality and the case study. In R. F. Ellens (Ed.), *Ethnographic research: A guide to general conduct* (pp. 238–241). New York, NY: Academic Press.

Putney, L. (1997). *Collective-individual development in a fifth-grade bilingual classroom: An Interactional Ethnographic analysis of historicity and consequentiality* (Unpublished doctoral dissertation). University of California, Santa Barbara.

Putney, L., Green, J., Dixon, C., Durán, R., & Yeager, B. (2000). Consequential progressions: Exploring collective-individual development in a bilingual classroom. In C. Lee & P. Smagorinsky (Eds.), *Vygotskian perspectives on literacy research* (pp. 86–126). Cambridge, England: Cambridge University Press.

Rex, L. (2001). The remaking of a high school reader. *Reading Research Quarterly, 36*, 288–314.

Sheridan, D., Street, B., & Bloome, D. (2000). *Writing ourselves: Mass-observation and literacy practices*. New York, NY: Hampton Press.

Smith, L. M. (1978). An evolving logic of participant observation, educational ethnography and other case studies. *Review of Research in Education, 6*, 316–377.

Spradley, J. (2016). *Participant observation.* New York, NY: Harcourt Brace/Waveland Press. (Original work published 1980)

Street, B. (1993). *Cross-cultural approaches to literacy.* Cambridge, England: Cambridge University Press.

Street, B. (2005). Introduction. In D. Bloome, S. Carter, B., Christian, B., S. Otto, & N. Shuart-Faris (Eds.), *Discourse analysis and the study of classroom language and literacy events: A microethnographic approach* (pp. ix–xii). Mahwah, NJ: Erlbaum

Wegerif, R. (2020). Introduction to the theory of dialogic education. In N. Mercer, R. Wegerif, & L. Mayer (Eds.), *The Routledge international handbook of research on dialogic education* (pp. 11–13). New York, NY: Routledge.

Yeager, B. (1999). Constructing a community of inquirers. *Primary Voices K–6, 7*(3), 37–46.

Yeager, B., Castanheira, M. L., & Green, J. (2020). Extending students' communicative repertoires: A culture of inquiry perspective for reflexive learning. In E. Manalo (Ed.), *Deeper learning, dialogic learning and critical thinking: Research-based strategies for the classroom* (pp. 84–104). London, England: Routledge.

Yeager, B., Floriani, A., & Green, J. (1998). Learning to see learning in the classroom: Developing an ethnographic perspective. In A. Egan-Robertson & D. Bloome (Eds.), *Students as researchers of culture and language in their own communities* (pp. 115–139). Cresskill, NJ: Hampton Press.

Yeager, E. (2003). *"I am a historian": Examining the discursive construction of locally situated academic identities in linguistically diverse settings.* (Unpublished doctoral dissertation). University of California, Santa Barbara.

Yeager, E., Green, J. L., & Castanheira, M. L. (2009). Two languages, one community: On the discursive construction of community in bilingual classrooms. In M. César & K. Kumpulainen (Eds.), *Social interactions in multicultural settings* (pp. 146–178). Rotterdam, the Netherlands: Sense Publishers.

CHAPTER 7

Examining Qualitative Data Using Spreadsheets: Constructing Analytical Narratives Around Talk, Action, and Practice

Judy Kalman, Patricia Valdivia, and Victor Rendón

THIS CHAPTER DESCRIBES our approach to using spreadsheets to analyze and interpret literacy data. It draws on a study of some everyday practices in a small cybershop located in an economically impoverished area of Mexico City (a cybershop offers customers access to Internet-linked computers, printers, photocopiers, and stationery supplies). We begin from the point where data transcription ends. Converting oral exchanges, graphic displays, and other data collected during fieldwork into text compose the first analytic step in research. We make decisions about what to transcribe, how to code these transcriptions, and what to describe about an artifact or photographic image. As we construct these written representations, we build our analytic methodology by conjugating our theoretical framing, our methodological stance, and our data. The same is true for systematically analyzing our data, establishing themes, interpreting events, and understanding the patterns we observe. Here the challenge is knowing what to do with transcriptions or fieldwork descriptions once we have them.

In this chapter, we share our process of constructing a database for qualitative data using spreadsheets, a tool common to most computers or freely available via Google Drive. An important impetus for designing our analytical procedure was Chris Hahn's 2008 book, *Doing Qualitative Research Using Your Computer: A Practical Guide*. As with various—often expensive—software packages developed since the 1990s to help researchers manage and analyze data, spreadsheets make data "searchable." Such computer applications make it easy to look for specific names or phrases, annotations, and data sets. They also allow the analyst to quickly locate and link data, codes, and notes; organize them according to purpose; and then retrieve them as part of refining codes, developing categories, and the like. The following pages contain a series of suggestions about how to organize written data using a spreadsheet and how to unpack talk, actions, and practice through contextualized analysis.

Background

Our current work studies the everyday uses of digitally mediated literacy practices in a poor urban neighborhood in Mexico's sprawling capital city. We want to shed light on the complexity of routine situations and the knowledge and know-how that go into making a photocopy or renting a computer in a cybershop. We also strive to carefully examine those situations that, for some reason, represent a particular challenge. Our corpus of data covers a wide range of cases and practices—from the evolution of official handwritten documents to the production of data-based and computer-generated ones, from self-generated language learning to the representation of electronic circuits in popular art. For this chapter, however, we develop and discuss an example from our data that examines the complexities of editing a hard-copy document in the process of reproducing it.

We began our fieldwork with two "big questions": What are some of the digital practices involved in participating in everyday literacy practices, and how are they accomplished? Because technology use often implies access to material and symbolic resources that poor people do not have, we wondered how people solve everyday digital needs such as filling out forms online or downloading documents. As our work progressed, we began to ask more specific questions about what factors facilitated or restricted technology use, in what ways did mediators intervene on others' behalf, and what kinds of knowledge and know-how are mobilized and displayed within the contexts we were observing.

New Literacy Studies is the theoretical starting point for our study. Its basic tenet, that literacies are situated complex activities that locate reading, writing, and other forms of representation within the context of broader social practices, is essential to our approach and understanding (see Street, 1984). New Literacy Studies emphasize the contextualized nature of reading, writing, and other meaning-making practices and underscores the importance of social relationships, material conditions, issues of power, and institutional arrangements as part of the mix (Barton & Hamilton, 2000; Street, 1995). Social practices are central to our inquiry.

Our understanding resonates with Reckwitz's (2002) notion of *practice* as both a way to signal human action (*praxis*) and as a way to focus on relatively stable forms of doing things (*praktik*). As such, *practice* often involves multiple interconnected parts: background knowledge, know-how, histories, ways of using the body, thought, language, different artifacts, situated contexts, and feelings. Being vegetarian provides a clear illustration of the notion of a specific practice. Preparing a meal, for example, implies a particular way of thinking about eating, the body, and health; it requires purchasing ingredients (fresh fruits and vegetables over frozen or canned goods), cooking in a certain way, adhesion to a kind of vegetarianism (vegans or lacto-ovo vegetarians), the type of utensils and machines used in food preparation (food processor, juicer, rice cooker, slow cooker, woks, Teflon-coated pans), and so on (Rendón & Kalman, 2017). Here we see how a particular articulation of know-how and beliefs (about health, what "counts" as vegetarian food, etc.), ways of doing (shopping for foodstuffs, cooking methods, how to use various kitchen tools), and processes come together to define a particular practice (i.e., vegetarian cooking).

The concept of *practice* refers to not only what people do but also what they think about what they are doing in the process of participating in the multiple events that make up social life (Hernández, 2015; Kalman, 2002; Schatzki, 2010). Practices therefore include beliefs and ways of thinking, but we cannot observe such things directly. So to examine and analyze practice, we therefore consider the observable arrays of human activities that connect materialities, actions, and purposes that occur in the context of events (Knorr-Cetina, Schatzki & Von Savigny, 2001). In this chapter, we are specifically interested in literacy practices and literacy events (see Jackobsen & Tønnessen, this volume). It is precisely in the intersection of activities and material arrangements at specific times and in particular places that social phenomena occur (Schatzki, 2010). One of the characteristics of any given practice is that it is often linked to other practices, forming sets or bundles of practices. This feature suggests that human activities are rarely a discrete sequence of actions but are more likely to be indeterminate, shifting, and interconnected (e.g., being a vegetarian includes cooking vegetarian meals and may also include choosing to wear nonleather clothing or growing one's food). Furthermore, we examine materiality within its *context of use* (de Certeau, 1984) and pay close attention to how people and cultures construct and assign meaning to artifacts. We want to know what these artifacts are made of, what you can do with them, and how they are used. Leonardi (2010) usefully points out that considerations of materiality—material things in the world—also include digital materiality and tangible artifacts, such as computers, tablets, routers, modems, mobile phones, video consuls made of plastic, circuit boards, microchips, and cables, along with perhaps less conventionally material (in an analog sense) artifacts such as programs, apps, and a variety of software.

The ongoing push to make services that we once stood in line for available through the internet—registering for a class, making a bank deposit, making an inquiry—has created the need to get to a computer, log in, and deal with bureaucracies, authorities, family members, and others in ways that for many are deeply unfamiliar. Often, people can be forced to engage with the shift to digital materialities regardless of their wants and concerns by dint of no face-to-face or pen-and-paper options being available. In our research, we set out to learn how people are challenged to adapt or work around existing and new procedures, troubleshoot when something goes wrong, and resolve breakdowns and crashes in situations of scarcity and fragmentation where electricity and connectivity fail, devices are made obsolete, and software might be bootlegged and buggy (Jackson, 2014; Prieto-Nañez, 2016).

We conducted our fieldwork in a variety of settings in one of the most impoverished areas of Mexico City; 39.2% of the population is poor; nearly 24% have not completed compulsory basic education (i.e., they have less than 9 years of schooling); 1% live in housing that has dirt floors, lacks running water, or has no indoor sanitation (Delegación Política de Tláhuac, 2015). We documented a series of micro-events in cybershops, government offices, and on the street; these events often lasted only a couple of minutes and are part of the continuous, ongoing *parole*—language in use—of literacy and technology, sites of learning and appropriation, and the place where technology users establish relationships with devices, infrastructure, social knowledge, and processes through their ways of using them (Chartier, 1984; Saussure, 1983; Sewell, 2005). The example we selected to illustrate how we use a spreadsheet to help manage our data analysis took place in Saíba, a cybershop (pseudonyms are used throughout). Saíba is an informal micro family business, with five computers for hire; photocopying, printing, and scanning services; and a small collection of stationery goods for sale. Also available are digital access services such as buying airtime for cell phones, activating accounts, and downloading needed documents from the Internet. The physical space is small in size; there is barely room to turn around in between the computers and the printer. Jocelyn, the main participant in our study, sits in the back at her computer, and her mother—the owner of the shop—usually is behind a small counter set up at the front.

Data Collection and Preparation

We observed participants while they were working, made notes, and documented their ongoing attention to customers and their continuous multitasking. When conditions allowed it, we were able to briefly interview Jocelyn and record it in audio or video. When she was too busy to interact with us, we depended on our ability to watch and develop our field notes to register what seemed to be significant events.

We transcribed all recorded data verbatim, using an abbreviated version of sociolinguistic annotation (see Kalman, 1999) and transcript preparation advice in Gumperz and Berenz (1993), Gee (2005), and Skukauskaite (2012). When transforming speech into written text, different forms of communication and meaning-making (interruptions, overlaps, elongations, intonations, silences or pauses, laughter, gestures, and actions) are easily lost. Written symbols to indicate *how* speakers say something make it easier to register not just what people were saying but what they were doing and what they most likely meant.

We followed Gee's (2005) proposal for how to prepare transcripts for analysis by dividing each participant's turns into stanzas or phrases by locating each clause on a different line and then grouping lines into stanzas. We based the separations of long turns or prolonged utterances on the presence of a verb, the coordinating conjunctions (copulative, adversative, disjunctive, distributive) or subordinates (causal, comparative, conditional, consecutive, concessional, temporary or final), and the elements to which they refer. We incorporated our field notes as much as possible into the transcripts as a way of contextualizing talk, clarifying certain aspects of events, and describing the nonverbal actions that occurred during interactions.

Setting up a Spreadsheet (Excel)

Once we transcribe our spoken data, we use Excel (2019) software to generate a workbook for each participant and titled it with their name or pseudonym. For this chapter, we present a selection from Jocelyn's case. The workbook, which bears her name, contains a total of 23 sheets, one for each of the 23 times we visited her (see Figure 7.1).

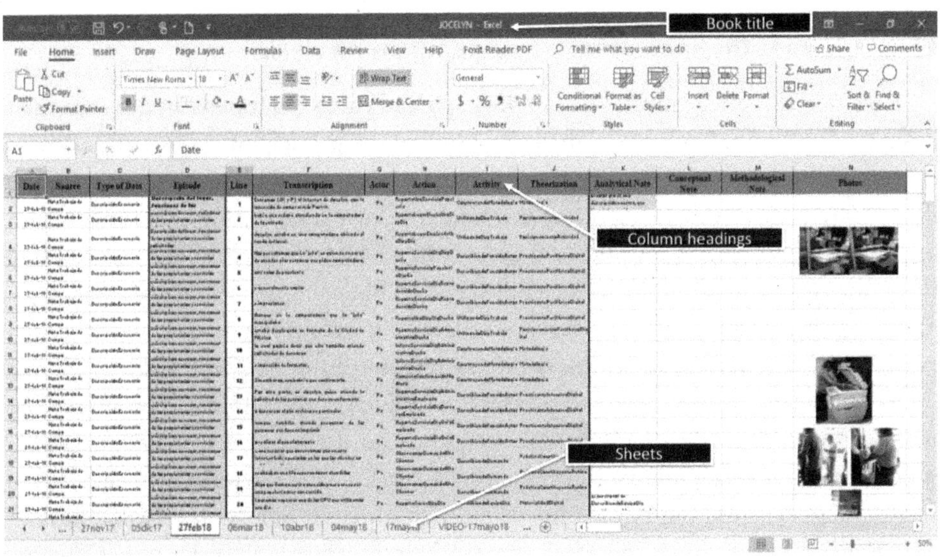

Figure 7.1. Setting up Jocelyn's spreadsheets

The next step is to label each of the columns in the spreadsheets (and using the same column headings for each sheet). The first few columns contain information about the data (date it was collected, data source, type of data, episode, line of the transcription, and actor). The next set of column headings reflects the theoretical framework that guided our analysis and therefore varies from study to study, depending on the data and purpose of a project. In our current study, we are interested in understanding the complexities of using digital technologies to meet everyday demands, participate in valued activities, and establish and maintain communication with others. Our analysis and reflections are guided by cultural-historical activity theory, theories of practice, and interactional sociolinguistics.

For this reason, our column headings focus on Actions (including speech) and Activities (see Cole, 1985). In the theorization column, we contextualize the data by situating them in broader social, historical, and cultural processes. For example, in this column, we identify those activities that are routine to cybershops like Saíba or standard ways of opening and closing everyday interactions. Finally, we assign cells for analytical, conceptual, and methodological notes. We also insert photographs to keep graphic materials close to the verbal interactions. In Table 7.1, we present the column headings and briefly describe and define each one.

To create the column headings, we place these labels in Row 1 of the spreadsheet. To be able to scroll down the spreadsheet without the titles disappearing, we freeze the first row by going to the *Home* menu, selecting *View*, and then activating the *Freeze upper row* option. In this way, the headings in Row 1 remain visible even when you scroll the spreadsheet down.

Placing Data in the Spreadsheet: Beginning the Analysis

Now that the spreadsheet is set up, we copy and paste the transcriptions into their designated column. Each row represents a line of the participants' discourse. People do not talk in lines like these; this is our written representation of their speech and the flow of interaction. The division into lines indicates the relationship existing between one line and another, and the broader activity in which these expressions are inserted (Gee, 2005). The horizontal relationships between the columns characterize, describe, and analyze each line while the vertical relationships contextualize and situate each participants' actions and activities within the ongoing flow of a given event.

As we read our data, we begin to get a feel for different moments in each event and the issues or topics that participants talk about and act on. To keep track of how an issue or topic develops, we tag different lines as part of an episode or set within an event (Dyson, 2006). These episodes can be continuous or discontinuous. For example, Episode A begins, and without ending, Episode B starts. When Episode B ends, Episode C begins. Without Episodes A and C ending, Episode D emerges. After Episode D ends, Episode A finishes, and Episode C continues until it is completed (see Figure 7.2).

We give each episode a name and label each line. In addition, we frame each episode with a dark border that makes it possible to identify the different episodes that make up an event. This visual marker helps to understand how participants develop their topics of interest (see Figure 7.2).

Table 7.1. Spreadsheet column headings for qualitative data analysis

Column headings in the spreadsheet (Excel)		
Column	**Column Heading**	**Content**
1	Date	Day when we collected the data in a day-month-year format.
2	Source	Name of the digital file where data is located.
3	Type of Data	Description of the type of data (written observations, audio transcriptions with notes about actions, or video transcriptions).
4	Episode	Thematic grouping of data that allows understanding the relationship between discontinuous fragments of data.
5	Line	Numbering of transcript rows to identify specific fragments.
6	Transcription	Text divided into simple lines according to Gee's (2005) methodological suggestions.
7	Actor	Identification of all participants involved in a given interaction and activity. Generally, each participant's initials are noted; this helps with keeping track of the different participants across their talk, action, and artifact use.
8	Action	Comprises the outcomes of a first close reading of data that describes what is happening line by line. Short sentences begin with a conjugated verb as a way of pointing out (1) who is acting (conjugated verbs in Spanish signal person, number and tense) and (2) a specific action (e.g., accept, comment, write, imagine, deny, ask, etc.). We add a direct object that gives specificity to the action (for example Accepts Suggestion, Imagines Procedure, Questions Cost, etc.).
9	Activity	This comprises a second level of analysis that groups several specific actions within a broader, organized activity (Cole, 1985) With this, we begin to construct the meaning and contextual purpose of what is being done at a specific time. The tags used are phrases composed of a verb in gerund form and a complement (Hahn, 2008) to signal an ongoing process. For example: Agreeing Digital Service, Building Product Possibilities, Filling out a Form, etc.
10	Theorization	Based on our theoretical framework (our understanding of guiding concepts such as speech acts, activity, social practice, literacy, digital culture, among others), we locate the activities within broader arrangements and signal possible explanations and interpretations of specific actions and activities in social-historical processes.
11	Analytical Note	Written comments during the analytical process as a way to record our ideas, questions, observations, or clarifications about our examination of the data.
12	Conceptual Note	Comments written to clarify or expand the theoretical notions referred to during the analytical process or include authors who address these terms.
13	Methodological Note	Written comments during the analytical process as a way to record researcher ideas, questions, and observations or clarifications about fieldwork and analytical procedures.
14	Photos	Digital files located at the height of the corresponding transcript fragment. Often during analysis, we examine photos to expand on or support certain information.

Source: Adapted from Kalman & Rendón (2016).

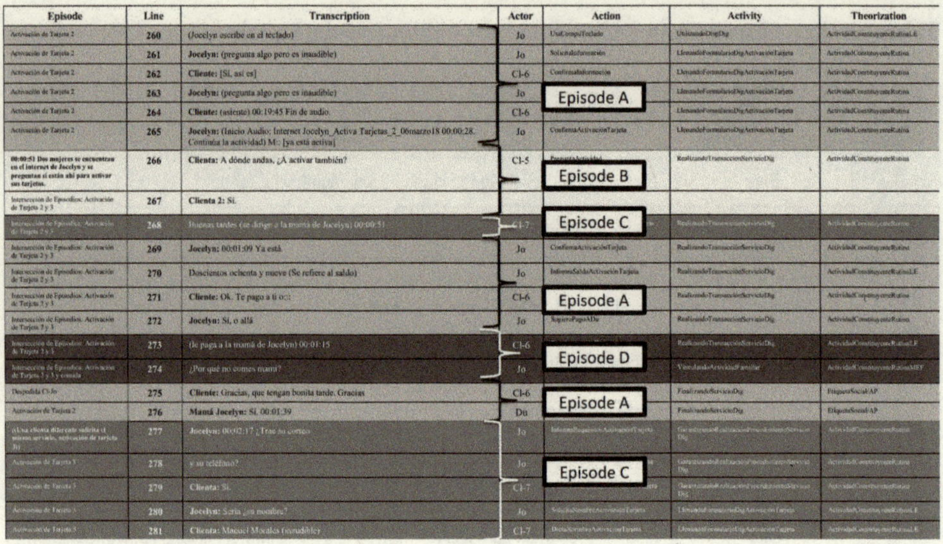

Figure 7.2. Episodes

In the line column, we number each row in ascending order; this helps when working with different fragments that make up the entire transcript. After the transcription column, we identify the speaker (actor). This shows the different shifts that occur during an interaction. We generally list the speakers' initials. Although the transcript identifies each participant at the start of an utterance, if we decide to divide a turn further, losing track of who the speaker is, is easy. As a safety measure, we reiterate who the speaker is in this column.

Spreadsheets also have a tool called Pivot Table, and as its name indicates, it reorganizes the rows and columns of any given table. Pivoting tables enables us to look at our data and analysis in a variety of ways so we can summarize, explore, compare, and present our analyses in various forms. To pivot a table, select all the cells or a range of data that you want to include. Including the headings of each column is always essential because the spreadsheet software will use the first selected line as the organizing label (see Figure 7.3). If you are not selecting all the data from the beginning, but the first row is frozen, select it along with the displayed data you wish to pivot.

Once the columns are selected, in the Insert menu, select the Pivot Table option. This will display a submenu where you choose the location of the pivot table: in a new spreadsheet or in an existing one (see Figure 7.4). We prefer a new spreadsheet because it is easier to manipulate the information fields and to keep track of the original spreadsheet.

Describing Actions and Talk

To begin our close-up examination of the talk, actions, and demeanor that make up people's participation, we use the Actions column. We create tags (descriptors that are

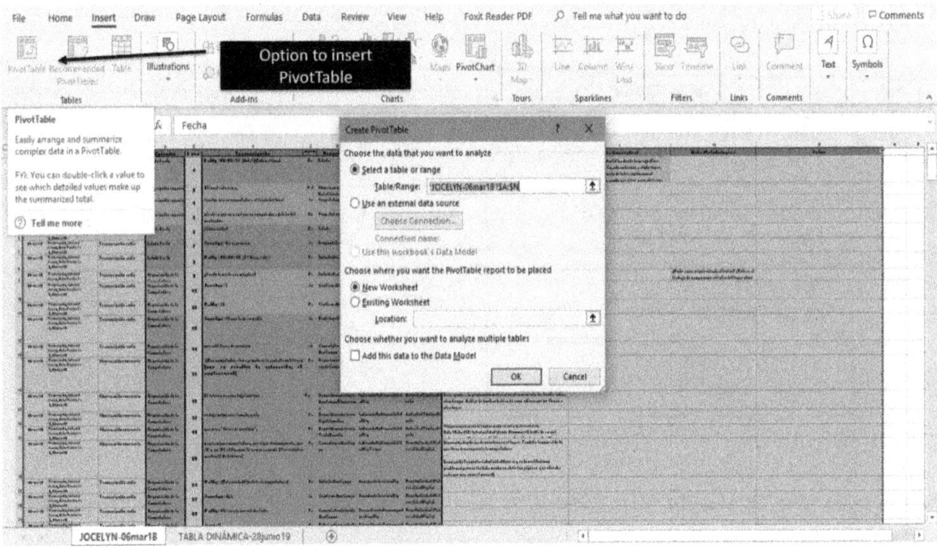

Figure 7.3. Setting up Pivot Tables

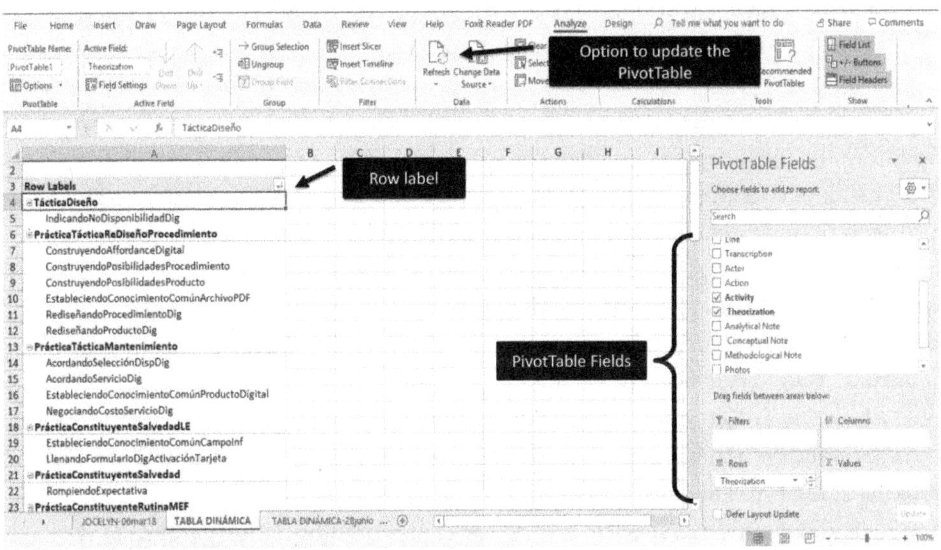

Figure 7.4. Pivot Tables in a new spreadsheet

abbreviated annotations) by identifying a transitive verb in third-person present tense and adding a direct object (a "last name" to give specificity to the different ways of participating; see Table 7.2). We start the beginning of a new word with a capital letter to facilitate reading and identifying the elements that make up the tags. Tags are similar

Table 7.2. Creating tags

Line	Transcription	Actor	Action
34	Client: two sets *Cliente: dos juegos*	Cl →	IndicatesQuantityCopies *IndicaCantidadCopias*
35	Owner: It would be::: four pesos... *Dueña: serian:: cuatro pesos ...*	Du →	CommentCostDigServiceReproduction *ComentaCostoServicioDigReproducción*
36	Both sides? *de los dos lados?*	Du →	QuestionDigIReproductionService *PreguntaServicioDigReproducción*
37	Client: Yes, please. *Cliente: Si, par favor.*	Cl →	NodsBothSides *AsienteDosLados*

to a simple sentence: *subject (in the actor column) + transitive verb in the present indicative + direct object*. For example,

34 C1 (customer abbreviation) + Indicates + NumberOfCopies
35 Du (owner's abbreviation) + Comments + CostServiceDigCopy
36 Du + [Tacit Question: Do you want?] + QuestionsDigReproductiveService
37 C1 + Nods + [Tacit complement: two sides]

In Table 7.2, there are two participants in this exchange, the customer (Cl—*cliente* in Spanish) and the owner (Du—*dueña* in Spanish). We use a tag to indicate their actions: The customer tells the owner how many copies he wants, and the owner responds by saying to the customer the cost and asking him how he wants his copies made.

We abbreviate "digital" as "Dig" in all the instances where we want to talk about anything digital, and we always use the same tag as part of the direct object (Lines 35 and 36). In the preceding examples, the abbreviation *Dig* is present in the tags CommentsCostDigServiceReproductions (*ComentaCostoServicioDigReproducción*) and AsksAboutDigitalReproductionService (*PreguntaServicioDigReproducción*). In a search over several days' data or between research participants, this tag would be useful for looking at the types of questions people ask. We could also use it to differentiate when the tag is about a specific service, artifact, or as part of information gathering. We have other tags such as Uses Digital Device (*UsaDispDigital*; device in Spanish is *dispositivo*) where we use *Dig*. What we decide to make explicit and specify in the direct object portion of our tag depends on what we are trying to make visible, our interests, and reflections. The same is true for the next column, the activity category. Activities are composed of multiple small actions (Cole, 1985), and, in this column, we identify the larger activity taking place.

One of the challenges of creating tags is to be consistent in the choice of words. When we first begin analyzing, we freely use verbs and direct objects as they come to mind.

Once we have examined several events, we collect all the verbs and scrutinize them for redundancies. For example, in some instances, we use "comments," and in another, we use "says." We then decide which verb to keep to signal the same action. This is especially important when more than one person is analyzing data. Being consistent in the tags makes contrasting and comparing easier and more precise. Figure 7.5 is a sampling of 11 verbs and their tags.

To check the complete collection of verbs that we use at the start of our analysis, we utilize the Pivot Table option. In the Field panel of the Pivot Table option, we select the descriptor column and deactivate the rest. This generates a list of all the descriptors that we place. This tool counts the number of descriptors and the number of times each one is used. But the most important feature is that it facilitates reviewing the tags and revising them in terms of doing away with synonyms or overlaps (when we inadvertently tag similar actions in different ways). For example, we have a descriptor ConfirmPasswordActivationCard and another ConfirmPasswordForActivationCard. In this case, we decide to omit the preposition and use the first one every time we come across this action as a way to make our tags more uniform and searchable. It also allows us to identify when there were two descriptors for the same action, for example, StipulatePasswordActivationCard and SpecifyPasswordActivationCard. We keep only the second tag and go back to the spreadsheet to replace the first tag with our chosen descriptor (i.e., SpecifyPasswordActivationCard). The spreadsheet has an option for finding and replacing all tags at once automatically, which makes changing tags easy and quick to do. Thus, our revisions and refinements take us from an original list of 119 tags to 65 tags for one day's data, an amount that is easier to handle for analysis. As we move to other data from a different day or another participant, we try to use existing tags as much as possible and create new ones only when none of the existing ones aptly describe what we are seeing.

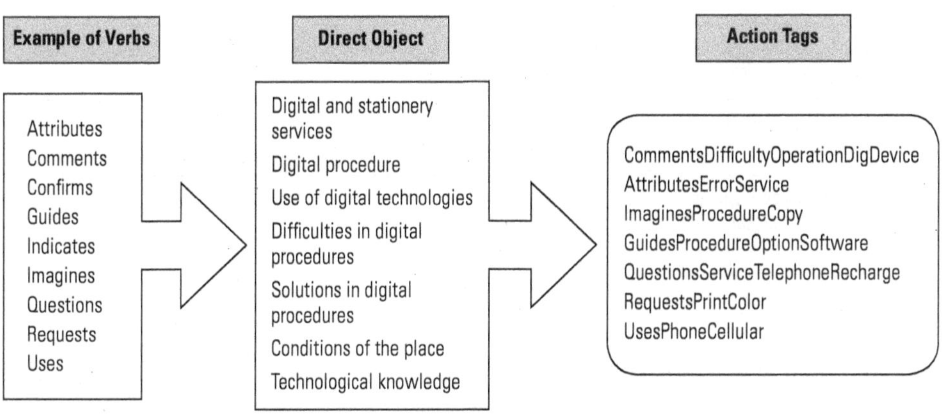

Figure 7.5. Sample verbs, direct objects, and tags

Constructing Activities

As a way of grouping descriptors, we identify the activities the participants constructed. The "Activity" category (and spreadsheet column) bridges the description of the actions we discussed earlier, and the theoretical dimensions of the activities (discussion follows). Here we use a verb in the gerund (after Hahn, 2008) to signal ongoing activity and to make visible how several actions interweave in complex processes. This enables us to examine multiple actions constituting an activity defined by participants' practices, specific meanings, and purposes. As in the case of the action tags, we complete the *–ing* verbs with a direct object as a way of giving specificity to the activities. For example, when two people fill out a form on a digital platform (activity), they execute several actions (confirm, dictate, specify, ask, write, request, and verify). Therefore, an activity can be analyzed in terms of the multiple actions that make it up, its purposes, how participants contribute, and so on. When Jocelyn and her clients filled out a form to buy airtime for their mobile phones, for example, the activity FillingFormDigRechargeTelephone (*LlenandoFormularioDigRecargaTelefónica*), is made up of several actions. We defined the form filling activity as *a collaboration process between participants to complete the required fields on a digital form necessary for requesting or obtaining a specific service.* In Table 7.3, we list the different actions that make up this activity:

Table 7.3. Action tags that make up an activity

FillingFormDigRechargeTelephone ***(LlenandoFormularioDigRecargaTelefónica)***
AsksCompanyRechargeTelephone *(PreguntaCompañíaRecargaTelefónica)*
SpecifiesCompanyRechargeTelephone *(EspecificaCompañíaRecargaTelefónica)*
AsksAmountRechargeTelephone *(PreguntaCantidadRecargaTelefónica)*
SpecifiesAmountRechargeTelephone *(EspecificaCantidadRecargaTelefónica)*
ConfirmsServiceRechargeTelephone *(ConfirmaServicioRecargaTelefónica)*
DictatesNumberRechargeTelephone *(DictaNúmeroRecargaTelefónica)*
UsesCompuKeyboard *(UsaCompuTeclado)*
AsksForConfirmationNumberRechargeTelephone *(SolicitaConfirmaciónNúmeroRecargaTelefónica)*
VerifiesNumberRechargeTelefone *(VerificaNúmeroRecargaTelefónica)*

The Pivot Table function is handy for integrating all the actions within one activity because it displays each activity (and its composite actions) as a separate entity. It also provides a way to review the activities themselves as an intermediate category halfway between the descriptor tags and more theory-informed categories. For example, in addition to selecting the activity column in the field table, we also drag across into the mix a given tag from the *Values Field*. This displays the number of times this tag is used in the pivoted table and helps identify which activities are the most common, as well as those activities that appear to be less common. In the latter cases, we review the data to see if combining those activities with other ones is possible, so that we can avoid or minimize ad hoc tags. This step is essential in revising and discussing how to conceptualize all the activities in what we observed and how each activity can be understood.

Another option in the spreadsheet is the use of filters. Filters display a list of tags in any given column and can be activated or deactivated for different reasons. If we are consistent in the way we tag activities and actions, we can appreciate the different variations of any given activity. For example, in the screenshot in Figure 7.5, there are three different activities related to filling out forms: FillingFormDigActivationBank-Card (*LlenandoFormularioDigActivaciónTarjeta*), FillingFormDigitalPayInformation (*LlenandoFormularioDigConsultaPago*), and FillingFormDigitalAirtimeMobile (*Llenand-oFormularioDigRecargaTelefónica*). Although each activity may involve similar actions, different artifacts and purposes are involved, and, as such, each activity—despite appearing at first glance to be similar—actually connects the participants to different institutions and social practices. In the example drawn on in our discussion here, Jocelyn is helping her customer activate a bank card, but other activities in our data concern buying air time for a mobile phone, downloading a financial statement, or repurposing a poster, to name just three.

To activate the filters on a spreadsheet, there is an option at the top of the screen that says "Sort and Filter." This option has a dropdown menu and you can select the "filter" option. Once this is turned on, you are able to select the tags you want to see. This includes a list that gives a glimpse of how the tags are grouped at present. If the tags have been constructed systematically, this also automatically clusters them in "families," that is, grouping together closely related tags that signal similar actions and activities.

Over time, we have had several interesting discussions about putting a verb in the gerund and concluded that doing so is not enough to depict broader activities. On the contrary, there is a risk of leaving the intermediate categories at the action level. For example, at one point we include as activity tags PayingStationeryProduct and ChargingStationeryProduct when, in fact, these are actions that can be subsumed into more complex activities. Using specific tags such as these actually fragments the data in a way that blurs what else is going on besides making a payment and collecting funds. This leads us to carefully reexamine what we are interested in highlighting and

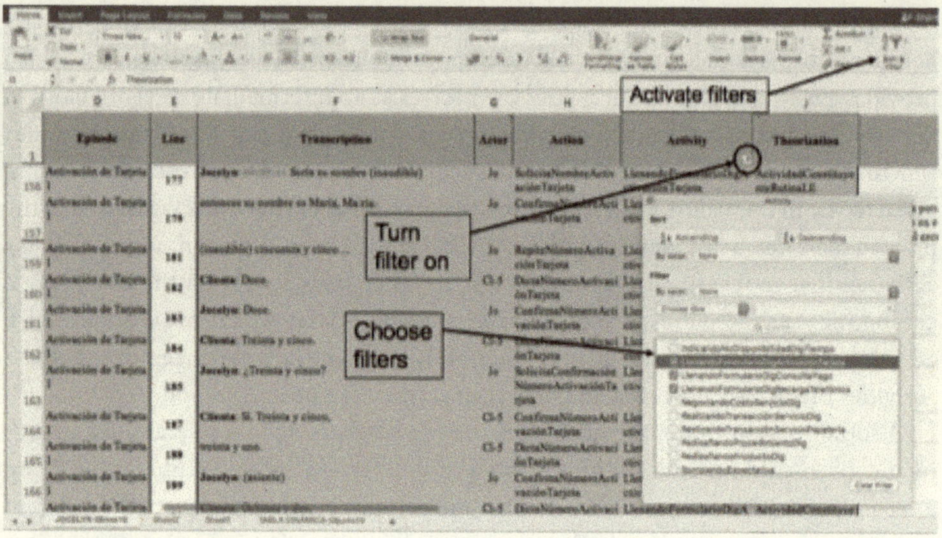

Figure 7.6. Using filters

to reconceptualize the activity as PerformingTransactionStationery (*RealizandoTransacciónPapelería*), which allows us to see and record aspects of the full activity.

Using the Pivot Table option, we created the following fragment of a larger event to illustrate how complex something as familiar as coming to an agreement about how to make a photocopy can be. In this case, however, it is not just a straight forward copy job. Prior to the selected data, two young women ask Jocelyn and the owner if they can scan a document, but they want them to eliminate an image when doing so. As the conversation moves forward, it becomes clear that what they want is a photocopy, not a scan of their document. We reorganize the data by pivoting the table so that the Activity column is put first, allowing us to identify all the actions that go into figuring out how to reproduce the flyer without the image (see Table 7.4). Immediately before this moment, one of the clients asks if there is a way to use whiteout to remove the unwanted section.

This exchange takes place in barely a minute and shows how four people interact to agree on how to reproduce a document when it does not involve a straightforward photocopy. What we have denominated as ConstructingPossibilitiesProcedure consists of imagining what the final product will look like, considering possible flaws, doing a trial run and accepting the expense, checking to make sure that the outcome is acceptable, and making the trial copy. Each one of these actions is expressed through talk and physical movements and involves using or referring to different artifacts such as the flyer, the printer, whiteout, extra paper, and so on. Due to their continuous occurrence and reiterations, small interactions in everyday events often look like nothing ever happens, when, in fact, a lot is going on.

Table 7.4. Building possibilities

Activity: BuildingPossibilitiesProcedure/*ConstruyendoPosibilidadesProcedimiento*	
Action	**Transcription**
ImagineProcedureCopy ImaginaProcedimientoCopia	((The client asks if she used whiteout on what they wanted to cover (a drawing), would it be in the copy of the document)) ((La clienta pregunta que si le ponía corrector a aquello que querían tapar saldría en la copia del documento))
ConsiderResultCopy ConsideraResultadoCopia	((Jocelyn tells her that sometimes the whiteout can be noticed Jocelyn le dice que a veces si se llega a notar el corrector))
ImagineProcedureCopy ImaginaProcedimientoCopia	**Client 2 (companion):** And if you cover it, and make a copy, do you think it will come out? **Clienta 2 (acompañante):** ¿Y si lo tapa, y le saca una copia, cree que salga?
MinimizeCost MinimizaCosto	**Jocelyn's Mom:** One peso. **Mamá de Jocelyn:** Un peso.
RequestConfirmationProcedureCopy SolicitaConfirmaciónProcedimientoCopia	**Customer:** What do you think? ((to his companion)) **Clienta:** ¿Cómo ves? ((a su acompañante))
SuggestProcedure SugiereProcedimiento	**Jocelyn's Mom:** Well, do the test. **Mamá de Jocelyn:** Pues hagan la prueba.
RequestProcedureAtypicalCopy SolicitaProcedimientoAtípicoCopia	**Customer:** Uhum. Yep. **Clienta:** Uhum. Sip.

Theorizing: Practices, Tactics, and Mediation

The preceding intermediate categories serve as the basis for developing theoretical concepts and insights. In developing our theoretical ideas, we try to think about our data in light of related concepts we have found in the literature, our interests, and the ideas that guide our analysis. For this research project, we developed the concept of *routine constituent activities* that characterize the usual goings-on of cybershop. However, we also developed a way of tagging and understanding what happens when an activity gets derailed and the precise moments where changes occur in routine procedures.

As in action and activity columns, we add "last names" to the theoretical tags. These are abbreviations that remind us of the events that we want to highlight. In this case, our interest lay in making visible the presence and flow of literacy within the context of routine activities. Many of the activities carried out in Jocelyn's cybershop are linked to written representations of meaning, establishing and maintaining social relationships, and communicative practices. In order not to lose sight of these, the abbreviation LE (*Lectura/Escritura* in Spanish) is placed at the end of the tag (e.g., ConstituentPractic-eRoutineLE/*PrácticaConstituyenteRutinaLE*) to distinguish those moments in which reading and writing are prominent in the flow of what we call a routine constituent activity (i.e., events that happen the same way over and over again) or tactical activity (e.g., after the work of de Certeau, 1995, and referring to its spontaneous and situated nature). For example, when Jocelyn reads a written document aloud, when a customer dictates information for filling out an online application, or when a customer requests a printed document such as a job application or a payment form, these moments are marked with LE.

In addition to highlighting literacy events, we also identify and tag those moments where certain aspects of informal microenterprises are evident (such as charging micro fees, attending to family issues while working, negotiating prices and procedures with clients). In these cases, we add the initials MEF (*microempresa familiar* in Spanish) at the end of the tags, for example, ConstituentPracticeRoutine becomes ConstituentPracticeRoutineMEF, as a way of keeping track of these examples.

For this study, we constructed several theoretically based categories, that were informed directly by the research literature. In the list shown in Table 7.5, we exemplify some of them, briefly discussing each one and giving at least one reference from the research literature.

Table 7.5.

Category	Definition + Reference
DigitalDeviceAccess	We conceptualize access as the conditions necessary for participating in social and cultural events. Access to digital devices refers to having opportunities to interact with other digital technology users and to learn know-how and how to appropriate different ways of using devices. Examples include situations such as how to rent and use a computer in Saíba, the cybershop run by Jocelyn. Access includes mediation by others, learning what people do, how to understand uses and meanings of digital devices. DigitalDeviceAccess emphasizes interaction with others in using digital devices (Capstick, 2016; Kalman, 2003).
ConstituentPracticeRoutine	A concept that identifies events that happen the same way over and over again. These events include defining activities that give identity to a given social space.
	Routines define different procedures and actions that follow a predictable course without mishaps. In this case it includes making copies, scanning, assigning computers, selling stationery products, printing, downloading documents from the Internet, and so on. For the most part, they are micro actions that occur through a series of quick interactions. Typically they include greeting, requesting, performing, delivering, paying, and so on (cf. Barton & Hamilton, 2000)
ConstituentPracticeRoutineLE	There are Routine Constituent Practices where reading and writing are especially salient and where they are actions that are fundamental to participating in an event. Some examples include where people are dictating from or reading what's on the screen, trying to understand an instruction, producing a document, or filling out forms (Street, 1995).
ConstituentPracticeRoutineMEF	Routine Constituent Practices capture the visible characteristics of being an informal micro family business. These routines articulate family matters and business operations, where the boundary between the two is blurry. An example of this is making sure family members have a meal while attending to customers (Kalman & Hernández, 2018).

Category	Definition + Reference
ConsituentPracticeCaveat	These are also routine practices, but they do not occur as expected. That is, in the process of performing a routine activity, a glitch arises that requires an immediate solution, such as changing the way a photocopy is made, troubleshooting an internet connectivity problem, how an online service is obtained. Those involved have to rethink their usual ways of doing things, but once the obstacle is resolved, the rest of the activities are uneventful (Rendón, 2019).
TacticContingency	These refer to practices in which the way to resolve something that does not work, and does not let the activity take its course. These contingencies can lie within objects, procedures, participants' understanding, and so on. TacticContingency refers to forms of appropriating digital technologies in order to respond to unexpected conditions that arise and must be corrected in order to be able to continue (cf. de Certeau, 1984).
TacticDesign	These are tactical practices in which the solution to a glitch involves designing a creative response to a problem. This could entail creating something such as a sign (it may involve a written or graphic object), adapting devices (connecting inkwells to outside sources), improvising pieces for a camera, using the body as an auxiliary to technology use, or holding a mobile phone against your face to see if it is overheating rather than testing the battery (Rendón, 2019).
TacticDesignProcedure	This concept comprises employing tactics in which the solution to a glitch involves reorganizing or inventing a *procedure* different from standard ways of carrying on by mobilizing available resources. These are often "work arounds," that is, coming up with creative solutions to common obstacles (e.g., an online form does not accept input information as valid and the user has to resort to workarounds or devising an alternative solution; see de Certeau, 1984).
ActivityTrajectoryPivot	This idea pinpoints the moment when an activity is interrupted. This may be a discrepancy between customer and attendant, or a glitch of some sort, for example. It is a pivotal moment when participants must make decisions about the activity and decide what course of action to follow due to an unexpected situation (Rendón, 2019; Scollon, 2004).

When we create the different tags (for actions, activities, and theoretical categories), we ask ourselves what aspect of the data do we want to make visible and emphasize. We try to put that characteristic first so that we can easily group into "families" all related tags using the pivot table or filter options. For example, for the theoretical category Constituent Practice, there are four variations: ConstituentPracticeRoutine, ConstituentPracticeRoutineLE (*Lectura Escritura*—literacy), ConstituentPracticeRoutineMEF (*MicroEmpresa Familiar*—micro family business) and ConstituentPracticeCaveat (comes with disclaimers). Each one of these add-ons at the end of the stem tag helps identify specific characteristics of what we see in the data. At the same time, we preserve the overarching idea of routine practices that recur and are part of what makes a social space identifiable as a cybershop, a library, or a restaurant.

Finally, the columns for our analytical, conceptual, and methodological notes are the place where we, as researchers, extend or refine our analysis, conceptualizations, or concerns regarding fieldwork and analytic moves. These columns usually include more elaborated observations and details regarding how we examine the data and that we do not want to lose. We also use this set of columns to identify different authors or papers that have come to mind when discussing the data analysis. It is a way to identify and pay attention to the different connections we make as we consider what we are finding.

Making Sense of the Analysis: Creating Analytical Narratives

Everyday events seem frequent, standard, and repeated, and it often seems as if nothing happens. We use spreadsheets as the basis for assembling analytical narratives (Kalman, 1999) of the different events observed. An analytical narrative is a contextualized reconstruction of an event that includes actors' words, actions, activities set within the theoretical framework that guides the study, along with the researchers' observations and insights. A person enters an establishment and asks for a photocopy; the person in charge takes the document to be reproduced, sets it in the copier, copies it, delivers it to the customer, returns the original, charges for the service, and then the customer leaves. The same happens with renting a computer, printing a page, or paying for airtime. At first impression, nothing happens, but after a more meticulous examination, the small details that constitute our daily lives appear. Within these routines lie knowledge and shared meanings that are visible in small phrases, actions, spaces, and materialities. To illustrate just how elaborate a reiterated routine can be, look at the following exchange between a customer and a business owner: the customer enters the premises, approaches the counter with two sheets of paper in his hand, and requests the photocopying service by asking for the number of copies:

34. **Customer:** Two sets
35. **Owner:** That would be:: four pesos
36. **Owner:** On both sides?
37. **Customer:** Yes, please (He delivers the copies, the customer pays and leaves)

One outstanding characteristic of this exchange is how much is accomplished through implicit understandings, starting with the absence of social etiquette for initiating and ending the interaction. There is no explicit opening or closing, and the participants accomplish a great deal through shared knowledge and implicit understandings. By arriving with two sheets of paper in his hand and directly asking for two sets of copies, the customer abbreviates the exchange, and the owner acknowledges that she understands what the customer is requesting by answering with the cost of the copies, setting the price, and defining the job at the same time. The question, "On both sides?" (Line 36) suggests a format for the photocopies, front and back, and the customer readily agrees. With this very brief exchange, they specify the terms the service, the cost, and the format for reproducing a document without mentioning the word *photocopy*.

The two participants collaborate through their socially-constructed, shared knowledge about what is done in a cybershop. The advertising on the storefront, the presence of computers and stationery, and photocopiers in sight at the entrance, come together to say "we make photocopies" to those who pass through the doorway. Interactions like this one happen over and over again throughout the day. Photocopying, printing, scanning, and renting out computers are continuous activities and key constituents of this small business.

When everything goes as expected, nothing seems to happen, but even if they are routine activities, they are not always smooth. A passing observer may only see the comings and goings of customers, but as analysts, our job is to understand what is said, what is done, what is thought of what is said and done, and how it connects to broader contexts and concerns. It is up to us to understand the choreography of movements, words, actions and artifacts in use, displacement in space, the modifications from one moment to another, and slight variations in the practices and to differentiate the routine situations from those that somehow go astray.

According to Jackson (2014), breakdowns, fragmentations, and detours often accompany the use of technology in precarious conditions. These chance events have to be resolved to move forward and achieve purpose-driven activities (cf. Cole, 1985). Jackson (2014) argues that when unexpected events occur, they often are marked by moments of creativity and inventiveness. Chartier (1984, p. 233) goes so far as to refer to these minute solutions in terms of "adaptations, trespassing, and subversions." We have found that glitches in the activity are also a time when knowledge and know-how become visible and mediation—the help and guidance of one user directed to another—flourishes.

What follows illustrates how we build analytical narratives from our analysis in Excel and how we reconstruct events using our observations and notes in the spreadsheets. In this case, there is an unexpected event, and the participants work together to solve it.

A Scan Becomes a Modified Photocopy

In the event we describe, we witness a discussion about what procedure to use to reproduce a printed page while removing a part of it without leaving any trace of its modification. We do not have access to the text itself or its final use. Instead, what we observe is how two customers approach the cybershop and ask for advice from the attendants on how to produce the document they wanted. What is interesting about the process is the collective redefinition of the activity and the redesign of a routine that seems at first to be straight forward. This results in an explicit explanation by Jocelyn concerning her knowledge about different digital procedures, clarification of the customers' specific requests, and demonstration of key criteria for making decisions about how to proceed on the part of Jocelyn and the two customers working together.

The reproduction of texts is a common act in a literate world: From medieval scribes to the present, the possibility of having several copies of the same piece of writing has been an engine for inventing and improving multiple reproduction technologies (copyists' procedures, printing, carbon paper, photocopying, scanning) in a world dependent on the circulation of written documents. Reproducing documents and distributing them occurs in schools, in public agencies, in social organizations, in religious institutions, in businesses, and in social life in general (e.g., party invitations, announcements, recipes). Within specific contexts of use, specific readers and writers share diverse interpretive and production practices concerning the reproduction and use of texts. Indeed, flyers and posters are an important part of the linguistic landscape (Blommaert, 2013) and their widespread use is characteristic of what Burrell (2012) and Spitulnik (2002) have called *small media* found in daily face-to-face interaction, such as in the public display of writing on signs and poster boards, in graffiti, and in the use of digital messaging, to name a few examples.

In the case of our study, the document the customers want to reproduce seems to be a flyer, a letter-sized sheet with text along the top and bottom of the page and with a drawing in the middle. Our interest in this example is in the material, discursive, and interactive conditions present in the process of reproducing and altering the original text (cf. Park & Bucholtz, 2009). In the fragment discussed, the two women customers look for a technical solution to partially reproduce a document. First, they ask Jocelyn if she can scan their text, and then they explain, more precisely, what they want to do.

290. **Customer 1:** Excuse me, do you scan?
291. **Jocelyn:** Uhum (nods).
292. **Jocelyn's mother:** Yes.
293. **Jocelyn:** Yes.
294. **Customer 1:** ((Begins to talk with her companion, then turns to Jocelyn)). She wants a scan because she wants to eliminate something from the sheet. ((A conversation begins between the customers and Jocelyn about how to hide the image)).
295. **Jocelyn:** It can only be scanned as PDF.
296. **Jocelyn's mother:** Right.
297. **Customer 2 (companion):** Will the drawing be visible in this [PDF] (inaudible)?
298. **Jocelyn:** Yes, yes because it almost comes out [identical]

Customer 1 seems to be mediating the discussion with the cybershop attendants for Customer 2. They confer among themselves, and then Customer 1 conveys what Customer 2 wants. The activity at first is a regular routine procedure in the cybershop except that the women want to reproduce the document in such a way that the drawing located in the middle of the sheet does not appear. There is some confusion about what the customers wants the attendants to do. They ask for a routine scan but at the same time are talking about a printed version of some kind. This leads Jocelyn to clarify that the product of a scan is an electronic PDF (Portable Document Format) file and not a paper copy, an example of the kind of knowledge Jocelyn has regarding the digital reproduction of documents. She explains that with a scan, the drawing would be included because a digital image of the document would be identical to the original. This moment represents a redefinition of the activity, the moment when the requested procedure is subverted and the participants pivot and change their minds; it links the idea of creating a PDF file with the production of a new document from an existing one. The need to produce a document without generating an electronic file implies making a tactical decision or transforming the activity (de Certeau, 1984). Here, there is a double redesign, one in terms of the document itself and, the other, in the way of producing it.

299. **Customer 2 (companion):** And if you cover it and make a copy, do you think it will come out?
300. **Jocelyn:** [It might]
301. **Customer 1:** (inaudible) Will you be able to see the black line??
302. **Jocelyn's Mom:** Sometimes you can
303. **Jocelyn:** Mmm:: Yes, you might:::
304. ((The customer asks that if she put a whiteout on what they wanted to cover, would it be noticeable in a photocopy of the document.))
305. **Jocelyn:** [sometimes]
306. **Customer 1:** What do you think? ((to companion))

This is the moment when the participants redefine the activity, and they move from the production of an electronic file to a paper version by making and manipulating a photocopy. The shared experience of the participants on the use of the photocopier becomes visible as they discuss how to remove a part of the original. All four participants understand that a document can be modified by "covering" some part of it and then making a photocopy—in this case, the reproduction of the document without the central drawing. They try to imagine a procedure to produce this edited version and adapt the photocopying procedure to their needs. Although the clients originally request a scan, the questions they ask and the solutions they propose (cover the photo, put whiteout on the "black line") refer to a printed version. All involved understand the meaning of the "black line" sometimes perceived in photocopies that have been modified (the black line is the shadow of the edge of the paper patch that is used to hide that part of a document you do not want to print). Their interest in this black line not being visible suggests that they do not want it to be evident that it is a reproduction of another document and that they are planning to circulate the modified document in some way (i.e., they want it to look polished to others' eyes). The proposal to use whiteout liquid over any black lines that appear is a technique left over from typographic processes. Their reasons could be esthetic but could also have to do with prescriptive notions regarding altering documents. School officials and government agencies prefer crisp documents over untidy ones, and modifying documents can call the text producer's legitimacy into question.

In the following lines, Jocelyn's mother convinces the customers to do a test run on a photocopy, covering up the unwanted content. She points out that it will only cost a peso:

307. **Jocelyn's Mother:** Well, do the test.
308. **Jocelyn's Mother:** A peso.
309. **Customer 1:** Uhum. Yep.

The idea of doing a scan is already lost at this point in the discussion, and all participants are now geared to photocopying. This implies both a change in the procedure and a different end product. The customers accept the idea of a trial run and make a copy with the image covered by a paper patch; the text comes out without the black line. Satisfied with the outcome, they pay a peso for the copy and leave.

The ways the clients talks about how to proceed is critical to understanding how they operate (de Certeau, 1984; Jackson, 2014). The preceding example leaves several questions open about why the customers are concerned about the black line and why they are trying to produce a document from an existing one rather than just putting together their own. Although we are not able to collect specific information regarding these questions, the data suggest at least three possibilities about the customers: first, that their working knowledge about the digital is somewhat limited. They know that scanning as a procedure exists but not necessarily that what it produces is a digital file. Second, they seem not to personally own or operate a printer, a scanner, a photocopier, or a computer and, for this reason, come into the cybershop. And, third, they are aware of certain mores regarding repurposing documents and what is considered socially acceptable and unacceptable. All these point to social knowledge and know-how regarding documents and their digital production and illustrate how the customers and attendants modify standard uses of technology and literacy to tactically produce a document that would fit the customers' needs and comply with what they all agree to be social expectations concerning the quality of documents.

In our project on the use of digital technologies in precarious contexts, we are writing up our analyses, such as the previous one, as a way to portray everyday activities that constitute the circumstances, routines, and uses of technologies and the ways that some practitioners mediate for others. One of our initial premises is that the conditions for using technologies (digital as well as analog) are less than optimal in our research site and that places like the cybershop are spaces where people can use technologies and get assistance with using them. Similarly, we also zoom in on those situations that break with the common and redefine the routine constituent activities by means of small deviations from the expected to overcome an unexpected situation: a web page that does not respond, a slow computer, a lack of connectivity, temporary suspension of electricity, an unusual requested service. Our goal is to present a version of how people use and appropriate digital technologies for everyday purposes (and not specialized ones) based on what they face and do.

It also allows us to examine the different uses of technologies that the focal participants reveal to us. For example, Jocelyn not only works in a cybershop but also takes advantage of any free time she has there to study Japanese, which involves technologies that are very different from those required by her work (e.g., using online translators to move among Spanish, English, and Japanese to validate her writing in Japanese). They illustrate traces of her school experience and are coupled with her aspirations and interest in Japanese language and culture.

We find detailed descriptions and explanations useful for making comparisons, and as ways to magnify the similarities between routine situations, the uniqueness of exceptions, and the many ways people create workarounds, come up with tactical solutions, or redesign procedures and uses. In the process, they also make their knowledge and know-how explicit, discover new affordances, and appropriate technologies for their uses. Each event that we analyze helps us understand how folks appropriate technologies into everyday interactions, meet societal demands, and accomplish new literacies. They also reveal creativity in minute actions, unexpected solutions, and complex, multilayered interactions.

Suggested Further Reading

Barton, D., & Hamilton. M. (2000). Literacy practices. In D. Barton, M. Hamilton, & R. Ivanič. (Eds.), *Situated literacies: Reading and writing in context* (pp. 7–15). New York, NY: Routledge.

Blommaert, J. (2013). *Ethnography, superdiversity and linguistic landscapes: Chronicles of complexity*. Toronto, Canada: Multilingual Matters

Excel (2019). *Microsoft Excel*. Retrieved January 7, 2020. https://en.wikipedia.org/wiki/Microsoft_Excel

Gee, J. (2005). *An introduction to discourse analysis: Theory and method*. New York, NY: Routledge.

Hahn, C. (2008). *Doing qualitative research using your computer: A practical guide*. Thousand Oaks, CA: Sage Publications.

Kalman, J., & Rendón, V. (2016). Uso de la hoja de cálculo para analizar datos cualitativos [Using a spreadsheet to analyze qualitative data]. *Magis: Revista Internacional de Investigación en Educación, 9*(18), 29–48.

References

Barton, D., & Hamilton, M. (2000). Literacy practices. In D. Barton, M. Hamilton, & R. Ivanič, (Eds.), *Situated literacies: Reading and writing in context* (pp. 7–15). New York, NY: Routledge.

Blommaert, J. (2013). *Ethnography, superdiversity and linguistic landscapes: Chronicles of complexity*. Toronto, Canada: Multilingual Matters

Burrell, J. (2012). *Invisible users: Youth in the internet cafés of urban Ghana*. Cambridge, MA: MIT Press.

Capstick, T. (2016). *Multilingual literacies, identities and ideologies: Exploring chain migration from Pakistan to the UK*. London, England: Palgrave.

de Certeau, M. (1984). *The practice of everyday life*. Berkeley: University of California Press.

Chartier, R. (1984). Culture as appropriation: Popular cultural uses in early modern France. In S. L. Kaplan (Ed.), *Understanding popular culture: Europe from the Middle Ages to the nineteenth century* (pp. 229–253). Berlin, Germany: Mouton.

Cole, M. (1985). The zone of proximal development: Where culture and cognition create each other. In J. Wertsch (Ed.), *Culture, communication, and cognition: Vygotskian perspectives* (pp. 146–161). Cambridge, MA: Cambridge University Press.

Delegación Política de Tláhuac. (2015). Programa delegacional 2015-2018 *"Tláhuac, por amor y Dignidad"* [Delegation program 2015-2018: "Tlahuac, with love and dignity"]. Mexico City, Mexico: Author. Retrieved from http://www.tlahuac.cdmx.gob.mx/wp-content/uploads/2017/01/PROGRAMA-DELEGACIONAL-TLAHUAC-2015-2018.pdf -122). Hillsdale, NJ: Erlbaum.

Hahn, C. (2008). *Doing qualitative research using your computer: A practical guide*. Thousand Oaks, CA: Sage Publications.

Hernández, O. (2015). *Trabajo, estudio y canto: Actividades cotidianas y la apropiación de prácticas digitales en una comunidad suburbana de la ciudad de México* [Work, study and song: Everyday activities and the appropriation of digital practices in a suburban community in Mexico City] (Unpublished doctoral dissertation). DIE-Cinvestav, Mexico City, Mexico.

Jackson, S. (2014). Rethinking repair. In T. Gillespie, P. Boczkowski, & K. Foot (Eds.), *Media technologies: Essays on communication, materiality, and society* (pp. 221–239). London, England: MIT Press.

Kalman, J. (1999). *Writing on the plaza: Mediated literacy practices among scribes and clients in Mexico City*. Cresskill, NJ: Hampton Press.

Kalman, J. (2002). La importancia del contexto en la alfabetización [The importance of context in literacy]. *Revista Interamericana de Educación de Adultos, 24*(3), 11–27.

Kalman, J., & Hernández, O. (2018). The making of survival: Technology, literacy, and learning in two microenterprises in Mexico City. *Information Technologies and International Development, 14*, 81–95.

Kalman, J., & Rendón, V. (2016). Uso de la hoja de cálculo para analizar datos cualitativos [Using a spreadsheet to analyze qualitative data]. *Magis: Revista Internacional de Investigación en Educación. 9*(18), 29–48.

Knorr-Cetina, K., Schatzki, T., & Von Savigny, E. (2001). *The practice turn in contemporary theory*. London, England: Routledge.

Leonardi, P. (2010). Digital materiality? How artifacts without matter, matter. *First Monday, 15*(6). Retrieved from https://firstmonday.org/article/view/3036/2567

Park, J., & Bucholtz, M. (2009). Introduction. Public transcripts: Entextualization and linguistic representation in institutional contexts. *Text & Talk: An Interdisciplinary Journal of Language, Discourse & Communication Studies, 29*, 485–502.

Prieto-Nañez, F. M. (2016). Learning through infrastructures: Cybercafes as spaces for digital literacy. In M. A. Peters (Ed.), *Encyclopedia of educational philosophy and theory* (pp. 1–5). Singapore: Springer.

Reckwitz, A. (2002). Toward a theory of social practices: A development in culturalist theorizing. *European Journal of Social Theory, 5*, 243–263.

Rendón, V. (2019). *Los chavos y las tecnologías: Apropiaciones de recursos digitales por jóvenes de la periferia verde de la Ciudad de México* [Kids and technologies: Appropriating digital resources by young people in the green periphery of Mexico City]. (Unpublished doctoral dissertation). DIE-Cinvestav, Mexico City, Mexico.

Rendón, V., & Kalman, J. (2017). Se quitan el zapato y allí lo meten: Consideraciones acerca de la materialidad digital en ámbitos educativos [They take off their shoes and leave them there: Considerations of digital materiality in education settings]. In O. Hernández, G. Ortiz, & D. Hernández (Eds.). *Comunicación, educación y tecnologías digitales: Tendencias actuales en investigación* [Communication, education and digital technologies: Current trends in investigation] (pp. 49–79). Lerma da Villada, Mexico: Juan Pablos Editor.

Saussure, F. D. (1983). *Course in general linguistics* (R. Harris, Trans.). London, England: Duckworth.

Schatzki, T. (2010). Materiality and social life. *Nature and Culture, 5*, 123–149.

Scollon, S. W. (2004). *Nexus analysis: Discourse and the emerging Internet.* New York, NY: Routledge.

Sewell, W. (2005). The concept of culture. In G. Spiegel (Ed.), *Practicing history: New directions in historical writing after the linguistic turn* (pp. 76–95). New York, NY: Routledge.

Skukauskaite, A. (2012). Transparency in transcribing: Making visible theoretical bases impacting knowledge construction from open-ended interview records. *Forum Qualitative Sozialforschung/Forum: Qualitative Social Research, 13*(1), Article 14. Retrieved from http://www.qualitative-research.net/index.php/fqs/article/view/1532

Spitulnik, D. (2002). Alternative small media and communicative spaces. In G. Hydén, M. Leslie, & F. F. Ogundimu (Eds.), *Media and democracy in Africa* (pp. 177–205). London, England: Routledge.

Street, B. (1984). *Literacy in theory and practice.* New York, NY: Cambridge University Press.

Street, B. (1995). *Social literacies: Critical approaches to literacy in development, education, and ethnography.* London, England: Longman.

CHAPTER 8

Methodology for Liberation: Doing Collaborative Participatory Research With Community

Joanne Larson and George Moses

COMMUNITY-ENGAGED SCHOLARSHIP IS a growing field in research universities that acknowledges the importance of seeing community members as authentic research partners. In education research, Gutiérrez and Penuel (2014) signaled this shift by articulating the crucial role problems of practice defined by communities plays in designing research that matters. Building on this trend, we—a collaboration between faculty and graduate students from the University of Rochester and residents of the Beechwood community of Rochester, New York—describe a long-term research partnership in all its messiness and transformation.

Flower (2008) refers to the intimacy of the term *community* in her research on urban community literacy. The term is often a sort of insider reference that indexes a shared perspective and relational closeness. We use the term in similar ways; however, "our" community has grown and changed over the years of our collaboration. In one sense, community means the residents of the Beechwood community who share the intimacy Flower describes. It is a predominantly African American neighborhood (63%) but also includes Latinx families (22%), and White families (15%). The larger Rochester community is fairly evenly split between White (46%) and African American (40%) along with Latinx (17%), Native American (1%), Asian (3%), and multiracial inhabitants (4%; U.S. Census Bureau, n.d.). However, due to high segregation, many areas of the city have concentrations of minoritized communities. Into this more geographic way of thinking about community, we deliberately weave a relationship-based sense of community. University of Rochester researchers along with their graduate students entered Beechwood to work alongside residents for emancipatory purposes. The university faculty were White; however, graduate students included international students, Asian Americans, and African Americans. All but one lived in the city of Rochester; one graduate student lived in the Beechwood neighborhood.

The most important thing to know about doing collaborative research with communities is that you have to build trusting relationships. The Beechwood community has faced a stream of researchers with "solutions" to their "problems" who leave when the grant money runs out or when the "study" is over. In communities like ours, researchers often enter with prior assumptions based on deficit ideologies about poverty that they think they can "fix." Yet nothing changes after they leave, except the community feels abandoned once again. What we describe in this chapter is how not to do this. We describe a community that views itself from an asset-based mind-set and that is grounded in the seven principles of *nguzo saba*: unity, self-determination, collective work and responsibility, cooperative economics, purpose, creativity, and faith (see Figure 8.1). These principles are rooted in the pan-African holiday of Kwanzaa founded by Dr. Maulana Karenga in 1966 to celebrate what it means to be African and fully human (Karenga, 2018). Northeast Area Development (NEAD) is a community development agency located in Beechwood and the local sponsor of Rochester's Children's Defense Fund Freedom School. The Freedom School builds on nguzo saba in its curriculum and service work. As such, our research evolved to include these principles in how we interpreted our work together. We drew on all seven principles (see Figure 8.1) at different times depending on the purpose and the context at the moment.

In this chapter, we describe how our collaborative research team came to know each other as co-researchers, co-authors, and co-implementers in ways we hope can guide others in similar work. We begin this telling with how we came to know each other. The research team included Joanne, with colleagues and graduate students from the University of Rochester, and George, along with neighborhood residents of Beechwood. We (Joanne and George) have worked together for about 15 years. First and still, we are friends. And we are friends who research together. As a collaborative research team, we are co-authors, co-researchers, and co-implementers composed of community residents, university colleagues, and graduate students. We describe in the following how we came to do research together, how we developed a large team of researchers, and how we have done analyses and publication as a team. We have developed terms such as *generative frictions* and *attunement* to explain the complexity of the process of relationship building that is critical to doing research with an emancipatory purpose (Larson & Moses, 2018).

Community members wanted to determine their own futures and, in their words, "wanted to be free." We all realized a collaboration with university researchers would

Umoja (unity)—to strive for and maintain unity in the family, community, nation, and race.

Kujichagulia (self-determination)—to define ourselves, name ourselves, create for ourselves, and speak for ourselves.

Ujima (collective work and responsibility)—to build and maintain our community together and make our brother's and sister's problems our problems and to solve them together.

Ujamaa (cooperative economics)—to build and maintain our own stores, shops, and other businesses and to profit from them together.

Nia (purpose)—to make our collective vocation the building and developing of our community in order to restore our people to their traditional greatness.

Kuumba (creativity)—to do always as much as we can, in the way we can, in order to leave our community more beautiful and beneficial than we inherited it.

Imani (faith)—to believe with all our heart in our people, our parents, our teachers, our leaders and the righteousness of our people.

Figure 8.1. Nguzo Saba

Source: Kwanzaa (n.d.).

help accomplish this goal. Specifically, by bringing two discourse communities together, university researchers could support community members in naming their work and getting evidence that policy makers and funders would recognize. Naming relates to the self-determination principle of nguzo saba. Our collaboration helped develop tools the community needed to meet their own goals. But this was not one-directional learning. University faculty and graduate students learned to question their assumptions about what counts as knowledge production and who counts as a researcher.

An example of how this occurred might be useful. After more than 10 years of working together, we began writing a book about the work. We will talk more about how this happened later, but at this point, how Joanne came to realize that she saw the principles of nguzo saba as a cultural artifact instead of part of our shared theoretical framework is relevant. While writing the chapter detailing the theoretical framework of the research, she kept running into stumbling blocks around where our data showed nguzo saba was a central part of how we were interpreting the data. It was a lightbulb moment when she realized that this was, in fact, part of our theoretical framework and not simply an object of research. Realizing this after more than 10 years of working together was humbling but remains an important moment and a moment among other moments in how we came to see how much we learned from each other.

Questions to Ask Yourself About Your Proposed Study

Are you positioning members' ideas and practices as artifacts of study? Reflect on this and come to see community members as co-researchers whose knowledge, practices, and theories are equally valuable.

Building on new directions in community-engaged scholarship, we call our work together *collaborative, participatory ethnography* in which all parties—university researchers, community organizers, and community members—are researchers/researched. The relationship between researcher and researched, the forward slash, is the main point. What happens in that relationship is where knowledge production happened. We produced community-defined evidence through collaborative qualitative analyses done in weekly research team meetings. Building on community-based participatory research methodology, we used a collaborative approach to research that actively and purposefully involved all partners in the research process and recognized the unique strengths that each brings and the challenges this uniqueness presented. Beginning with a research topic important to the community, community-based participatory research aims to combine knowledge and action to achieve meaningful change (Israel, Schulz, Parker, & Becker, 1998; Kellogg Health Scholars, n.d.).

Participatory ethnography seeks to decolonize research, understanding that it has traditionally been a ground for the colonization of discourse and culture (Harrison, 1991; Hemment, 2007; Paris & Winn, 2013; Patel, 2016; Reyes Cruz & Sonn, 2011). Used in complex corporations (Darrouzet, Wild, & Wilkinson, 2009), participatory ethnography aligns with the critical literacy framework of Freire (1971) we used in our theoretical framework. Specifically, we focused on researching with participants, not *at* or *for* them (Kinloch, Faulstich Orellana, & Lewis, 2016). Participatory ethnography builds understanding within the system, alongside the participants, and positions all parties as knowledge builders and actors of change within the system. Furthermore, the critical participatory stance we adapted to this methodology explicitly positions the research as emancipatory and the researchers as full participants in that emancipatory work. This stance aligns with the nguzo saba principle of collective work and responsibility and builds on our research goals of epistemic equality (Fricker, 2007; Postma, 2016). Other research designs, such as participatory action research, are similar. It's not so much about the name of the design. We posit a difference in our work because of our shared focus on liberation and epistemic justice. The point is to see all parties as fully human and capable of producing knowledge that leads to authentic transformation for everyone working on the research project together. You need to use the design strategy that best suits your context.

Examples of what this looked like in the moment can be found across our research team meetings. These moments show what happens when two very different discourse communities, an academic community and the local community, come together to build new understandings and see each other as fully human. For example, while developing our interdependence model, the research team was talking through what we thought it all meant. One of our doctoral students at the time, Courtney Hanny, brought up Deleuze and Guattari's (1987) concept of rhizome as a possible way to interpret what we were seeing. Community members immediately asked what on earth she meant and proceeded to look it up on their smartphones. When George saw the images of plants and the explanation about how they put out offshoots, he said, "Oh, we call that grass-roots." Once this connection was made, the team adopted *rhizome* as our shared term. This is one of many examples where all knowledge and understanding counted in the knowledge production process and aligns with our commitment to epistemic justice.

The Research Context

Although Joanne and George knew each other before beginning to research together through participating in other citywide meetings, our official co-researcher relationship began in the fall of 2011, when a group of community organizers at the NEAD purchased a corner store across the street from their office building. Building on the nguzo saba principle of cooperative economics, NEAD wanted to address Beechwood's status as a food desert and keep monies earned in the neighborhood. The NEAD staff lived in Beechwood and hired community residents as employees for the market, focusing on building capacity in the neighborhood workforce. The market is located on a major thoroughfare and bus route so customers come from all over the city. George, NEAD's executive director, reached out to Joanne, a University of Rochester faculty member and researcher, to discuss how we could document the work at the store. George and the NEAD staff wanted to investigate the processes of change that they predicted would take shape through their work at this urban corner store and wanted to learn how to document the work in ways that would be considered "evidence" to policy makers. They wanted to define what counted as evidence on their own terms. And they wanted to learn the privileged discourses to which policy makers might respond.

Based on a shared history of having been exploited or let down by university researchers or well-intentioned funders, the NEAD staff were determined to collect their own evidence—to *research* rather than always be the *researched*. They were long tired of the steady stream of researchers or nonprofits with grants who sought to "rescue" their community. Our collaboration was formed to document the community produced processes that sought to transform a typical corner store into the cornerstone of its community—the Freedom Market (Larson & Moses, 2018). This would be the first corner store owned and operated by African Americans living in Beechwood (a food desert with 63% African American residents and 94 corner stores). Community members talked about their neighborhood as a food swamp because there were food options, but the food was of poor quality and would kill them. They wanted to be able to provide evidence for this claim and how they would use the principle of cooperative economics at the store to transform their neighborhood.

> **Takeaway**
>
> Be willing to work through assumptions together. Stay when it gets hard.

Of key importance here is that the community did not actually see themselves as "in poverty." As we began our collaboration, university researchers had to confront their own discourses around positioning urban communities in deficit terms, and community members had to ask themselves whether to participate in their discursive production as "in poverty" or to challenge it. We all chose to have the difficult conversations needed for the university participants to move past deficit discourses.

Community members, specifically the elders, pointed out that when they grew up, they were not inundated with the words *poverty* and *trauma* that have become ubiquitous in contemporary public discourse. In their initial attempts to secure funding, they tried to use asset language, but funders did not respond. They shifted to using poverty data in grant proposals to play the game with funders, but their primary agenda was to show they could transform their community on their own terms. Together, we developed expertise in the privileged discourses around funding which gave space for the community to show transformation could be done and that they were capable agents of change. As a collaborative team, we were able to document the work done and to publish about it. George's reflection on this process captures a significant learning point for all of us: "Don't start off as the Black Panther Party." We took this to mean that working slowly and purposefully, rather than bulldozing our way through, would have a longer lasting transformative effect. This realization did not deter our passion or commitment but did help us develop more impactful strategies. Community members knew from elders and practical experiences that the African American community has had numerous models of collective work and responsibility. However, based on other's knowledge or lack of knowledge regarding past liberation movements in the community, we would show the principles and model the behaviors and norms. In this way, we facilitated different introductions and understandings in what we called Sankofa (bringing the lessons from the past forward) moments rather than just saying what we were fighting for up front.

What It Looks Like in Practice

Our research team often shares the story of the time Robert, NEAD's director of economics and a Beechwood resident, challenged Joanne, her colleagues, and the doctoral students about the role they were playing. They had begun the research as they always had—participant observation and taking field notes, interviewing, and so on—while doing some "teaching" to community members about how to analyze qualitative data. During a research team analysis session, Robert questioned why the university team members were asking all the questions about them and pointed out the community members knew very little about the university researcher members of the team. It was a powerful moment that dramatically changed our relationships and afforded us the opportunity to be more personally vulnerable. We began holding meetings at university team members' homes and developing authentic relationships outside of academic armor. University team members "worked the store"—managing the cash register, stocking shelves, selling lottery tickets. There were many laughable moments when Joanne, for example, did not know the price of something and the customer had to tell her or when customers explained how the lottery machine worked. But this shift in roles was critical for community residents to begin to trust us as human beings who were not there to hurt or exploit them. We discussed this event and our subsequent reflection at length in the book we wrote together, claiming that in this case,

> the challenge of unidirectionality caused us to rethink, collectively, how we understood (or failed to understand) participatory research. It wasn't enough simply to be physically present observing, or to "share" our skills, or "teach" our methods. Such assumptions, in fact, can mask epistemological inequities—valuing some forms of knowledge and failing to recognize others. That is, even the most progressive and justice-minded approaches to social and educational research frequently maintain tacit assumptions that the "knowledge" produced by the research will be filtered through and validated by extant paradigms as determined by academic institutions. The presumption that we, as university researchers, were to teach community researchers how to do research and how to recognize what counts as evidence was a false premise, grounded upon an unjustifiable epistemological hierarchy. (Larson & Moses, 2018, p. 36)

As our research developed over the next decade, understanding the epistemological equity of all parties proved to be difficult but worthy work.

Takeaway: It's All About Relationships!

Participate authentically in the community beyond traditional researcher roles of notetaker or interviewer. Attend community and family events as a participant and let go of academic armor.

Being Co-Researchers

We began our collaborative research like most ethnographic research teams do: weekly meetings to discuss what was going on during the previous week of data collection. In the beginning, Joanne and colleagues were asked to teach the community members how to do qualitative research. Not surprisingly, they went about enacting their university professor identities to explain interpretivism and discussing how to seek participant meanings, to gather data, and to conduct qualitative analyses. Once we had interview transcripts, we began to work through how to code and analyze data. We began with constructivist grounded theory procedures (Charmaz, 2014) of open coding, constructing categories, and building themes. It was not long before we realized that as formally designated "researchers" investigating food deserts we were, instead (or additionally), participants in the research—our research team meetings were part of the data. At these meetings, Robert challenged university folks' positionality, for example. How we came to develop shared discourses and to understand each other was the focus of the work after all.

Alongside coming to see the research and each other in more complex ways, we accomplished a number of important scholarly steps over the years as we all developed as researchers and as new insights emerged in our work. We started our analyses by collaboratively coding field notes and interview transcripts. Each team member would have a paper copy of the data and code independently. At our weekly research team meetings, we shared our coding and, through discussion, we agreed on codes, categories, and themes. The developmental trajectories and transformational pathways indexed in our continually evolving framework we called our "interdependence model" (see Figure 8.2) were the result of this collaborative analysis process. We called it the interdependence model realizing that, although they are each independent nodes, the collective nodes are interdependent, in many cases utilizing the same people.

At the beginning of our thinking, we thought we were researching one space: the market. During our initial coding and analysis sessions, we constructed categories we came to call developmental trajectories: belonging, building relationships, being family, building community, becoming, and communicating. During one of our team meetings around constructing these categories and struggling over how they worked together, the conversation around using the rhizome metaphor happened, for example. It was then we realized that there were more spaces than the market that were a part of our work together.

Over time, we realized we were all at different spaces in the community but it was "all the same people" at those different spaces. Many of us began our day at Freedom School, then went to the market, to NEAD, and the university to work. We often saw each other at other citywide meetings or events. We ran into each other at the "million hoodie march" after Trayvon Martin was killed. Talking through how we found ourselves in similar spaces helped us to name what we called transformational pathways (political, economic, educational, social, research, and, eventually, health) through which we moved in, around, and through during our daily lives. We came to see what was happening (the people and spaces) as a collection of nodes (see Figure 8.3 for node detail) in a continually evolving rhizomatic network of relationships (Deleuze & Guattari, 1987; Larson et al., 2017).

In addition to the Freedom Market, several research partnerships evolved and became new nodes in the model: Freedom School, East Freedom parts 1, 2, & 3; Growing a Healthy Community; ENGOAL project; and, Sankofa Communiversity. As part of the national Freedom School network sponsored by the Children's Defense Fund, the

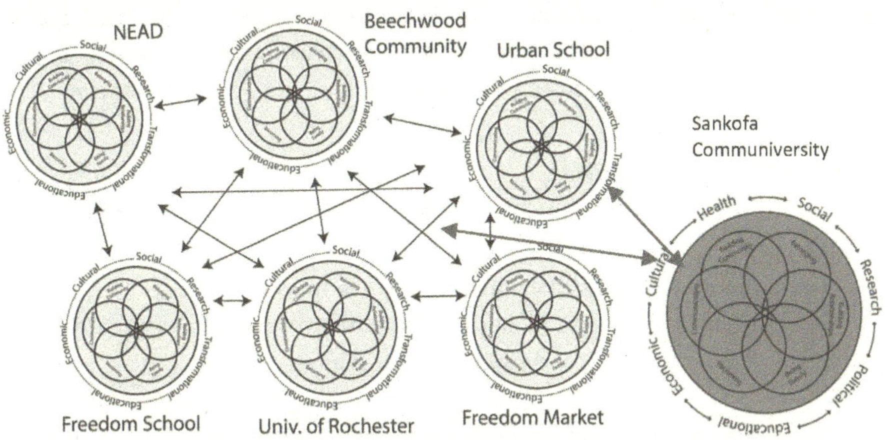

Figure 8.2. Our interdependence model

Source: Adapted from Larson, J., & Moses, G. H. (2020). *Community literacies as shared resources for transformation* (p. 23). New York, NY: Routledge. Permission granted by publisher.

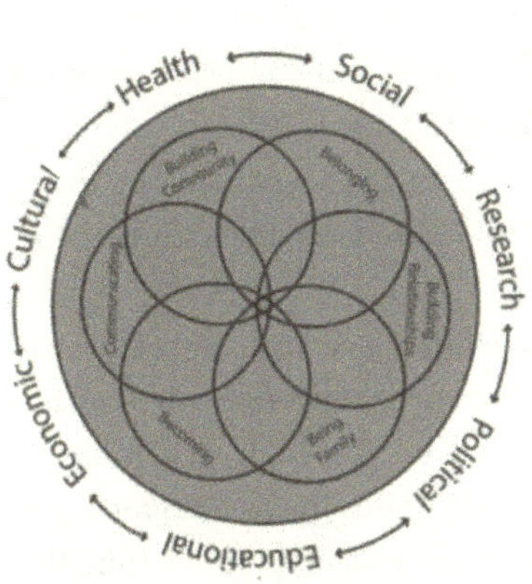

Figure 8.3. Node detail

Freedom School had been serving the children and youth in Rochester for many years in its Afrocentric summer reading program. The NEAD contracted with a local high school on several projects designed to serve students who struggled in traditional classrooms (East Freedom). Joyce Duckles, a university colleague, took the market work in the direction of health research and deepened her relationship with community members, specifically with community elders (Growing a Healthy Community and EN-GOAL). Sankofa Communiversity evolved from her work into the most recently added node of our interdependence model. After about 10 years, Joanne shifted her primary role to working with the local high school in a unique university/school partnership but maintained a relationship with the research team for presentations while finishing the book; the school also became a new node in the model. All the nodes in the model remain active and in relation to each other. We note several principles/actions for others to consider that proved critical across all our collaborative projects and over time:

- Working across difference
- Staying within contentious and contested spaces, negotiating multiple identities
- Recognizing the generative potential of these spaces
- "Stagnation is not an option" because as community activists we share goals of meaningful local action for social change

All these principles are connected—mutually constituted, if you will. Each of us drew on our theoretical principles and our experience working together to develop these principles. Community members drew on the nguzo saba principles, specifically unity, self-determination, and collective work and responsibility, to focus on how we could work together to improve the community. Working across difference meant we stayed no matter what and worked through difficult conversations. It was more than agreeing to disagree. University researchers brought Ziarek's (2001) concept of *dissensus* to describe the process of staying in discussion when consensus was not the goal. We intentionally prioritized dissensus to highlight the importance of struggle and contestation in the work we do. Building relationships and coming to understand one another is a dynamic process with no predetermined answer. The point is to go into process together and to stay when it gets hard. Together we understood that all major transformation occurs through conflict and not through the avoidance of it.

A key example centered around what it meant to be feminist. As one part of an interdisciplinary theoretical framework, Joanne and the university folks drew on feminist theories of intersectionality to understand the data and our evolving relationships. Community members saw feminists negatively, based on stereotypes from 1960s' popular culture and viewed feminists as anti-male. There really was no place or time that we came to a shared understanding of what "feminist" means. Many heated arguments, some ending in tears, ensued. Restorative justice work facilitated staying in the relationship, but dissensus remained.

Grounded in Foucault's (1978/1990) theory of power as force relations, we came to see these spaces and moments as *generative frictions* that produced new knowledge and understanding and that deepened our relationships and our commitments to each other (Larson & Moses, 2018). This process is not finished. The term *feminist* continues to provoke friction. We connect these ongoing discussions to the nguzo saba principle of self-determination (to define ourselves, name ourselves, create for ourselves, and speak for ourselves). Even though community members might agree with intersectional feminist ideology (Crenshaw, 1990) and perhaps follow some of the principles in practice, they continue to resist being "named" by language outside the community.

Of crucial importance in our evolution as a research team was confronting the barriers to collaborative research with the community presented by the university's ethical clearance board. It seemed that only having community members sign consent forms perpetuated the epistemological injustice we had uncovered and were trying to change. We challenged the ethical clearance board to help us reform this practice. We developed a process where community members were trained using the same materials university faculty used to pass the ethical clearance board's ethics exam to receive an identity code authorizing access to the online human subjects research proposal submission system. Once community members passed this exam, we were able to add them as study personnel who could martial the consent process and collect data. Thus, our co-researcher relationship became authentic across our different professional spaces.

Being Co-Authors

Learning to write together followed a similarly circuitous path as learning to research together. Joanne and colleagues came with assumptions about academic publishing and histories of co-authoring practices that privileged revising written text with things such as track changes or using a shared Google Doc for collaborative composition. Academic writing is a complex genre that does not easily translate outside of its discourse community. Community members had very different experiences with "writing." These differences produced another generative friction.

George pointed out our different starting points during a research team meeting after Joanne began to express frustration, feeling that people were not "writing." We had been working for several months to produce the book by the deadline. We met every week to talk about what had been written that week. Joanne and colleagues did their usual work; they read literature, revised text using these new ideas, gathered data as warrant for claims, and wrote interpretive commentary. We shared all of this via a Google Drive folder to which everyone had access. Community members printed out the drafts and read them. Some made marginal notes but did not enter text into the document. Joanne perceived this as "not writing" and felt pressure to produce written text. When she began to express frustration about what she thought was a lack of writing, George interrupted, saying, "Who here has ever written a book before?" Only Joanne's hand went up. Point taken. We had a generative conversation about what counts as writing and whose writing practices were perceived as privileged. Community members pointed out they "wrote" collaboratively while discussing ideas in a free-flowing conversation.

As a result of this generative friction, we developed a process of writing that included everyone's strengths and histories of literacy practices. Academics composed, did literature reviews, revised, and so on, continuing to share everything in our Google Drive folder. Community members read each iteration, most often downloading it and printing it. During our weekly meetings, we talked about what was written that week and brainstormed revisions. Whiteboards were a key interactive artifact in this collaborative composition process. As ideas were talked about, anyone with an idea wrote or drew on the whiteboard. Many times, university folks simply wrote down everything a community member said, especially when they were recounting a memory of important historical events. The university co-author of a particular chapter took pictures of these discussions and put the ideas into academic text. We used this cycle for well over a year to complete the book. And we met the deadline!

As a group, we committed to making sure the book, or any other means of disseminating our research, was accessible to neighborhood residents. We developed a variety of forms of dissemination that included flyers, photo arrays, short videos, spoken-word poetry, murals, and slide presentations. We presented at research conferences and community-based organization meetings nationally and internationally. A community member always attended, including when one group went to Singapore to present at an academic conference.

After the book was published, a group of elders joined the research team when Joyce began to focus on elders and community health to form our newest node, *Sankofa Communiversity.* One elder woman, Miss Addie, read the history chapter with fervor, highlighting passages and marking pages with Post-it notes. At one team meeting, she pointed out that the person we talked about in the section on the Rochester 1964 riots was her family member. She emotionally recounted those events and the consequences for her family. Seeing herself and her history in a published book was transformative.

When our work was accepted at a national ethnography conference, Miss Addie and two other elders, Miss Maxine and Miss Pam, came with us to present along with other team members, including George's youngest son. George rented a passenger bus and an intergenerational team of about 12 drove together to the conference in Philadelphia. Miss Addie brought her now-well-worn book and used her presentation time to tell the story of reading about her history.[1] She asked George's son to sit opposite her while she told the story. She explained to the audience that she did this to illustrate how elders pass on history to the young. It was a powerful moment where the idea of Sankofa—reaching back to frame the future—came into being for all present.

Being Co-Implementers

The idea of being co-implementers emerged as we set about doing the work of community transformation. This work included education (Freedom School, partnerships with neighborhood schools), health (Freedom Market, ENGOAL, garden project), and economics (Freedom Market, Speedy Slice). All this work was based on the seven principles of nguzo saba and the concept of Sankofa. Sankofa Communiversity enacted these principles across generations and spaces. We define Sankofa Communiversity as an intergenerational, collaborative community of research, scholarship, and social activism. Journeying together, we are grounded in our histories, our shared knowledge, and our faiths. The team developed a logo using the image of the Sankofa bird from a mural we painted on the NEAD office building (the nguzo saba principle of creativity; see Larson, et al., 2017). Together, the team collects data, teaches each other and the community, and does the labor of transformation (running the market, serving on school committees, sharing the research, developing new relationships).

However, transformation is not only within the neighborhood. The university also needed to change, especially around the reward system for researchers. There may be new opportunities for university faculty to take on this work. Joanne serves on a new university committee that is working on adding language to the official university handbook section on criteria for promotion and tenure that includes counting community-engaged scholarship as valued for tenure. It was already the case that the university benefited from community-engaged research that faculty in the medical school and the school of education, among others, was doing. This work enabled the university to say it was involved in the community to the public. Yet the labor of faculty tended to be considered as service or activism, not as research. Following a national push to change this, this committee is doing work to educate colleagues and implement this change.

Making Sense of the Work

We have learned some lessons we think may help others do the collaborative research we have described in this chapter. To researchers, qualitative and quantitative, who have said they want to do this kind of work with communities but do not know how to start, we suggest learning the rhythms of the community (we have called this *attunement*) you wish to serve by showing up to, and spending time at, community events as an entry point to building relationships and earning trust before doing any research. This is more than "building rapport" discussed in research methods textbooks. Get to know people, their families, their beliefs, and what concerns them and let them get to know you—be vulnerable. Value everyone as fully human and fully capable as knowledge producers. Develop research questions and research studies with the community. There are several existing research methodologies you might consider: Youth participatory action research (cf. Fine & Torre, 2019; Mirra & Garcia, 2016), action research (cf. Herr & Anderson, 2015), and social design experiments (cf. Gutiérrez & Jurow, 2016) are all good starting points.

For early-career faculty, this work can be more difficult given the academy does not yet reward community-engaged research, although this may be changing. It remains the case that you will need to publish in research journals to get tenure, and we are not arguing that this is not important and valuable work. You could negotiate with your collaborative community (or school) partners when publishing and let them know you will need some publications to be solely authored. For senior faculty, we suggest a continued and forceful challenge to the academy to appropriately value community-engaged scholarship, especially research with an emancipatory purpose. Community members have asked us, "Why is the university sleeping?" We all need to wake up the academy so that the impact of our research is useful in real time and in real places.

A Final Word

Know this work is not for everybody; it is a choice you have to make. We ask you to consider the ethics of working with communities who work against systems of oppression, especially if you are only there to "study them" to build an academic career. You need to ask yourself whether you can sustain the trusting relationships needed for authentic collaborative work with communities. It does not make you a bad person to say you are not in a place to do this work. As we look back at the history of the Beechwood neighborhood, we see a trail of well-intentioned researchers with programs and initiatives they believed would make a positive impact. However, when the grant ended, they left. The problems remained and the community was disrupted. For community members (or teachers, administrators, students, and their families) working for emancipation whose lives are already disrupted and inconsistent, adding inconsistency is simply unethical.

Suggested Further Reading

Gutiérrez, K. D., & Jurow, A. S. (2016). Social design experiments: Toward equity by design. *Journal of the Learning Sciences, 24*(4). https://doi.org/10.1080/10508406.2016.1204548

Patel, L. (2016). *Decolonizing educational research: From ownership to answerability*. New York, NY: Routledge.

Paris, D., & Winn, M. (2014). (Eds.). *Humanizing research: Decolonizing qualitative inquiry with youth and communities*. London, England: Sage Publications.

Mikesell, L., Bromley, E., & Khodyakov, D., (2013). Ethical community-engaged research: A literature review. *American Journal of Public Health, 103*(12), e7–e14. https://doi.org/10.2105/AJPH.2013.301605

Note

1. A video of our full presentation can be found at https://www.youtube.com/watch?v=-LQFOKwbznk&t=221s.

References

Charmaz, K. (2014). *Constructing grounded theory.* Thousand Oaks, CA: Sage Publication.

Crenshaw, K. (1990). Mapping the margins: Intersectionality, identity politics, and violence against women of color. *Stanford Law Review, 43,* 1241–1300.

Darrouzet, C., Wild, H., & Wilkinson, S. (2009). Participatory ethnography at work: Practicing in the puzzle palaces of a large, complex health organization. In M. Cefkin (Ed.), *Ethnography and the corporate encounter: Reflections on research in and out of corporations* (pp. 61–94). New York, NY: Berghahn.

Deleuze, G., & Guattari, F. (1987). *A thousand plateaus: Capitalism and schizophrenia.* Minneapolis: University of Minnesota Press.

Fine, M., & Torre, M. E. (2019). Critical participatory action research: A feminist project for validity and solidarity. *Psychology of Women Quarterly, 43*(4), 433–444 https://doi.org/10.1177/0361684319865255

Flower, L. (2008). *Community literacy and the rhetoric of public engagement.* Carbondale, IL: SIU Press.

Foucault, M. (1990). *The history of sexuality: An introduction.* New York, NY: Vintage. (Original work published 1978)

Freire, P. (1971). *Pedagogy of the oppressed.* London, England: Penguin.

Fricker, M. (2007). *Epistemic injustice: Power and the ethics of knowing.* Oxford, England: Oxford University Press.

Gutiérrez, K. D., & Jurow, A. S. (2016). Social design experiments: Toward equity by design. *Journal of the Learning Sciences, 24,* 565–598. https://doi.org/10.1080/10508406.2016.1204548

Gutiérrez, K., & Penuel, W. (2014). Relevance to practice as a criterion for rigor. *Educational Researcher, 43*(1), 19–23.

Harrison, F. V. (1991). *Decolonizing anthropology: Moving further toward an anthropology for liberation.* Washington, DC: Association of Black Anthropologists.

Hemment, J. (2007). Public anthropology and the paradoxes of participation: Participatory action research and critical ethnography in provincial Russia. *Human Organization, 66,* 301–314.

Herr, K., & Anderson, G. (2015). *The action research dissertation: A guide for students and faculty* (2nd ed.). London, England: Sage Publications.

Israel, B. A., Schulz, A. J., Parker, E., & Becker, A. B. (1998). Review of community-based research: Assessing partnership approaches to improve public health. *Annual Review of Public Health, 19,* 173–202.

Karenga, M. (2018, December). Reimagining and remaking the world: A Kwanzaa commitment to an inclusive good. *Los Angeles Sentinel,* A1. Retrieved from https://lasentinel.net/annual-founders-kwanzaa-message-reimagining-and-remaking-the-world-a-kwanzaa-commitment-to-an-inclusive-good.html

Kellogg Health Scholars. (n.d.). About. Retrieved from http://www.kellogghealthscholars.org/about/community.php

Kinloch, V., Larson, J., Faulstich Orellana, M., & Lewis, C. (2016). Literacy, equity, and imagination: Researching with/in communities. *Literacy Research: Theory, Method, and Practice, 65*(1), 94–112. https://doi.org/10.1177/2381336916661541

Kwanzaa. (n.d.). Nguzo saba: The seven principles. Retrieved from http://www.officialkwanzaawebsite.org/NguzoSaba.shtml

Larson, J., & Moses, G. (Eds.). (2018). *Community literacies as shared resources for transformation*. New York, NY: Routledge.

Larson, J., Hanny, C., Duckles, J., Pham, H, Moses, R., & Moses, G. (2017). Expressing community through freedom market and visual connections. *Pedagogies: An International Journal, 12*(1), 4–20. https://doi.org/10.1080/1554480X.2017.1283999.

Mirra, N., & Garcia, A. (2016). *Doing youth participatory action research: Transforming inquiry with researchers, educators, and students*. New York, NY: Routledge.

Paris, D., & Winn, M. (Eds.). (2014). *Humanizing research: Decolonizing qualitative inquiry with youth and communities*. London, England: Sage Publications.

Patel, L. (2016). *Decolonizing educational research: From ownership to answerability*. New York, NY: Routledge.

Postma, D. (2016). Open access and epistemic equality. *Education as Change, 20*(2), 2–10.

Reyes Cruz, M., & Sonn, C. C. (2011). (De)colonizing culture in community psychology: Reflections from critical social science. *American Journal of Community Psychology, 47*, 203–214.

U.S. Census Bureau. (n.d.). Quick facts: Rochester City. Retrieved from https://www.census.gov/quickfacts/rochestercitynewyork

Ziarek, E. P. (2001). *An ethics of dissensus: Postmodernity, feminism, and the politics of radical democracy*. Stanford, CA: Stanford University Press.

CHAPTER 9

Theorizing With (a) Difference: Fanfiction, Literacy, and Neurodiversity

Allison Dziuba, Rebecca W. Black, and Jonathan Alexander

Allison Dziuba (AD): Thank you, Rebecca and Jonathan, for talking with me about the role of theory in your research. I'm particularly interested in your recent work on representations of autism in *Harry Potter* fanfiction. In this study, you find that the interactive and audience-driven medium of online fanfiction can provide a space for writers to center the experiences of people with autism spectrum disorder (ASD) and, potentially, to contest stereotypes. My own research examines self-sponsored literacy practices among college students, many of whom identify as members of historically marginalized populations so I'm especially interested in your research approach and findings.

Jonathan Alexander (JA): Thanks, Allison. It was a lot of fun to work on that project with Rebecca Black, Vicky Chen, and John Duarte. The article we wrote, "Representations of Autism in Online Harry Potter Fanfiction," was published in the *Journal of Literacy Research* in 2019. In this work, and after providing an overview of the scholarly literature on both the representation of autism and neurodiversity in a range of media, as well as the value of fanfiction and participatory media more broadly for cultivating robust and even critical literacy practices, we turn to an analysis of a set of stories written by fans of *Harry Potter* in which the authors introduce characters who are autistic, neurodiverse, or otherwise identified as having ASD. As we say in our abstract, "findings suggest that these online narratives diversify available representations of autistic characters; moreover, the interactive nature of the online publishing forum allows readers to respond to and potentially disrupt stereotypical thinking and common fictional tropes surrounding autism" (Black et al., 2019, p. 30).

AD: Fascinating! I hope to learn more about how one undertakes a scholarly project like yours. To start off, could you tell me about your project's genesis?

Rebecca Black (RB): It's actually an interesting story that is pretty relevant to the topic for this chapter. In 2016, I received an email from a high school student who was interested in conducting research on fanfiction. This student sent me a literature review and had some really good insights into the fanfiction community; however, when it came time for him to design a project for us to work on together, it became clear that we were approaching the study of fanfiction from two completely different research paradigms. The initial proposal that he sent was grounded in a positivist paradigm; specifically, the proposal had an experimental design aimed at measuring the impact of writing and reading fanfiction on autistic people's empathy and theory of mind. While it was a well-constructed and well-researched proposal, I read it as grounded in a deficit mindset in relation to ASD, and as theoretically and methodologically distinct from the kind of work that I do. For me, it doesn't make sense to try to objectively measure the impact of writing and reading fanfiction; my work instead has focused on the ways that fanfiction authors and readers, particularly those from marginalized backgrounds, construct meaning as they write and read fanfiction. It's about the empowerment and agency that fan communities and participatory culture can afford. So, we reworked the proposal together and came up with a study focused on understanding the ways that autistic people and their friends, family members, and advocates represent ASD in their fanfiction writing. So, in a nutshell: How do they construct meaning around autism?

AD: It's really helpful for me to hear the story of how research projects like yours get started. You've noted how your theoretical and methodological commitments affect the kinds of studies you pursue. Could you say a bit more about how these commitments inform your research questions?

JA: Both Rebecca and I have a strong professional commitment to valuing the importance of both participatory cultures and self-sponsored literacy practices. Rebecca has researched and written extensively about fanfiction and fan practices, and most of my scholarly career has focused on literacy sponsorship in the co- and extracurriculum. Following the work of Deb Brandt, in *Literacy in American Lives* and other publications, I attempt to pay close attention to how different literacy practices are "sponsored" by a variety of organizations and cultural formations outside of formal, school-based instruction. Brandt (2001) defines sponsors as "any agents, local or distant, concrete or abstract, who enable, support, teach, model, as well as recruit, regulate, suppress, or withhold literacy—and gain advantage by it in some way" (p. 19). At a time of increasing proliferation, at least in the United States, of media and communication technologies that allow individuals and groups to create, upload, and disseminate a variety of content, we need to expand our understanding of how literacies and multiliteracies are sponsored to include forms of self-sponsorship, particularly as young people consume multimedia narratives and then create their own content in response to them. Fanfictions and other forms of fan media constitute a significant example of what I call such "self-sponsored" forms of literate and multiliterate practice.

Such self-sponsorship links to the growth in participatory cultures, or the many ways in which fans and others are actively invited by producers and media makers to offer feedback on mass-produced culture, and the ways in which fans produce and disseminate their own content *about* mass-produced culture through a variety of platforms, from Fanfiction.net to YouTube. I recently published a book, *Writing Youth: Young Adult Fiction as Literacy Sponsorship* (Alexander, 2017), that looked both at how young adult novels modeled different acts of literacy (think of the kids at Hogwarts learning a magical language that they use both to defend themselves and potentially transform their worlds—making the *Harry Potter* series a form of literacy narrative) *and* created their own content, including at times full-length movies—that reproduced, modified, extended, and sometimes even challenged some of their favorite young adult narratives. Young people in particular, especially ones who are savvy users of media, often feel particularly free to use existing mass-produced narratives to tell their own stories, or versions of existing stories that make more sense to them, to grapple with topics that are important to them that often *aren't* present in the initial narratives, or to fill in the gaps in those narratives. Inserting LGBTQ characters into fanfiction set in the *Star Trek* universe, for instance, is a common kind of participatory practice that expands that universe to imagine characters and plots that haven't typically been part of it. Ditto for the *Harry Potter* universe, whose associated fanfictions and fan media were originally a cause for debates over intellectual property rights, but which were ultimately approved by the *Harry Potter* intellectual property holders given that such fan work constitutes a kind of free advertisement for *Harry Potter*. More pointedly, academic, media theorist and "acafan" (his term, referencing being a fan and an academic) Henry Jenkins (1992) has called such fan participation an important form of engagement with a major contemporary "mythology"—especially given that the *Harry Potter* story is one that a wide variety of folks across multiple generations, walks of life, cultures, and even nations can share in the absence of other formerly shared narratives, such as religious story and belief.

In our article, we also attempted to bridge participatory culture with an expanded sense of participation for those often marginalized or elided in mass-produced culture. The autistic or neurodiverse have often been portrayed as damaged, pathological, or even inhuman, so focusing on fanfiction about them—often written by those invested in rehabilitating or offering alternative and more positive portrayals of individuals with autism—allows us to see how participatory cultures expand and diversify cultural production and representation. In the following paragraph, we make this particular theoretical turn, which the remainder of the article picks up on in its analysis of stories from the Fanfiction.net archive:

> Jenkins' [Puroshotma, Clinton, Weigel, & Robison's] (2006) notion of participatory culture pushes for an expansion of the vision for new and digital literacies beyond technical skills to include an array of social skills and dispositions when engaging in online literate practice. Fanfiction is a particularly robust example of such dispositions. For example, the typical activities of online fanfiction, such as engaging in collaborative or networked writing tasks, shifting between writerly/readerly and expert/novice roles, and accessing distributed sources of knowledge, require certain social skills and cultural competencies as well as technical knowledge of print-based literacy and digital devices. In addition, fanfiction authors are a clear instantiation of "prosumers" (a portmanteau of *producer* and *consumer*) who go beyond the structural constraints of consuming mass media to actively engage in the production of media content and the "diversification of cultural expression" (Jenkins et al., 2006, p. 34). (Black et al., 2019, p. 34)

AD: It makes sense to me that you would choose to study *Harry Potter* fanfiction given the popularity of the books and movies and your previous research on the series, Jonathan. What else about this series makes it a rich resource for examining participatory culture?

JA: The desire to focus specifically on the *Harry Potter* universe ties into our theoretical commitment to examining how participatory cultures extend themselves at times to include the marginalized and underrepresented. Note our explanation in the following paragraph:

> The study team chose stories set in the *Harry Potter* universe for several reasons. First, the immense popularity of the series makes it a likely candidate for fanfiction authoring. Following the adventures of a group of friends through their middle and high school years attending Hogwarts, a school for witches and wizards, the action alternates between the real world and the wizarding school. Students with innate magical tendencies are recruited to attend Hogwarts, while "normal" nonmagical people, called Muggles, are often amazed or disconcerted by the powers of the wizarding world. In the series, much attention is focused on the various trials of growing up as "special," as someone who does not quite fit in. As such, the series appeals as both a fantasy (kids developing special powers and abilities as they grow up)

> and as a story of the difficulties of being an outcast (a condition with which many teen readers can likely empathize). Thus, a fundamental interpersonal dynamic of the series—nonnormative wizards trying to find acceptance or at least tolerance among normative "muggles"—might appeal as a trope that could be played with by fanfiction writers interested in exploring autism in their stories. Indeed, fans have noted how "Harry's feelings of relief after being 'diagnosed' as a wizard are similar" at times to "feelings of relief after being diagnosed with autism" (Harrington-Kane, 2007, para. 4). Thus, the overarching narrative and the Hogwarts school setting seem to call for a focus on how young people navigate their identities, confront a range of psychological and physical differences, face social pressures to conform, and identify opportunities for self-reflection, resistance, and agency. (Black et al., 2019, p. 38)

As you can see, the choice of *Harry Potter* fanfiction allowed us to focus on a world that already invited writers to "navigate," as we put it, issues of identity and normalization. So, in addition to constituting a large and popular archive of fanfiction, *Harry Potter* fanfiction already thematized some of the theoretical issues we were interested in exploring.

AD: Moving from the texts' content to their venue, I'm curious about how you selected Fanfiction.net. What informed your choice of textual analysis, of approaching the online fanfiction repository as an archive? And what are some of the affordances and limitations of such an approach?

RB: Because we were interested in the empowerment and agency that participation in a fandom and participatory culture affords—or as Jonathan mentioned, sponsors—we wanted a site that, like most participatory cultural spaces, had low barriers for entry and participation. We outline some of our reasoning in the following excerpt:

> Because the study focused on the potential that online fanfiction might offer for reaching a broad audience of readers with varying levels of knowledge about ASD and involvement in fandom (i.e., sites that might have the broadest popular reach), we limited data collection to fictions posted on Fanfiction.net. Fanfiction.net is arguably the largest online fanfiction archive, is widely known and technically easy to join and navigate, and has a diverse community of members in terms of age, location, language, level of fandom involvement, and interests. (Black et al., 2019, p. 36)

That excerpt didn't exist in the first draft of our article, but one of the reviewers asked us why we didn't include sites like Archive of Our Own (AO3), which also have dedicated sections for fanfiction focused on ASD. While I think it would be worthwhile to explore sites like AO3, I feel that sites like AO3 have higher implicit barriers to participation. They are more insider fandom communities, while Fanfiction.net is very much an "entry-level" fanfiction site. This makes it easier for first-time authors to feel comfortable contributing, and it increases the chances that an author's story will be read by a wider audience. And, because at this point we were interested in what the texts themselves could offer in terms of alternate forms of representation, it made sense to do an archival analysis rather than one that incorporated interviews. In a later iteration of this study, I think it could be really useful to expand to include sites such as AO3 and to interview fanfiction writers to get a better sense of their intentions when representing ASD and autistic characters in specific ways in their stories.

Theoretically, we also were interested in the tensions between the structural constraints of stereotypical representations of ASD in mainstream media and the agency of fan-created depictions of characters on the spectrum. So that led us to focus on an even smaller subsection of Fanfiction.net:

> Next, because the study team was interested in the potential that online fanfiction might offer to challenge mainstream representations of ASD by autistic people or those with close, personal experiences with autistic people, we focused on fictions archived in the "Neurodiverse and Differabilities" subsection of Fanfiction.net. These subsections are intended for stories that feature a character with some sort of neurological difference. (Black et al., 2019, p. 36)

Our hope was that fanfictions posted in a subsection with a clear focus on neurodiversity might be more likely to present ASD in ways that challenge mainstream media representations.

AD: I see that there wasn't a Fanfiction.net subsection titled "autism" or "ASD." My understanding is that some definitions of "neurodiverse" and "ASD" overlap but that the terms aren't synonymous or without debate over their meanings. How did you navigate issues of naming when collecting data?

JA: Indeed, we needed to acknowledge in the article that writing about "autism" is tricky because ASD covers a "spectrum" of conditions, experiences, and abilities. Some people reject the pathologizing and disabling connotations of "autism" in favor of what they call neurodiversity. We accounted for this difference in the following paragraph:

> In recent years, there has been a groundswell movement in the autism community toward understanding autism as a form of neurodiversity, or the idea that "neurological differences like autism and ADHD [attention deficit hyperactivity disorder] are the result of normal, natural variation

> in the human genome" (Robison, 2013) and should be treated as a valuable part of human history (Silberman, 2015). Rather than focusing on a cure for autism, proponents of a neurodiversity paradigm emphasize understanding and accommodation for neurodiverse individuals living in a "neurotypical" society. Such a paradigm also recognizes the strengths that can be conferred by autism, such as attention to detail, high levels of concentration, forthrightness, dedication, and strong memory skills, to name just a few (Loftis, 2015; Silberman, 2015). (Black et al., 2019, p. 31)

What's theoretically important—and challenging—here is our need to cast a wide enough net with data collection so that we can account for differences *within* a community of folks on how they understand, and wish to have represented, a subject about which they care deeply and with which they identify. Interestingly, when Rebecca and I wrote about this research study for a popular publication, we met with some resistance and questioning from someone who maintained that autism is not a difference but a disability. Part of what we needed to do in finding stories was ensure that such scope for contention within a community wasn't unnecessarily elided or silenced, given that it's part of the internal dialogue that animates a community.

RB: Also, in terms of naming, we tried to use the terms that the fanfiction writers and reviewers chose to describe themselves and their loved ones. This meant, however, that we had to clearly acknowledge the problematic nature of some of the terms, such as Asperger's.

AD: I'm seeing how your theoretical framework informed your data collection process. How did you then select specific stories for further examination, and what was your method of data analysis?

RB: In terms of story selection, we included only those stories that made explicit claims about focusing on ASD and that were written by fans who self-identified as autistic or as family members, friends, or advocates of those with ASD, and we also analyzed all reader reviews of these stories. In terms of analysis, our theoretical interest in the tensions between structure and agency informed how we approached the study and our qualitative analysis of the data. On one hand, we conducted close readings of the data with an eye to the ways in which stereotypical representations of ASD were present. But on the other hand, we also conducted close readings of the data with an eye to ways that the authors might be offering alternative representations of autistic characters and pushing back against common stereotypes. We describe this process here in the following excerpt:

> The team began by conducting a literature review that explored elements of both structure (e.g., commonplace and stereotypical representations of

> individuals of varying ability in popular culture) and agency (e.g., fandom and participatory culture) in relation to popular media. Drawing from this literature review, the team developed a reading protocol to focus our attention on specific aspects of the fanfiction texts and facilitate comparison. For example, the protocol focused attention on narrative elements of the story, such as characterization, setting, conflict, catalyst, and resolution, to gain an overall sense of the plot. The protocol also focused attention on how autism and autistic characters were discursively positioned in the narrative by looking at story elements such as characterization, dialogue, and literary devices (e.g., metaphor, pathetic fallacy). The protocol also served as a reminder to attend to the research questions and how elements of the fanfiction texts might intersect with or depart from the cultural constructions of ASD identified in our literature review. (Black et al., 2019, p. 39)

AD: As you detail in your article, the study team was composed of multiple individuals at different points in their scholarly journeys and with different personal interests in literacy practices. How did you approach collaboration in your coding and discussion of findings?

RB: I think working together to develop the reading protocols was key in this respect. It helped more novice members of the study team to focus on the research questions and specific elements of the texts. Actually, I think it was helpful for *all* members of the study team. Reading and observation protocols, especially when they are developed with your underlying theory in mind, can be quite helpful when there are aspects of your analytic process that are strengthened by systematicity. While the reading protocols provided some structure in the early stages of analysis, the other bits of the coding process aren't really something that I would describe as neat and systematic. We tried to capture some of the messiness and back-and-forth that took place during this part of the process in the following excerpt:

> While reading, each team member engaged in first-cycle coding that included descriptive and in vivo coding, and taking analytic memos (Saldaña, 2009). The first pass at coding yielded an overwhelming number of diverse codes, often clustered around the same brief segment of text. During the first post-coding meeting, the study team worked on defining codes based on relevance to the research questions and literature review. During this process, we decided to collapse initial descriptive, in vivo, and literary codes into more general conceptual codes that were applicable across texts, author's notes (A/N), and reader reviews. Because the goal of this study was to understand the possibilities that fanfiction texts might offer for diverse representations of autism and autistic people, our goal was not to achieve any

> quantitative measures of consensus (i.e., interrater reliability) but rather to converge on possible readings of the texts. If several members of the team had markedly distinct readings of a textual element, then that element was not included in the coding scheme or subsequent thematic patterns. After refining the coding scheme, all members of the study team then returned to the data and began an iterative process of rereading, coding/recoding, and memoing. (Black et al., 2019, p. 39)

So, as you can see from the write-up, there was a lot of discussion among our interdisciplinary team about how to develop and operationalize codes that aligned with our sometimes subtly distinct but still related interpretations of the texts.

JA: As someone with a humanities background, having been trained many years ago in literary and textual analysis, I was particularly interested in noting how our writers "talked" at the level of specific words about ASD and neurodiversity. Unsurprisingly, given that how one *identifies* autism or ASD—is it a disability? a neuro*diversity*? something else entirely?—the choice of words matters a great deal and is often thematized in the stories themselves. I was particularly drawn to a passage in one story that seemed to highlight how people *talk* about ASD as distinctly related to possibilities for empowerment and agency amongst the neurodiverse. Here's our analysis of that passage:

> Fan authors also use the interior struggles and evolution of the characters themselves to challenge dominant cultural representations of difference in relation to ASD. For example, in the following excerpt, Harry Potter has just been admitted to Hogwarts and is engaged in a conversation with headmaster Albus Dumbledore and teacher Severus Snape about what makes him different. The excerpt begins with Harry's thoughts on the notion of difference.
>
>> Different. He knew that word. Oh, he loathed that word. It was another way of saying special. A polite way of calling him a retard that seemed socially acceptable. Harry, however, did not think it was. A scowl twisted his face. "Aspergers, the doctor said." He answered, deciding to watch Severus out of the corner of his eye. Why was the man's mouth doing an upside-down smile?
>>
>> Severus knew that word. Years of dealing with young Slytherins had taken him to camping in muggle libraries once in a blue moon. He was damn sure he almost had a degree in psychology now. "Autism, Mr. Potter?" He clarified, exhaling upon Harry's nod.

> "But Harry," Albus reiterated his question. "What do you think, makes you different?" This was a special school, he thought. I can't be the only one different. "I like writing and science. Mrs Greenwood said I was good at them, she did."
>
> Through this exchange, the reader is given a window onto Harry's sense of frustration with the use of culturally sensitive language when it is not accompanied by a broader paradigm shift (i.e., a paradigm in which neurodiversity is viewed as a strength rather than a deficit). However, when asked to define difference on his own terms, Harry elects exceptional academic ability as a marker of one thing that sets him apart from others, relegating ASD to the background. (Black et al., 2019, p. 44)

Looking back on this passage, I am reminded that a strength of working collaboratively on a research project comes in no small part from being able to mobilize a range of previous scholarly experience and expertise in working with complex texts. In this case, our coding scheme allowed us to understand this passage as exemplifying an important theme around empowerment and agency, and our various abilities in textual analysis helped us underscore the ways in which a sensitivity to language is intimately tied to larger ideological paradigms around ability. How we talk about something, that is, reveals our values and biases, conscious or not. As researchers committed to the expansive power of participatory cultures to bring marginalized voices and issues to the fore, we very much appreciated how this individual author had thematized *within a fanfiction itself* the intimate connection between language and ideology.

AD: What were the key patterns that the research team identified through this process?

JA: Our coding and discussion process helped us identify three major themes that seemed important to the authors whose stories we analyzed: the importance and the power of speaking about one's difference; the intersections amongst different kinds of difference, especially other differences as they intersect with ASD and neurodiversity; and the desire to move away from models and paradigms of dis-ability and toward empowerment and agency.

AD: Were there any points during the data analysis when your theoretical framework and methods were in tension? How did you decide to proceed?

RB: This is an interesting question. Much of Jonathan's and my work has been grounded in a theoretical focus on the agency that young people are able to exercise when they engage in self-sponsored, online literacy practices. This theoretical orientation lends itself to an inductive approach to the data, with a focus on identifying the ways that participants are using their texts to construct narrative worlds in particular ways. So the process of coding the data is bottom up, where we closely read the fanfiction texts and reader reviews and generate new codes to describe what we are seeing in the data. For example, we noticed that in the texts, ASD was often depicted as intersecting or being collocated with other forms of difference or exceptionality (e.g., attention to detail, high intelligence, obsessive-compulsive disorder). We initially settled on the code of "intersectionality" for these types of collocated characteristics; however, a reviewer's comments led us to think more deeply about the literature around intersectionality. And, although the construct of intersectionality was helpful for thinking about some of our examples, it wasn't well aligned with others; in particular, the ones focused on exceptionality and dual medical diagnoses. Ultimately, I think we settled on the term "intersecting" to capture how we were seeing this pattern in the data. So, that's some insight into our inductive coding process. But for this article (i.e., Black et al., 2019), we also needed to focus on structural constraints—in the form of stereotypes—and how such constraints might be manifesting in participants' writing. I don't know about Jonathan, but for me this was a challenge when coding; I don't often use deductive approaches to coding. I think that's one of the reasons that having the reading protocol was so helpful. It served as a reminder to consistently attend to these structural constraints from the top down, systematically applying the a priori codes that we developed based on the literature and our research questions to the data. Our reading protocol had some broad literary categories that helped us to focus on patterns in how the stories were constructed, such as point of view, catalyst, denouement, and so on. It also had coding categories based on stereotypical representations of ASD that experts in this field have identified. We discuss this in the article:

> For ASD in particular, many mainstream media representations rely on reductive representations (Rozema, 2014) and metaphorical concepts for autism that are tied to a pathology paradigm and grounded in a deficit mind-set (Gross, 2012; Loftis, 2015; Thibault, 2014). Gross (2012) outlines several of the most prevalent metaphors used in relation to autism: military (war against autism), kidnapping (autism stole my child), barriers (child is trapped behind a barrier of autism), and death (parents grieving over an autism diagnosis). Similar metaphorical constructs for autism are prevalent in children's and young adult literature. Bartmess (2015) groups such metaphors into three common and problematic tropes and suggests that the perpetuation of such tropes can have significant consequences for cultural constructions of autism and how neurotypicals (individuals without autism) and autistic people view autism. (Black et al., 2019, p. 31)

Bartmess's (2015) tropes include (1) autistic people "being described or treated as less real than non-autistic people," (2) "autism being shown as a debt [individuals with autism] have to repay to others around [them]," and (3) autistic characters "portrayed as only looking or acting certain ways" (para. 6). As we were coding, we found that it was sometimes difficult to disentangle the structural constraints that we'd identified in the literature—these stereotypical representations—and the agency that writers were showing as they depicted characters with ASD in their stories.

JA: Indeed, I felt that we often had to walk a fine line between honoring these writers' sincere engagement with autism and neurodiversity while also being aware that even the best-intentioned description and representation can produce and reproduce stereotypical notions.

AD: Among the stories analyzed, only one is authored by someone who self-identifies as ASD or neurodiverse. You explain in your article that this data set risks "parallel[ing] how the larger public discourse about neurodiversity is still driven by descriptions *about* those on the spectrum as opposed to discourse *by* such individuals" (Black et al., 2019, p. 47). What role do politics of representation play in your research project?

JA: In our Discussion section, we return to the theoretical "stakes" that we laid out at the beginning of our article, particularly around the issue of "participation." We definitely felt the need to clarify that, however well intentioned many of these stories might be, they also can be critiqued for (in our words) "how some unfortunate tropes are reproduced" (Black et al., 2019, p. 46). In particular, we had to note that most of the stories were "skimpy" on the representation of interiority, or the deeply felt interior experiences of autistic and neurodiverse characters. In retrospect, we are struck by the fact that narrating such interiority might be difficult for *any* young writer of fanfiction, particularly given that such narration is a fairly advanced writing technique. With that said, we were concerned that most of the individuals whose stories were analyzed did *not* identify themselves as autistic or neurodiverse. Here's how we grappled with that important dimension of this research:

> There is also the question of who gets to tell these stories. This study focuses on a mix of authorial sources, from those who identify as neurodiverse to those who claim to be writing in sympathy for loved ones. Findings from the study can draw attention to the potential that new media and fan culture offer for marginalized groups to define themselves on their own terms through writing, reading, and interacting in online participatory cultural spaces. The importance of ASD-identified individuals writing from the perspective of their own experiences and interactions in the world cannot be understated, particularly for those on the spectrum. Gross (2012) asserts that "as with all autism-as-separable [from personhood] metaphors, autistic people are not considered to have the agency to take up arms against their

> own condition—the war is fought by non-disabled relatives, professionals, and organizations" (p. 260). (Black et al., 2019, p. 46)

We recognized that we could not make claims for "participation" when those whose identities and experiences were being represented in these stories were not always—or even often, in our case—authors of their own stories. As such, we recommended that "data collection in future studies . . . extend to sites such as AO3 that, while having a more limited audience, may provide a richer data set of fictions authored by autistic individuals" (Black et al., 2019, p. 46).

RB: And, although this doesn't address the issue of participation in the fanfiction community, we did enlist some help in terms of representation throughout the process of conducting the study:

> We also sought feedback from two external readers. One is a young adult who self-identifies as being on the spectrum and participates in the *Harry Potter* fanfiction community. The other is an associate professor who self-identifies as autistic and whose academic area of expertise is fictional representations of autism in the media. The first external reader provided feedback on an early draft of the manuscript in terms of our data collection and choice of media canon, as well as the overall focus of the article. The second external reader provided feedback on a later draft of the manuscript in terms of theoretical grounding, analysis, and specific language used in the article. (Black et al., 2019, p. 38)

So our external readers, in addition to contributing their disciplinary expertise, also helped us to be mindful of how we were constructing our study and of ensuring that the language we used reflected our theoretical and ideological alignments. And, say what you will about Reviewer 2, we received some excellent feedback from our reviewers that forced us to revisit, if not always change, the choices that we made in terms of representation. For example, one of our reviewers inquired about the use of "person-first" (person with ASD) versus "identity-first" (autistic person) language in our manuscript. This was a worthwhile point to consider, as some are strongly in favor of foregrounding the shared personhood of an individual with ASD versus leading with a potential difference. Ultimately, we ended up using identity-first language for much of the paper, but this choice was made because it aligned best with the ways in which the writers and readers, including those who self-identify as being on the spectrum, were foregrounding aspects of their identity as a point of knowledge and a source of pride.

AD: I appreciate your reflections on how research methods can unintentionally (and, at times, intentionally) reinforce normative ways of talking and writing about a population. So, theory informs methods, but methods and findings also inform theory, yes?

JA: The work of theorizing doesn't stop! We theorized not just that participation from autistic and neurodiverse writers might "thicken" the representation and accounting of experiences of neurodiversity. We theorized that such might create interesting opportunities to question normative understandings of self and subjectivity:

> Far from chipper, several of these fanfiction stories offer a compelling and challenging portrait of navigating life with autism and inviting readers to learn more. But is such an invitation also . . . part of the work of destabilizing assumptions about "normal" minds? Are the stories transgressive? Well, the study team's conclusion is that it is kind of complicated. (Black et al., 2019, p. 47)

In our language, you can hear the "tightrope" walk that we are trying to navigate—one of the ways in which theorizing can generate alternative views on your objects of study! We want to believe that such writing in the world is undertaking not just the work of inclusion, of expanding the kinds of authors who contribute to such platforms as well as the kinds of stories they can tell, but also expanding our sense—or perhaps challenging our sense—of what passes for normal.

AD: There seem to be these layers of knowledge production—popular media, fans' rewritings, fanfiction writer and reader conversations, and scholarship. Where do you see knowledge producers challenging dominant scripts about ASD and neurodiversity?

JA: Curiously, some of that work of challenging might play out in how stories such as the ones we analyzed are picked up in formal literacy education. Our final thoughts about autism and neurodiversity in fanfiction tie together the theoretical value we place on participatory cultures and self-sponsored forms of literate engagement with some potential ramifications for more *formally* sponsored literacy education, such as within education systems. In our article, we advocate for the use of fanfiction texts in classroom instruction, and we provide some guidelines for how that work might be generatively incorporated:

> *Identifying representations of disability:* There are numerous representations of physical and neurological difference in participatory cultural spaces (e.g., Tumblr, Memebase, Wattpad, An Archive of Our Own). These representations range from callous and erroneous all the way to poignant and eye-opening. Having youth compare and contrast such representations of

> disability with popular media representations and their own prior knowledge can encourage critical thinking about the multiple fronts on which cultural constructions of difference take place.
>
> *Becoming an active audience:* Nearly all participatory cultural spaces offer ways for audiences to communicate directly with content creators. Youth can compose responses that question, challenge, or commend content creators for their choices in representing difference and have the opportunity to engage in civic discourse with content creators and other audience members in a semipublic forum.
>
> *Contributing to cultural constructions of personhood:* Youth can choose participatory cultural spaces and text types (e.g., fanfiction, memes, Tumblr posts, tweets) and specific characteristics (e.g., ability, gender, sexuality, race) or associated social issues (e.g., bullying, racism, sexism) of personal interest to them and publicly post texts that explore and contribute to public conversations on such topics. (Black et al., 2019, p. 48)

For us, a key component of participatory culture is, well, in a word, *participation*. And although we remain fascinated by and keen observers of a range of young people's engagement with multiple media and genres of storytelling, we also recognize that participation is a skill set that can be taught, made more critically robust, and actually contribute to how young people understand themselves—and their potential and agency—in the world. Our theoretical framework and our method of paying attention to the self-sponsored writing activities of young people also challenges us as educators, specifically as *literacy educators*, to think critically and creatively with students about what participation means, how we might foster it, what it teaches all of us, and how it enhances our development of personal and collective agency through literacy.

AD: These questions about participation will stay with me as I move forward with my research. Participation can mean very different things for different writers; your earlier point about the accessibility of different online platforms demonstrates that medium and venue influence who participates, and how. I want to continue to think about the different ways that people practice literacy and engage in cultural production and about what I, as a teacher and researcher, can do to further these lines of inquiry. Again, thank you!

Suggestions for Further Reading

Black, R. W., Alexander, J., Chen, V., & Duarte, J. (2019). Representations of autism in *Harry Potter* fanfiction. *Journal of Literacy Research, 51*(1), 30–51.

Curwood, J. S., Magnifico, A. M., & Lammers, J. C. (2013). Writing in the wild: Writers' motivations in fan-based affinity spaces. *Journal of Adolescent & Adult Literacy, 56*, 677–685. doi:10.1002/JAAL.192

Loftis, S. F. (2015). *Imagining autism: Fiction and stereotypes on the spectrum*. Bloomington: Indiana University Press.

Thomas, E. E., & Stornaiuolo, A. (2016). Restorying the self: Bending toward textual justice. *Harvard Educational Review, 86*, 313–338. doi:10.17763/1943-5045-86.3.31

References

Alexander, J. (2017). *Writing youth: Young adult fiction as literacy sponsorship*. Lanham, MD: Lexington Books.

Bartmess, E. (2015, December 18). Autistic representation and real-life consequences: An in-depth look. Retrieved from http://disabilityinkidlit.com/2015/12/18/autistic-representation-and-real-life-consequences/

Black, R., Alexander, J., Chen, V., & Duarte, J. (2019). Representations of autism in online *Harry Potter* fanfiction. *Journal of Literacy Research, 51*(1), 30–51.

Brandt, D. (2001). *Literacy in American lives*. New York, NY: Cambridge University Press.

Gross, Z. (2012). Metaphor stole my autism: The social construction of autism as separable from personhood, and its effect on policy, funding and perception. In J. Bascom (Ed.), *Loud hands: Autistic people, speaking* (pp. 258–269). Washington, DC: The Autistic Press.

Harrington-Kane, E. (2007, July 24). What Harry Potter can teach us about autism [Blog entry]. Retrieved from https://blog.easterseals.com/what-harry-potter-can-teach-us-about-autism/

Jenkins, H. (1992). *Textual poachers: Television fans and participatory culture*. New York, NY: Routledge.

Jenkins, H., Puroshotma, R., Clinton, K., Weigel, M., & Robison, A. (2006). *Confronting the challenges of participatory culture: Media education for the 21st century*. Cambridge, MA: MIT Press.

Loftis, S. F. (2015). *Imagining autism: Fiction and stereotypes on the spectrum*. Bloomington: Indiana University Press.

Robison, J. E. (2013, October 7). What is neurodiversity? *Psychology Today*. Retrieved from https://www.psychologytoday.com/blog/my-life-aspergers/201310/what-is-neurodiversity

Rozema, R. (2014). The problem of autism in young adult fiction. *Language Arts Journal of Michigan, 30*(7), 26–31. doi:10.9707/2168-149X.2039

Saldaña, J. (2009). *The coding manual for qualitative researchers*. Thousand Oaks, CA: Sage Publications.

Silberman, S. (2015). *Neurotribes: The legacy of autism and the future of neurodiversity*. New York, NY: Random House.

Thibault, R. (2014). Can autistics redefine autism? The cultural politics of autistic activism. *Trans-Scripts, 4*, 57–88. Retrieved from https://www.academia.edu/7234120/Can_Autistics_Redefine_Autism_The_Cultural_Politics_of_Autistic_Activism

CHAPTER 10

Following Texts, Bodies, and Objects in Everyday Practice: Thinking With Actor Network Theory

Jason F. Lovvorn and Kevin M. Leander

EDUCATIONAL THEORIES, LIKE many social theories, largely remain people-centered. At the same time, they often inherit and maintain structuralism's penchant for particular forms of stability, sorting experience and creating order out of disorder while prioritizing humanistic patterns of interpretation. In part, such tendencies derive from the inherently human associations, no doubt created and sustained by humans, that surround educational practice. Teachers teach. Students learn. Administrators administer. In this disposition, agents of practice and agents of change are grounded in psycho-social-cultural perspectives wherein human intentions take center stage and material objects exist largely as tools (e.g., Cole & Engestrom, 1993; Engestrom, 1999). In such models, shaped by what Latour (2005) calls a "strong 'socio-logy,'" human subjectivity reigns supreme, and people own the verbs put into play.

More recent scholarly efforts, however, challenge human primacy, going so far as to suggest an active, equal footing for nonhuman materials. This "posthuman" turn (Barad, 2003; Braidotti, 2013) posits that nonhumans share ability and should share credit for work in the world, including the knowledge work of educational practice. In this context, a posthuman "New Materialism" (Barrett & Bolt, 2013; Coole & Frost, 2010; Dolphijn & van der Tuin, 2012) has emerged across multiple disciplines, focusing attention on the ways in which *things* hold sway. In this vein, "thing theory" (Brown, 2001) has helped scholars reorganize the ways in which we understand agency and accountability (Bennett, 2010; Brown, 2004; Lamb, 2011). *Vibrancy* and *vitality* are descriptors ascribed to nonhuman objects in these new accounts where things possess force (Bennett, 2010). Here, objects share verbs traditionally wielded by humans. Spaces mark. Bodies influence. Things shape.

A specific strand of materially-oriented work drives this chapter. As part of the shift toward an "object-oriented" (Harman, 2009) philosophy/ontology in social research, Actor Network Theory (hereafter abbreviated as ANT) originated with ethnographic efforts to understand how scientific knowledge arises across identifiable contexts (Latour, 1987, 1993; Latour & Woolgar, 1986). This work in the sociology of science considers how various agents, both human and nonhuman, are distributed in complex networks, making possible certain forms of knowing. For example, in thinking about Einstein's famous equation $E = mc^2$, an ANT account would consider Einstein's genius as merely one factor contributing to this breakthrough. Besides the intellectual tradition preceding Einstein, ANT might also describe nonhuman actors, such as the city and university libraries in Bern, a drawer in the Bern patent office where Einstein kept his notes, and even the equals sign itself, a symbol that did not come about until the 16th century. Bruno Latour (1988), a key originator of ANT, in fact, examines Einstein's theory of relativity with an eye toward what he calls the "sociology of delegation," wherein the origins of the treatise stretch widely across a range of objects and humans. In this regard, Latour lists among the important "actants" (his term for *any* element that *acts*) the following: rods, a train, Trafalgar Square, a raven, fixed stars, lightning, a marble table, a railway carriage, stones, and a note emitted by an organ pipe.

ANT therefore requires of the researcher an ability to level distinctions between people and things. This flattening—whether the metaphor is delegation (Latour, 1988), distribution (Bennett, 2010), or symmetry (Callon, 1986; Spinuzzi, 2015)—insists that objects be granted agency equal to that which humans enjoy in people-centered descriptions of activity. As Spinuzzi (2015) succinctly defines it, such symmetry is "the principle that human and nonhuman actants are treated alike when considering how controversies are settled" (p. 23). Three important implications arise from this line. First, as already noted, humans and nonhumans share agency. Second, the interconnections and play of these varied "actants" shape how knowledge settles into view. Third, such settlings are not predetermined; they involve shifts and struggles as actants play off one another and therefore require careful tracking at the ground level. Combined, such ideas push us from ANT as social theory toward a more layered understanding of this domain as both theory and methodology.

As a tool in the employ of the literacy researcher, ANT defies easy categorization. Part theory, part method, it signals an attitude toward activity at the same time it recommends descriptive techniques. Its originators recognize as much. Latour (1999a), for instance, notes, "For us, ANT was simply another way of being faithful to the insights of ethnomethodology: actors know what they do and we have to learn from them not only what they do, but how and why they do it" (p. 19). Thus, even though "theory" is foregrounded in ANT's name, just as much emphasis rests on *how* researchers might trace significant elements in activity. More recent scholarship echoes this sentiment. For example, Nespor (2012) points out that ANT is both "a set of assumptions and conceptual tools for studying them" (p. 2), and Hamilton (2012) positions this work as a "conversation between theory and data" (p. 41). Fenwick and Edwards (2012) stretch these insights even further, noting, "ANT is not 'applied' like a theoretical technology, but is more like a sensibility, a way to sense and draw (nearer to) a phenomenon" (p. ix). Invariably grounded in case studies, ANT forces a simultaneous consideration of theory and data, often asking investigators to consider novel ways to categorize and understand data. Such was the case in our prior examination of literacy practices in and out of school, the centerpiece for the methodological discussion that follows.

As a kind of sensibility, our attraction to ANT in this work was largely based on wanting to try and understand something that felt very abstract (space-time relations and literacy) in the more material and embodied experiences of using literacy. At the time of this research (approximately 2004 to 2006), it was unclear how conceptions of in-school, out-of-school, or other setting-based separations provide powerful distinctions for understanding differences among practices of literacy learning, teaching, and thinking. Largely, we think these puzzles are still with us, although we have made some progress and like to think of this study as one contribution. Literacy theory, we want to point out, always engages some theory or concept of space-time, and, as Brandt and Clinton (2002) have argued, we must acknowledge the "heavy hand literacy has had in building networks across time and space" (p. 347). Texts, a mainstay of literacy research, coordinate and structure space-time within a given activity and space-times across diverse activities. For researchers interested in understanding this reach, an important theoretical and practical task is to interpret the configurations, circulation, and translations of texts in relation to other actors in activity. ANT offers both theory and method for doing so.

Moreover, practices of reading and writing are invariably interwoven with other forms of activity. Literacy doesn't only exist in some set of "events" that are separate from the events of everyday living and moving and doing all manner of things—this idea was becoming a mainstay finding in the New Literacy Studies. In moving social practice theories of literacy (Gee, 1990; Street, 1984) forward, we argue, researchers need to develop a view of the social that includes an understanding of how a wide range of actors (e.g., humans, texts, technologies, and objects) are brought into relationship with one another, with a careful eye on how these relationships have unique space-time qualities. This movement will also extend emerging conversations about how literacy and texts participate in social–material configurations (Fenwick & Edwards, 2012) and encourage researchers to broaden the scope of what is meant by *literacy*.

Actor Network Theory in Action: Summary of "Literacy Networks"

"Literacy Networks" (Leander & Lovvorn, 2006) is a particular kind of research article that differs somewhat from typical article norms, including posing a research question or questions, selecting a theoretical lens for the question(s), and then applying this lens for the analysis of the data. Rather, the study was more of an investigation of theory and data together, in an attempt to create new ways of understanding these data, with the hopes that these new ways might have some traction in the field beyond. In that sense, then, the connections among theory, method, and data were messy in this study, and we try to offer an unsanitized view of this messiness in our account as we move along.

The questions guiding the study, although they are more implied than stated outright in publication, were the following:

1. How might the study of networks, drawing on ANT, help us to think about literacy practices and their relations to space-time? Can we conceptualize something like a "literacy network?"
2. How might the analysis of literacy networks (if we can pull that off) help us to understand the engagement, agency, and identity of one youth across his different practices with literacy?

Looking back on these questions and directions now, more than 13 years since the study's publication, they seem ambitious and complicated, which we think also "locates" this study as a kind of exploration across theory, method, and data—as an attempt to open up some new ways of thinking—without reaching something like "tested" arguments for seeing the data one way over all others. In that sense, work in the study was sometimes more divergent than convergent and drew on our sense of imagination as well as our analytic capacities.

Findings reported in our "Literacy Networks" article (Leander & Lovvorn, 2006) resulted from a case study that was part of a larger study called "Synchrony," itself structured as a set of seven case studies that followed youth participants across school and online contexts. Synchrony was an effort to understand how the use of (then "new") information and communication technologies, such as instant messaging, chat, e-mail, searching the Internet, building websites, and online gaming was related to youth literacy practices, to their social networks, and to their identities in offline contexts, including but not limited to school. Synchrony was not only fascinating but also difficult and very messy to write about at any scale, and one way to deal with this messiness was to select individual cases, such as the case of "Brian" presented in "Literacy Networks." Brian was a 13-year-old youth during the time of the research and lived with his brother and parents outside a small town (population 6,000) in the mid-South of the United States. Of all the cases in Synchrony, Brian's was the most robust, in part, because he was the most willing to engage in the research and stayed with it longer than the other participants.

We collected data to develop a case study of Brian's activities with literacy across school and home contexts through standard ethnographic methods: participant observations, document collection, interviews, small surveys of his classmates, and field notes. To record Brian's online activity, which, in his case, was nearly entirely from home, we used software for the digital capture of online interaction, and we videotaped his online interaction using a digital video camera typically placed over Brian's shoulder. Brian was observed at least once per week in his English and history classes from February to June 2003, and his course work from these classes was collected during these visits. Biweekly home observations of online literacy practices, including computer gaming, also began in February and continued through August 2003, with less frequent follow-up visits extending for several months.

Brian had little competition from family members for access to a recent model PC with a cable modem. He spent, on average, two to three hours per day in online activity, which primarily involved playing massively multiplayer online games (MMOGs). During the summer months, Brian's online activity often increased to five or more hours per day as he began to play Star Wars Galaxies: An Empire Divided (Lucas Arts & Sony Entertainment, 2003), an MMOG based loosely on the *Star Wars* milieu.

Analysis in Practice: Bringing Constructs From Theory and Selections From Data Into Dialogue

Before we launch into the nitty-gritty of our analysis-in-practice, it seems important to note a few things that had an important influence on our analysis but may not be explicit in reading the original paper alone. "Literacy Networks" (Leander & Lovvorn, 2006) is a study out of a larger study (Synchrony) that was exploring literacy practices situated in and out of school, on one hand, and online and offline, on the other. So a first observation about our larger method is that we were engaged in a comparative method within our ethnographic work—looking for differences and similarities across these boundaries (in/out, online/offline). We had chosen schools where there was at least some engagement online, so by design, we had two sets of comparisons going that did not neatly map onto one another.

In addition to this comparative method, and inspiring it, was a concept from spatial theory that we were continually thinking about: *How can we think beyond the notion of activities simply being "situated" in space and time? Or how does literacy relate to space-time?* The idea of literacy as "situated" was a major idea in Literacy Studies when we wrote the article (and still is). The idea of situatedness, in fact, was itself pushing back on something more traditional. The New Literacy Studies had pushed away from abstract or "autonomous" theories of literacy and subscribed instead to "ideological" theories (Street, 1984). Part of the meaning of thinking about literacy as "ideological," in the New Literacy Studies, was to consider how literacy was "situated" in the everyday lives of people. This situatedness often was taken up through a focus on local practices, such as is the bread and butter of much of anthropology. Through a nascent critique of "situatedness," we were inclined in the larger study to keep thinking about space and time relations, including the movements of people, things, and texts. So, space, time, and movements were key mindsets or forms of "framing" with which we continually looked at our data. In our analysis, we wanted to mess with "situatedness," and especially with container-like views that simply saw texts or practices with literacy as being located somewhere.

In service of our larger question about how literacy may be actively involved in producing space-time relations (and not just situated in "contexts"), and in service of the more focused questions of the study, we developed for our analysis five related constructs. These constructs were informed by our reading of ANT, but our reading of the theory was also related to our questions and to our data. These constructs need emphasizing because it would be inaccurate to say that the following five qualities somehow appeared wholly formed and ready to use in the theory, as a kind of "model" or template for analysis. It would also be inaccurate to say that we created a theoretical model outside of the context of having data and thinking about these data—like a ready-made "toolkit" or "lens" to apply to the data. Rather, these five constructs were our attempt to put part of the theory to work for us—to clarify for ourselves how and when we would "see" ideas within the data that we had already collected but were still selecting cases and ideas from. We see data collection and selection, theory development, and data analysis as deeply intermingled in this work.

We developed five analytic dimensions from ANT during the course of the study (see Leander & Lovvorn, 2006, pp. 305–306):

1. Translation
2. Heterogeneity of space-time representations
3. Movements and positions of texts in circulation
4. Rhythms and speeds of circulation
5. Network continuity

Although we referred to these dimensions as a "framework" in the original article, we hesitate to do so here because a framework implies something more static and completely formed.

We mainly addressed textual translation, although in ANT, "translation" can apply to many kinds of practices and objects. Our analysis considered how texts spoke for, stood in for, or seemed to mobilize other texts, objects, or bodies. A paper text in the form of a student assignment, for example, was seen as "[mobilizing] the body and thoughts of the student... [continuing] the circulation of the student toward the teacher, where the student could be examined and evaluated" (Leander & Lovvorn, 2006, p. 305).

The heterogeneity of space-time representations, the second dimension, is related to translation. Because texts express particular versions of space-time (time-space or chronotopes; Bakhtin, 1981; Leander, 2001), we looked for the kinds of space-times particular texts produced and organized linguistically, imagistically, and by other means. In the process of coding and contrasting data, we focused especially on texts that offered participants "representations of their activity that were global in scale with respect to their locally embodied activity" (Leander & Lovvorn, 2006, p. 305) and asked how, by introducing these representations, texts produced multiple time scales (heterochronies; Lemke, 2000) and multiple spaces (heterotopies; Foucault, 1986).

We hoped also to describe a *geography* of texts in activity, through the third dimension, by analyzing how material texts move and fall into order with other actants in activity. By considering the "space-time prepositional relations" (e.g., before, after, during, on top of, besides, behind) of texts to other objects in activity, we could see, for example, that in some forms of activity, the text "is placed" as the final result or curve of what came before (such as writing a summary of a presentation), whereas in other situations texts are "overlaid with activity" (Leander & Lovvorn, 2006, p. 305). Sometimes the space-time relation of texts to other actants may collapse into a text–actant fusion or hybridity. For example, containers that have measurements printed on them, or whose measurements have become routine in a particular practice—such as a half cup in baking—are simultaneously implements and texts of measurement for routine practice (Berg, 1997). According to Berg (1997, p. 420), such "small crossings" are essential for understanding how participants traverse the apparent gap between the formal–textual and practical and, consequently, how material hybridity allows researchers to conceive of texts as acting among a "myriad of little powers."

Unlike the dimension of movement and position, which foregrounds a spatial dimension of displacement, the analysis of rhythm and speed—the fourth dimension—focuses more directly on temporality. In some kinds of activity (e.g., some computer games), texts and the space-times they mobilize "are placed in frequent and rapid relation to other actants in circulation," and within such practices, the human participants "appear to beat out a rapid rhythm of texts and action" (Leander & Lovvorn, 2006, p. 306). The speeds are much slower in other kinds of human activity, and the periods between beats may be long.

Finally, with respect to network continuity, texts or other objects in a network might seemingly circulate without end, while other networks are cut off by various means. Where circulations *could* be traced, we gave them "a God's-eye view" and connected "select, observed locales with myriad other nonobserved locales in space and time" (Leander & Lovvorn, 2006, p. 306). Even from the constrained perspective of a participant, however, some networks are much more continuous than others. By way of comparing Brian's literacy practices, we considered how his relations to the texts he was reading and writing appeared to be either "more or less extended and continuous" (Leander & Lovvorn, 2006, p. 306), or "cut" (Strathern, 1996).

Selections From Data

The following data from our research is presented in a form that is somewhat "raw," although, of course, we have already made many analytic moves through processes of recording field notes (and video), selecting these episodes, and summarizing the data. It is also important to reemphasize that for the original article these data were selected from a larger set of ethnographic data, spanning participant observations of several months in Brian's various classrooms and about a year and a half in his home. We note this because, with the broad look at practices in this research, we attempted in our selection of these episodes to make evident typical social practices and patterns and, thereby, to get at typical ways that literacy was involved in space-time relations in schooling and gaming (our research questions). In this sense, *all* the data (that we are not explicitly writing about) are every bit as important to our thinking as *these* data, because they inform our selections, inform our thinking about the whole, and inform our use of specific constructs from the theory. Although it has been said many times before in relation to ethnography, there is no substitute for sustained engagement over time.

In what follows, we present two summaries of practices from Brian's classroom and field note summaries from two episodes of video game play at home. These data representations will enable us to illustrate our analytic method subsequently.

1. History Class Lecture and Notes Routine

In his history class, Brian's teacher, Mrs. Quinn (pseudonyms are used throughout), would present to the class on most of the observed days with a style that combined lecturing with storytelling. When the students arrived in class, their task was to copy questions from the whiteboard pertinent to that day's lecture (e.g., "How did muckrakers hope to eliminate social evils?"). Students were also to copy vocabulary terms from the whiteboard. To receive credit in class, the overall tasks for the students were to capture the answers to the questions that were prestructured for them and to define the vocabulary terms. Once their notes were completed, students were also to mark their answers to the questions with a highlighting pen to save Mrs. Quinn time in checking over their notes. Lecture notes and defined vocabulary accumulated from day to day, and students were supposed to end up with a large set of notes from which to study for each unit test. Brian enjoyed Mrs. Quinn's stories during the lecture quite a lot and described history as a "real active class." However, he was uninterested in taking notes and only did so for class credit. Brian seemed to labor with handwriting while note-taking, often falling behind, and was often missing answers to questions and vocabulary definitions. Brian's notes were also poorly organized in his notebook, and he reported never using them to study. Nevertheless, Brian was able to earn a B+ in history because, despite his poor performance with note-taking, his test scores were high.

2. *English Class Research Project*

Brian was uninterested in English class, seeing himself as one who never did well in it. At the same time, Brian never spoke about English class as being challenging. Ms. Marshall (pseudonym), Brian's English teacher, assigned the students a research project in early May that she hoped would help them with their writing. Because of time constraints, the teacher eventually decided that the students would not be able to write the paper and would only complete notecards and an outline. When the class topic was bracketed as "historical periods," Brian chose World War II, because he "just thought there would be a lot of information on it." The students received handouts from Ms. Marshall on how to paraphrase and how to create notecards and made visits to the library and computer lab over a few days. Brian mostly talked with friends in the library and then completed his notecards in his study hall. His notecards offered scanty detail and many of them included information that Brian already knew. One card, for instance, listed "WWII" and then underneath this heading, "Pearl Harbor," followed by "Japan bombed Hawaii." On the day that the cards were due in class, Brian had forgotten about the outline but was able to hastily draft up an outline while Ms. Marshall was circulating around the room and collecting other students' projects. Brian received a B– on the project, scoring full credit for handing it in on time and having completed most of the note cards.

3. *(At Home) Video Game Play Episode 1*

Observation 2, July 2. Just a week previous to this episode, Brian had created a virtual character for game play, Tiumbe, using a set of tools built into the game. He had also done a bit of exploring around the planet Tatooine. In this session, Brian decided to explore a different planet, Naboo. Brian had already sold the first gun he had purchased, replacing it with a custom-built gun from someone in the game "who [was] really good at building them." Brian had also given Tiumbe new armor on his legs and a new backpack. Tiumbe's exploration of Naboo was motivated by Brian's desire to find a place for his future house, and because Naboo was full of waterways and islands, exploration consisted of a good deal of swimming and walking long distances. Few characters and creatures existed in the areas that Tiumbe explored. Although Tiumbe covered 6,000 meters, as measured on the planetary map, day and night cycled every hour in real time. Brian decided that the islands that Tiumbe explored were too far from the city (and thus other players, shopping, transportation, and other services). Tiumbe headed back to the city to catch a ship to Tatooine while simultaneously communicating with another player whose character was on a different planet in the game. Using a chat screen, he asked how to autorun (make Tiumbe run across the landscape automatically). The other player did not know. Tiumbe then made his way to the starport and, while waiting for his ship, browsed auction listings on a computer terminal located near the star port.

4. (At Home) Video Game Play Episode 2

Observation 3, July 10. Brian began by noting the house of a friend, who was a rich player in the game. Tiumbe toured the house and shopped for a sofa among the various items this other player offered for sale. After Tiumbe moved outside, Brian provided a brief explanation of experience points and hunting to the researcher. Tiumbe then teamed up with another player, Ben, to conduct a hunt. The two engaged a giant peko peko bird but were overpowered. To recover, Ben made a camp, but the camp actually disappeared temporarily—an occurrence that Brian explained as a bug in the game. To work around this and other game bugs, Ben decided to log off temporarily. Tiumbe then showed the researcher a new guildhall—a central meeting space for fellow guild members and him. When Ben logged back in, the pair briefly aided other hunters and then successfully hunted a falumpasset (large four-legged creature) by themselves. After the two harvested animal parts, Brian made camp by drawing out a ready-made campsite from Tiumbe's inventory and noted another game bug: Tiumbe sometimes did not sit directly on the camp chair. Following some surveying work, Tiumbe helped Ben defeat two ikopi (horse-like creatures). After harvesting resources from the animals, the two were beset by rabid shaupauts (kangaroo-like creatures). During this attack, Brian noted, "I'm trying to get experience for trapping," and so Tiumbe employed traps to help defeat two waves of shaupauts while Brian distinguished between the various types of traps and their effects. Brian then discussed and demonstrated trap crafting, using the resources collected from animals. Tiumbe and Ben then went on additional hunts for other animals, set up a new camp, and crafted additional traps.

Analysis in Practice: Making Sense of the Data and Theory

These data look like quite a mess at first glance, so one impulse might be to tame them with different kinds of models or frames. For instance, for one set of goals, coding themes across the data would be perfectly acceptable. But in this case, we're trying to keep some of the mess alive, keep looking at materials, and keep looking at movements. We're keeping our focus on circulations that may give some clues as to the relations between literacy and space-time. To illustrate our process, let's consider the second dimension of our concept list from ANT: "Heterogeneity of space-time representations." We believe that not every dimension will work well for all the data, and each dimension may need a lot of refinement for our analysis and for that of others going forward. The eventual description of "Heterogeneity of space-time representations" in our 2006 article arose from our work with the dimension. When we began, what we knew was to look for "heterogeneity of representations." That concept, then, would come to mean something for us in the context of our work, so one goal became making its meaning clear to others. (Whether our meanings about it may transfer well to other research, we can't say yet.)

In looking at these data now, with the benefit of hindsight, what we really see are heterogeneous representations (e.g., local and global texts coming together) and heterogeneous mixes (e.g., local actions being combined with more global texts). The simplest case to think with in this dimension is that of the note cards for the English research project. In this case, Brian copies relatively abstract propositions, coming to him from distant sources (e.g., authorities in the library, sources online) and renders that information still more abstract through the processes of making note cards and an outline for an essay. This abstraction and extraction process seem linked to a testing/evaluation economy, as evidenced by Ms. Marshall's concern for the standardized writing assessment and by her use of standardized guides for practices such as note cards. In this regard, Brian's schoolwork in history is quite similar—he extracts notes from the history lectures to answer pregiven questions and predetermined definitions. The knowledge that Brian is tasked with transcribing/re-presenting is given as general, timeless, and spaceless knowledge.

On the other hand—and this contrast lit up as really important to us—Mrs. Quinn, Brian's history teacher, weaves personal stories into her lectures of history. These stories juxtapose abstract representations of the past with local and personal accounts. Brian loves these stories—they are what seem to move him to keep engaged. These local–global connects (Brandt & Clinton, 2002) seem, in ANT terms, to "enroll" Brian as a history student. Although Mrs. Quinn's verbal stories and anecdotes don't continue in the circulations of papers and tests in the classroom, they serve to help Brian continue as an identity pulled into and moved by history. This difference between Brian's English and history courses also illustrates, again, the power of a comparative method for research, in this case not assuming that work practices and circulations look the same merely because they are situated in school. Rather, the two classes, at least in these selected activities, create different relations of space-time to literacy.

The gaming episodes we recorded in our data involved much more heterogeneity of space-time representations than did the classroom data—in fact, we could readily say that this heterogeneity, in terms of local and global perspectives on activity, was the norm. In the episodes summarized earlier, for example, Brian (as Tiumbe) explored Naboo in virtual embodied form, swimming and walking long distances. Within these navigations (yet not recorded in the excerpt above), Brian used waypoints that would connect map-based goals to his local, over-the-shoulder view of his character, and he continually circulated between a map (overhead, more global) perspective and his localized, first-person or over-the-shoulder perspective of his character. Moreover, Brian communicated with other players on other virtual planets while playing, thus giving more global reach to his activity and permitting him to multitask with local and more distal concerns. We further noticed how Brian often circulated between a local form of activity and some broad sense of his goals. For instance, in the middle of the camping scene depicted, Brian mentions wanting to get experience points for hunting. With the click of a button, he would very often make available to his view a menu that showed his point totals for different types of experience. Thus, he engaged in local/global perspectives that involved more than just navigation—they also involved a sense of how local activity types related to developing identity goals.

Contrasted with making notes in English or history, these ways of reading texts, seeing oneself in relation to the world, and thinking locally and globally during activity, seemed striking to us. They made us wonder, even more than before, how diverse representations of space-time in activity, and especially forms of connection between the local and global, may be related to Brian's senses of himself as an actor in the world. The contrasts in this regard also made clearer how it wasn't just the representations that were of interest but also the ways in which the texts that Brian used were juxtaposed with different types of activity that made such sharp distinctions between gaming and schooling for Brian. For the most part, schooling for Brian involved the circulation of one text to another—such as from the information in the teacher's talk to the notes on his paper or from the library book to his note card. Materially speaking, the work of taking up a text was to produce a different text. In gaming, however, texts were present frequently, but these texts (as images and words) were posed in relation to all types of activity (e.g., navigating, fighting, hunting) and appeared as embedded or dynamically connected to these forms of activity.

Our thinking about the data through the lens of heterogeneous space-time representations (Dimension 2) led us naturally to think about them through the lens of movements and positions of texts in circulation (Dimension 3). One would expect these relations because it's important to keep in mind that these different dimensions don't exist in the world as separate ideas. Rather, they are heuristics or little tools that we have used to tease out some different ways of thinking and seeing from complicated theory. One analytic method that helped us even further consider contrasts related to the movements and positions of texts was to create small sketches for ourselves. Over time, we have come to have a lot of faith in sketching relations as a means to understand data. Sketching can, of course, involve visually organizing data or making provisional models of some concept in relation to the data. In this case, we used sketches at a more basic level—we simply drew lines between texts, other materials, and people in the circulations of Brian's classroom activities and game play. In the backs of our minds was a quote by some educational sociologist (whom we couldn't recall and never quoted in the paper) that the circulation of school was mostly good at producing garbage—vast amounts of student work that ended up in dumpsters. So, we thought, trace that back . . . Where does the garbage come from? Who makes the first text or object? What does it turn into (Translation, Dimension 1) next? Our sketches were powerful tools for helping us understand how the gaming circulations set up incredibly different relations of texts to action and, additionally, created an entire game-based economy related to texts, objects, and activity. Each world Brian was in, of course, had its own economy, and to understand these circulations, we needed to visualize them.

One issue that we found incredibly intriguing as we contrasted and spent time with our data, reading and rereading, sketching and pondering, was how certain material objects in Brian's game play functioned as what we came to call "text-objects." The animal traps in the second game episode presented earlier are a good example of this phenomenon. Analytically, we want to note that the traps did not attract our attention because we were looking through a theoretical "frame," because we were coding something, or even because we were focused on the question of space-time. The traps were just cool. (Sometimes the data just scream for your attention. They even seem to mock you: "Okay, make sense of ME now, will ya buddy?") On one hand, the traps are representations, both visual and textual. During the middle of an attack by shaupauts, Brian accessed various images of traps in a help screen, clicking on them to pull up more screens that were filled with textual information about the effects of the traps. The traps themselves also provided Brian access to information concerning how many experience points each one would give him—capital toward his identity goals as a player. And, like texts more than objects, the traps could be packed along with all of his gear and seem to have no volume or mass. On the other hand, however, when he needed them, the traps were Brian's faithful tools in the struggle—they functioned like real materials in the scene of the hunt. The ways in which the text–object ontology made a difference in game play really struck us as we considered it, and we worried, "Are we just describing virtual reality? Wasn't all this most obvious?" Perhaps that was the case, but in these parts of the analysis, we have learned over time to trust our instincts in terms of what we find surprising, powerful, or of a striking contrast. The traps, and many other objects in the game, including Brian's own virtual body (as Tiumbe), were not merely texts or merely objects; they functioned and were used as something in between. Their being-in-the-world, or ontology, was different.

The text–object relation was somewhat captured in the third point of our space-time dimensions: "movements and positions of texts in circulation." Within that dimension, we came to describe how there could be a "fusing or hybridity of text–actant" wherein a text and a non-textual actant circulate in strong, rapid fashion (Leander & Lovvorn, 2006, p. 306). From ANT, we could see the text-object as not only *within* a circulation (around the game world) but also, itself, *was* a circulation. We were reminded that one theorist of ANT (Latour, 1991) said to notice how every actant is itself a network, a circulation. The traps, then, seem like a chain of semiotic and material relations (S-M-S-M-S-M) in how they are taken up in the game. On one hand, this seemed like a possible "definition"—a possible holding place for the analysis. Yet, it also felt incomplete—we were (and are) still bothered by the traps, still bothered by how to understand virtual bodies and materials and their relations to meanings and doings. A series of new questions opens up. Is the limit *Actor Network Theory*? Maybe. We are intrigued by how some of the newly-developing work in new materialisms might guide us. Is the limit *the data we have*? Perhaps. Now, and especially with artificial intelligence, we have still newer problems to consider around text–objects in our lives, problems that we find both puzzling and exciting.

Moving Forward: Helpful Stances for Literacy Researchers Employing ANT

We'd like to conclude with a short consideration of some stances that we believe are useful to researchers who want to think with ANT. Obviously, we don't believe that thinking *with* ANT is close to being settled in the field, nor do we feel a great deal of confidence that this list is somehow complete. Yet these are qualities that we believe will help you orient to the data in ways that will make more evident the kinds of things ANT is good for—showing human/nonhuman relations, for example, or making clear how different relations of literacy to space-time are created through different forms of circulation. As we have indicated throughout our discussion, we also see these forms of thinking with ANT as contributing potentially to the theory and to the data analysis—they are in some kind of dance of meaning, some kind of circulation. This stance contrasts with some other stances that would ask one to look through the theory as an established lens that is separate from the data.

- **You should value an ethnographic attitude.** In line with Latour's earlier comments about "ethnomethodology," Hamilton (2012) points out that "ANT's preferred method is ethnographic" (p. 43). But as already noted, any ANT ethnography must incorporate an expanded sense of the social to include material elements (Latour, 2005). Researchers accustomed to collecting human-centered data must stretch their gazes and pay greater attention to objects. As far as the nuts and bolts of collecting data, much has been made of Latour's (2005) call to "follow the actors" (p. 68), but ANT researchers often begin with traditional methods of qualitative research, common to ethnography, as ways to identify the actors worth following. Moreover, ANT shares with ethnographic reporting a bias toward storytelling, although ANT's stories often involve narratives of things such as vacuum pumps, laboratory slides, or scallops.
- **You should be attuned to connections and resulting networks.** In "Technology Is Society Made Durable," Latour (1991) writes, "We are never faced with objects or social relations, we are faced with chains that are associations of human (H) and non-humans (NH)" (p. 110). In an ANT account, these *relations, chains,* or *associations,* also captured

more broadly with language such as *assemblages* or the eponymous *networks,* are actually what give rise to the work traditionally ascribed to human intention. ANT consistently emphasizes relations and relational sets, and researchers therefore ask questions like the following: *How* are associations among people and things accomplished? (Nespor, 2012), and what do texts and objects *do* in their respective "assemblies or gatherings"? (Fenwick & Edwards, 2012, p. xi). An ANT researcher must function, to some extent, as an on-the-ground detective, tracking and tracing relations as they arise, and seeing where they go.

- **You should become comfortable with complexity.** ANT acknowledges complexity by granting notions of agency and collaboration that are highly varied and often densely intertwined. Speaking to this issue, Mol and Law (2002) write:

  > Much recent work in the sociology of science, history of technology, anthropology of medicine, cultural studies, feminism, and political philosophy has been a revolt against simplification. The argument has been that the world is complex and that it shouldn't be tamed too much—and certainly not to the point where simplification becomes an impediment to understanding. (p. 1)

  Law (2004) continues to press this line in social science research, pointing out how "standard research methods" sometimes produce the reality they seek to understand (p. 4), and he instead advocates for approaches to data that entertain divergent explanations and a wide range of accepted evidence. Indeed, ANT researchers may wind up tracking multiple relations and multiple networks, sometimes with no clear convergence in sight.
- **You should pay attention to texts and to their relations to other objects and to activity**. ANT has an affinity for texts that literacy researchers, in particular, would be well served to notice. In ANT accounts of scientific and technical activity, inscriptional devices and the texts they produce hold special places, in part, because these elements render static entities more mobile and allow traces of their perception to circulate in ways previously impossible. Such "immutable mobiles" impart certain kinds of power—cognitive, rhetorical, political and otherwise—to those who bear them and use them for various kinds of analyses (Latour, 1990). In one instance, Latour (1999b) tracks a scientific expedition to the Amazon, highlighting ways in which a savanna–forest border is sampled, translated into representations via a

range of scientific devices, and eventually moved off-site into laboratories and, later, into journal pages. This "material-semiotic" account, in which the physical world is reduced to symbolic stand-ins, is replete with texts at the same time it showcases ANT's preoccupation with how inscriptions often gather up elements and transport them (or *translate* them) across space and time (Law, 2008).

- **You should be attuned to spatiotemporal considerations.** Nespor (2012) observes how, in addressing various "hybrid collectives" (networks, assemblages, etc.), ANT focuses on "the movement of their constitutive associations across time and space" (p. 2). Indeed, metaphors of mobilization (Callon, 1986) and circulation (Latour 1999b) are integral to ANT's origins, and as we noted in our prior study, "to be an actant involves shifting in time and space, which involves the translation of actants as they circulate, are recruited, organized, and hybridized with other actants" (Leander & Lovvorn, 2006, p. 296). The ANT researcher, therefore, must be alert to such movements, seeking to understand how uptake and transport create longer chains of association between people and things.

Suggested Further Reading

ANT has a very large corpus by now, although much less so in educational research. We recommend reading the following texts as a substantial way into this means of thinking with ANT about literacy.

Fenwick, T., & Edwards, R. (Eds.). (2012). *Researching education through actor-network theory*. Oxford, England: Wiley-Blackwell.

Latour, B. (2005). *Reassembling the social: An introduction to actor-network-theory*. Oxford, England: Oxford University Press.

Law, J. (2004). *After method: Mess in social science research*. London, England: Routledge.

References

Bakhtin, M. M. (1981). Forms of time and of the chronotope in the novel (C. Emerson & M. Holquist, Trans.). In M. Holquist (Ed.), *The dialogic imagination: Four essays by M. M. Bakhtin* (pp. 84–258). Austin: University of Texas Press.

Barad, K. (2003). Posthuman performativity: Toward an understanding of how matter comes to matter. *Signs: Journal of Women in Culture and Society, 28*, 801–831.

Barrett, E., & Bolt, B. (Eds.). (2013). *Carnal knowledge: Towards a 'New Materialism' through the arts*. London, England: I.B. Tauris.

Bennett, J. (2010). *Vibrant matter: A political ecology of things*. Durham, NC: Duke University Press.

Berg, M. (1997). Of forms, containers, and the electronic medical record: Some tools for a sociology of the formal. *Science, Technology, and Human Values, 22*, 403–434.

Braidotti, R. (2013). *The posthuman*. Cambridge, England: Polity Press.

Brandt, D., & Clinton, K. (2002). Limits of the local: Expanding perspectives on literacy as social practice. *Journal of Literacy Research, 34*, 337–356.

Brown, B. (2001). Thing theory. *Critical Inquiry, 28*(1), 1–22.

Brown, B. (Ed.). (2004). *Things*. Chicago, IL: University of Chicago Press.

Callon, M. (1986). Some elements of a sociology of translation: Domestication of the scallops and the fishermen of St. Brieuc Bay. In J. Law (Ed.), *Power, action, and belief* (pp. 196–233). London, England: Routledge.

Cole, M., & Engeström, Y. (1993). A cultural-historical approach to distributed cognition. In G. Salomon (Ed.), *Distributed cognitions: Psychological and educational considerations* (pp. 1–46). Cambridge, England: Cambridge University Press.

Coole, D., & Frost, S. (Eds.). (2010). *New materialisms: Ontology, agency, and politics*. Durham, NC: Duke University Press.

Dolphijn, R., & van der Tuin, I. (2012). *New materialism: Interviews & cartographies*. Ann Arbor, MI: Open Humanities Press.

Engeström, Y. (1999). Activity theory and individual and social transformation. In Y. Engeström, R. Miettinen, & R-L Punamäki-Gitai (Eds.), *Perspectives on activity theory* (pp. 19–38). Cambridge, England: Cambridge University Press.

Fenwick, T., & Edwards R. (2012) Introduction. In T. Fenwick & R. Edwards, (Eds.), *Researching education through actor-network theory* (pp. ix–xxiii). Oxford, England: Wiley-Blackwell.

Foucault, M. (1986). Of other spaces. *Diacritics, 16*(1), 22–27.

Gee, J. P. (1990). *Social linguistics and literacies: Ideology in discourses*. London, England: Falmer Press.

Hamilton, M. (2012). Unruly practices: What a sociology of translations can offer to educational policy analysis. In T. Fenwick & R. Edwards, (Eds.), *Researching education through actor-network theory* (pp. 40–59). Oxford, England: Wiley-Blackwell.

Harman, G. (2009). *Prince of networks: Bruno Latour and metaphysics*. Melbourne, Australia: re.press.

Lamb, J. (2011). *The things things say*. Princeton, NJ: Princeton University Press.

Latour, B. (1987). *Science in action: How to follow scientists and engineers through society*. Cambridge, MA: Harvard University Press.

Latour, B. (1988). A relativist account of Einstein's relativity. *Social Studies of Science, 18*(1), 3–44.

Latour, B. (1990). Drawing things together. In M. Lynch & S. Woolgar (Eds.), *Representation in scientific practice* (pp. 19–68). Cambridge, MA: MIT Press.

Latour, B. (1991). Technology is society made durable. In J. Law (Ed.), *A sociology of monsters* (pp. 103–131). London, England: Routledge.

Latour, B. (1993). *We have never been modern*. Cambridge, MA: Harvard University Press.

Latour, B. (1999a). On recalling ANT. In J. Law & J. Hassard (Eds.), *Actor network theory and after* (pp. 15–25). Oxford, England: Blackwell.

Latour, B. (1999b). *Pandora's hope: Essays on the reality of science studies*. Cambridge, MA: Harvard University Press.

Latour, B. (2005). *Reassembling the social: An introduction to actor-network-theory.* Oxford, England: Oxford University Press.

Latour, B., & Woolgar, S. (1986). *Laboratory life: The construction of scientific facts.* Princeton, NJ: Princeton University Press.

Law, J. (2004). *After method: Mess in social science research.* London, England: Routledge.

Law, J. (2008). Actor-network theory and material semiotics. In B. S. Turner (Ed.), *The new Blackwell companion to social theory* (3rd ed., pp. 141–158). Oxford, England: Blackwell.

Leander, K. M. (2001). "This is our freedom bus going home right now": Producing and hybridizing space–time contexts in pedagogical discourse. *Journal of Literacy Research, 33,* 637–679.

Leander, K. M., & Lovvorn, J. F. (2006). Literacy networks: Following the circulation of texts, bodies, and objects in the schooling and online gaming of one youth. *Cognition and Instruction, 24,* 291–340.

Lemke, J. L. (2000). Across the scales of time: Artifacts, activities, and meanings in ecosocial systems. *Mind, Culture, and Activity, 7,* 273–292.

Mol, A., & Law, J. (2002). Complexities: An introduction. In J. Law & A. Mol (Eds.), *Complexities: Social studies of knowledge practices* (pp. 1–22). Durham, NC: Duke University Press.

Nespor, J. (2012). Devices and conceptual change. In T. Fenwick & R. Edwards (Eds.), *Researching education through actor-network theory* (pp. 1–22). Oxford, England: Wiley-Blackwell.

Spinuzzi, C. (2015). Symmetry as a methodologicial move. In P. Lynch & N. Rivers (Eds.), *Thinking with Bruno Latour in rhetoric and composition* (pp. 23-39). Carbondale: Southern Illinois University Press.

Strathern, M. (1996). Cutting the network. *Journal of the Royal Anthropological Institute, 2,* 517–535.

Street, B. V. (1984). *Literacy in theory and practice.* Cambridge, England: Cambridge University Press.

CHAPTER 11

Design, Theory, Analysis, and Interpretation in a Study of Early Internet Memes

Colin Lankshear and Michele Knobel

THIS CHAPTER REPORTS key steps in the research process we followed to undertake an exploratory study of a sample of successful early internet memes (see Knobel & Lankshear, 2007). We hoped the research would contribute to an empirical investigation of participating in Internet memes as a "new" literacy practice. At the same time, the project was informed and shaped, in part, by our wider interests in, and experiences with, advising university graduate research students and working with teacher researchers who are not enrolled in research degree programs. We conceived a kind of exploratory "try it on" project that we envisaged as precisely the kind of study that relative newcomers to academic research could pursue as a first step in learning how to think and act like a particular kind of qualitative researcher.

To this end, we put an emphasis on four things. First, we focused on coming up with a manageable and justifiable research design: to conceptualize a study that would let us address our research purposes as effectively as possible. Second, we wanted to identify some elements of theory that were relevant to and appropriate for addressing our research purposes and to develop from these a set of ideas and constructs that was sufficient to guide the research while avoiding unnecessary complication and being as economical as possible. Third, we aimed to use these theory bits to generate some simple but powerful tools and techniques for analyzing our selected memes. Finally, we sought to interpret the results of our data analysis in ways that could enhance existing knowledge of Internet memes as a cultural phenomenon.

By way of additional background information, some further points are worth noting about "where we were at" in our research interests and thinking at the time the study was conceived. Our primary interest so far as literacy studies research was concerned was in meaning-making practices within nonformal education settings and, particularly, within online popular cultural spaces. We were intrigued by Internet culture generally, as an emerging and rapidly evolving social phenomenon, and had developed a particular interest in what we thought of as characteristic kinds of Internet humor. We spent quite a lot of time hunting down hilarity online, and so far as Internet memes were concerned, we thought we had a pretty good feel for what was out there in the English language (especially the U.S. culturally oriented) memesphere. We had read Richard Dawkins's (1976/2006) founding work on memes, along with a reasonable amount of serious Memetics literature, and knew that what had become known as Internet or online memes were only analogously like the phenomena Dawkins and fellow memetics researchers regarded as memes (see the next section). Finally, by the time we undertook this study, we had been pondering for several years what might reasonably be counted as "new" literacies in a more significant sense than just thinking in terms of inscribing practices that involved digital technologies of various kinds. Specifically, we were interested in the kind of collaborative ethos that characterized what Henry Jenkins and colleagues (2006) called participatory culture and the kinds of communicative exchanges and meaning-making that went on among peers within what James Gee (2004) called affinity spaces.

Against this broad background, we decided to undertake our exploratory study of online memes.

Our Research Purposes

At the most general level, we wanted to contribute to the scholarly understanding of social practices of propagating Internet memes as one dimension of cultural production and transmission. Informed by Dawkins and memetics, we identified memes as contagious patterns of cultural information that get passed from mind to mind, influence ways of thinking about the world, and shape significant kinds of actions and behaviors within social groups. They get passed on by imitation and stay largely intact—with relatively minor mutations—over long periods.

With the arrival of the Internet, the very concept of a meme itself mutated into the idea of passing on something catchy by using the Internet to spread it through networks, forums, interest groups, and so on and, especially, by passing it on in a different but recognizable way rather than as "intact" as possible. And so, for example, early on people with an interest in photoshopping would pass on, say, digitally-edited images of the same tourist standing in front of major disasters, and others would contribute their variations on the idea (e.g., Tourist Guy with a plane crashing into the World Trade Center, leaving the *Titanic* as it sinks, when the Hindenburg zeppelin catches fire; see https://knowyourmeme.com/memes/911-tourist-guy). Internet memes got acknowledged as such if they gained sufficient traction to "get known online," and—since these early days—sites such as KnowYourMeme.com have sprung up to archive and provide information about them.

We were interested in questions to do with what kinds of Internet memes exist, what kinds of people enjoy what kinds of internet memes, and what kinds of qualities or features might help to explain why some Internet-mediated ideas and artifacts get sufficient traction to achieve recognition. Our research purposes included the following:

1. To identify a pool of successful memes that would provide a sufficient data set for an exploratory and provisional study
2. To identify and examine qualities that seem to constitute each exemplar as a *successful* online meme
3. To consider the degree of fit among the characteristics of longevity, fidelity, and fecundity that Dawkins attributes to (successful) memes, and the qualities of successful Internet memes suggested by our analysis of memes in our data set
4. To establish some categories of successful Internet memes that may help us better understand the online "memescape" in terms of the kinds of purposes those who participate in online memes may have, the kinds of things that appeal to them, and the kinds of uses to which they put online artifacts. In other words, we aimed to develop a typology of memes that would allow us to identify likely patterns of purpose, use, and take-up within and across different affinities and affinity spaces
5. To consider possible points of significance that our research findings might have for literacy education

The Theoretical Orientation

The theory informing the study came from four mutually-compatible perspectives. The first was the Darwinian biologist Richard Dawkins's original theory and concept of memes as units of cultural evolution and related contributions from memetics scholars. In 1976, Dawkins (2006) theorized that human evolution was both biological (genetic) and cultural (memetic). At the biological level, the unit of replication was the gene, and human organisms were the vehicles that "housed" these replicators. Over time, genes mutate to a greater or lesser extent, and some genes survive while others die out. The trajectory of human biological evolution is the outcome of this process. Gene replication and survival are consequences of three main characteristics, which Dawkins (2006, p. 35) called "fidelity," "fecundity," and "longevity." The more faithfully a gene is replicated (copied), the more quickly and abundantly it is replicated, and the longer the gene survives, then the greater its evolutionary footprint.

Dawkins argued that an analogous process occurs in human cultural evolution. He called the unit of cultural replication or imitation the "meme" and identified tunes, good ideas, catchphrases, clothing fashions, ways of making pots, or building arches as typical examples (see Knobel & Lankshear, 2007, p. 199). In his original sense, memes are contagious ideas, styles and modes, and ways of doing things that spread from person to person within a culture. In addressing how it is that cultures get to be and abide over time with so much continuity and recognizable shape, "Dawkins proposed a substantial evolutionary model of cultural development and change, grounded in the replication of ideas, knowledge, and other cultural information through imitation and transfer" (Knobel & Lankshear, 2007, p. 200). And, as with genes, the memes that leave the greatest cultural footprint are those that share the characteristics of fidelity, fecundity, and longevity.

A second component of our theoretical orientation was the widely-subscribed idea of literacies as social practices, and the idea that, with the emergence of the Internet, the concept of meme had morphed from the status of contagious ideas, styles, and modes that happen to catch on and get replicated to a conscious cultural practice of actively aiming to "invent" or "create" artifacts and then disseminate them online. For Dawkins (1976/2006), memes were a function of practices through which they were passed on, but there was no *practice* of meme-ing as such. In cultural evolution, the memes *themselves* are in control, and they are replicated because of their efficacy in the life of social groups. In *naming* memes, however, Dawkins unleashed a meta concept concerning how cultures get "made," and this, in turn, unleashed a way of thinking about how the Internet can be used to create and disseminate cultural items by "accident" or by design (i.e., deliberately creating something designed to "go viral"). From this perspective, meme-ing has all the features of a social practice: purposes, use of tools and technologies, development and application of appropriate kinds of knowledge and skills and know-how, shared values and criteria for competent performance, appreciation, and so on (cf. Kalman, Valdivia, & Rendón, this volume; Rish, this volume; Scribner & Cole, 1981).

Third, because we were interested in memes from the standpoint of meme-ing as a new literacy practice, we wanted to understand how particular memes as artifacts were related to the larger lives and identities of those engaging in meme-ing as a practice. One way of doing this is by drawing broadly on a version of discourse studies that privileges a *functional* approach to language, communication, and social semiotics based on the pioneering work of Michael Halliday (Halliday, 1978; Halliday & Matthiessen, 2004). This approach tries to understand how meanings are made, communicated, and negotiated by reference to three "systems" known, respectively, as the "referential or ideational" system, the "contextual or interpersonal" system, and the "textual" system.

We modified the textual system to focus explicitly on the relationship between the referential (content) and relational dimensions of memes and the ideologies and worldviews seemingly hailed by these memes. This let us home in on the kinds of *values and ideologies* communicated in the memes and better accommodate the mix of static and moving images in those memes. Such tinkering with Halliday's systems has many precedents (cf., Burn, 2008). This dimension of our theoretical orientation would inform our approach to analyzing our selected memes as *data*.

Finally, we believed that one of the risks associated with taking a discourse studies approach to understanding how meaning work is done within social and cultural life is that phenomena are often inadvertently reduced to static text(s) and the analysis becomes too text-centric. To avoid this potential issue, we drew on Gee's (2004) concepts of affinities and affinity spaces to help ensure that our analysis also focused on memes as parts of larger sets of social interactions and ways of getting things done and achieving our (social) purposes. Affinities and affinity spaces emphasize people participating; collaborating; sharing expertise and interest; relating to each other and each other's goals, purposes, needs, and resources; and so on. These are integral to the idea of engaging in and with memes as a social practice—a social practice of a *new* literacy. Affinities, obviously enough, are pursuits that people have an affinity for: a shared interest or endeavor that ties various people together and makes up part of who and what they are as people—like a shared interest in baseball (that brings together baseball fans and players), knitting, succulent gardening, or a video/computer game such as Call of Duty or Minecraft. Affinity spaces are purposefully designed spaces, whether physical or virtual, that have been built to resource people who share a particular affinity and enable them to participate in that affinity to whatever extent, level of proficiency, and so forth, they choose. It could include a bookshop and reading room attached to a church or some kind of specialist museum (for geologists, rock collectors, etc.), or it could be something like an online fanfiction site or dedicated photoshopping space, where people can get together; interact with and relate to others; and share knowledge, enthusiasm, expertise, and pleasure around their common affinity. As Gee notes (2004), like affinities themselves, affinity spaces and their resources—including knowledge and expertise—are "distributed and dispersed across many different people, places, Internet sites and modalities (magazines, chat rooms, guides, recordings)" (p. 73).

The Study Design and Methods

In short, the idea for our study was to generate a pool of memes that were all recognized as successful and that would constitute our dataset. We would then analyze these memes using some theoretically informed purpose-built techniques and procedures informed by the four elements of our theoretical orientation outlined earlier. Based on our analysis, we would identify our main results or outcomes, and we would then interpret these outcomes in the sense of describing what we saw as their significance or "so what-ness."

Sampling and Selecting Memes for the Data Set

We began by generating criteria to guide our data collection. Four main criteria were used. First, we wanted memes from the 5 years between 2001 and 2005 so that our pool reflected memes that postdated the widespread take-up of online practices by the general public within that part of the memesphere we felt competent to deal with, namely, English language and, primarily, grounded in North American Internet culture. It is widely recognized that in this "world," access to the Internet increased markedly from 2000 onward. Although this meant that some popular early online memes were excluded from our data set (e.g., Dancing Baby, Hampster Dance), these *types* of memes were nonetheless well represented in our final selection.

Second, the memes had to be more or less entirely transmitted *electronically* (by website, e-mail, chat spaces, online discussion forums, etc.).

Third, memes would be surveyed in the light of suitably-modified versions of Dawkins's (1976/2006) ideas of longevity, fecundity (along with people's susceptibility), and fidelity. For example, in Internet time, remaining popular over 2 years or more might qualify a meme for longevity. Gaining traction rapidly on a large scale was used to indicate fecundity. And replications that stayed true to what seemed like the "spirit" of the meme while nonetheless assuming quite different forms, might nonetheless qualify for fidelity. So, for example, in the case of The Lost Frog meme (see lostfrog.org), having Hopkin show up on a photoshopped Absolut vodka label as Absolut Hopkin and a photoshopped Error 404 Not Found image might be seen as faithfully replicating a quirky style of Internet humor shared by a strata of recognizable "usual suspects" who hang out in "the usual haunts" (think photoshopping forums, game forums, usenet forums, etc.).

Fourth, the memes could be deemed *successful* in the sense that they were able to garner online and offline broadcast media attention. This would include anything from sidebar mentions to full-fledged articles in newspapers, general-audience magazines and trade publications, and/or television coverage in news or talk shows.

Generating the Meme Pool as a Data Set

The criteria we employed for *successful* memes meant that we could use a range of well-known online search engines for maximum coverage of the most likely meme conduits at the time, such as website archives, weblogs, and broadcast media sites. Mostly we used Google.com for websites, Technorati.com for blogs, Wikipedia.org, popular image and animation forums and archives (e.g., Fark.org, Somethingawful.com), and resources such as WilsonWeb, ProQuest (ABI/Inform), and Lexis-Nexis for media reports.

We ended up with a data set comprising 19 memes. In chronological order of release, these were the Pancake Bunny (2001); Nike Sweatshop Shoes (2001); All Your Base Are Belong To Us (2001); Bert is Evil (2001); Tourist of Death (2001); Bonsai Kitten (2002); Ellen Feiss (2002); Star Wars Kid (2002); Black People Like Us (2002); Every time you masturbate . . . God kills a kitten (2002); "Girl A"/Nevada-tan (2003); Badger, Badger, Badger (2003); Read My Lips' "Bush-Blair Love Søng" (2003); the Tron Guy (2003); Lost Frog/Hopkin Green Frog (2004); JibJab's "This Land is My Land" (2004); Numa Numa Dance (2004); Dog Poop Girl (2005); and Flying Spaghetti Monster/Flying Spaghetti Monsterism (2005). We are writing here as though all readers will have a shared knowledge of the memes we talk about; at the same time, we're well aware that these memes are very much "of their time." Readers unfamiliar with these memes might like to pause here and look some of them up on KnowYourMeme.com to build background knowledge that will prove useful in reading later sections of this chapter.

Developing the Analysis

As previously noted, our study purposes and design committed us to analyzing our data by means of two complementary kinds of analysis. One would involve using a discourse studies approach—broadly construed—based on the theoretical constructs of three distinct systems integral to meaning-making and exchange in social settings. The other would scrutinize memes from the standpoint of affinities and affinity spaces. This would involve using appropriate kinds of tools and techniques consistent with their informing theories. The approach we used involved identifying and using two different sets of *prompt questions* based on our understanding of the constructs in question.

Analytic prompt questions are a hallmark of discourse analysis studies that prioritize discourse over grammar (cf. Cazden, 1988). The Discourse Studies field covers diverse orientations to investigating language-in-use, and there is no single "best" way of "doing discourse analysis" (cf. Gee, 2012). The research goal is to understand which "level" of analysis best suits the research purpose. We were less interested in fine-grained analysis of linguistic choices made by meme creators and more interested in meme *content*, the ways a meme appealed *relationally* to people and possible reasons why, and what *values or worldviews* were "encoded" into our memes, whether they were e-mail texts, websites with linked pages, or videos. Generating sets of prompt questions enhanced the systematicity of our analysis across memes.

First, for conducting the discourse analysis of the memes, we developed three prompt questions for each of the "systems" as follows.

The "referential or ideational" system focuses on the content and meaning of the meme. To get at this we used the following questions:

- What is the idea or information being conveyed by this meme, and how do we know this?
- How is the meme conveying this idea or information?
- What does this meme signify or mean at this moment in time, within this space, for particular people, and how do we know this?

These questions assume that meaningful configurations of images, video, gifs, text, audio, music, and the like, collectively represent something about the world. They were designed to help us unpack ostensive meanings of our memes and to help track the fidelity of a meme across its various instantiations or remixes. Making sense of memes-in-use involves examining their *situated* meanings. We believed this would help us understand the ways the meme itself was construed in terms of its design and meaning-bearing components and how it was used by people drawn to it (e.g., the Pancake Bunny meme used to suggest a given comment on a discussion board was nonsensical). These questions required us to act *anthropologically*—to try to read each meme as "insiders" (or those who spontaneously "get" and appreciate the meme) likely would.

The "contextual or interpersonal" system focuses on social relations within meaning exchange. Our prompt questions were:

- Where does this meme "stand" in terms of the relationship it assumes, enacts, or implies between people who are susceptible to it? What is it about the meme that tells us this?
- What does this meme seem to tell us about the sorts of settings within which it "catches on" and "infects" people and proves to be (highly) replicable?
- What does this meme seem to assume about truth or knowledge within these particular settings, spaces, or contexts?

Discourse analysts emphasize the ways texts and language carry meaning when shared with others in socially recognizable or "acceptable" ways. With memes, it is important to analyze the kinds of images chosen and the grammatical or visual moves used to signal what the meme poster assumes readers/recipients to be like as people (or fans, or practitioners of a certain sort, etc.), and the kind of identity (or identities) the meme poster might be enacting by sharing a given meme with others. Examining the "kinds of people the meme poster assumes will read and get it" can tell us a lot about the kinds of spaces in which each meme circulated (e.g., gamer spaces, photoshopper spaces, social news chat spaces). Within such spaces, matters like "what counts as funny," "which claims about how the world works are given credence or endorsement," and "what groups who aren't like us believe to be true" are determined by the group ("truth"). Our questions let us focus on what might make a given meme fecund (i.e., in terms of a given group of people being susceptible to it) and could tell us a lot about larger social practices in which the meme is circulating, referring to, or what it is critiquing (e.g., the Bonsai Kitty meme sardonically critiqued the myriad do-it-yourself home decor blogs of the time).

The "ideological or worldview" system focuses on values, beliefs, and worldviews. We used these prompt questions:

- What are the larger or deeper ideas, positions, or themes being conveyed by this meme or these memes?
- What do these ideas, positions, or themes tell us about different social groups?
- What does this meme or these memes tell us about "the world," or about some particular "version" of the world?

Language and meaning are never neutral but are shaped and informed by values, mindsets, and worldviews. The preceding questions aimed to tap into larger values and ideologies "encoded" into a meme, in part, to understand the longevity (or not) of an online meme. We also believed these questions might provide another angle on what makes memes contagious and people open to carrying them. For example, in the case of the Dog Poop Girl meme, shared values concerning personal responsibility and communal cleanliness were violated by the woman on the train, and public shock and outrage fueled the spread of this meme. The Nevada-tan meme—based on a schoolgirl murderer—tapped into countercultural values that celebrated gore and violence. Understanding as far as possible the values or mindsets assumed within a meme would help us to understand their contagiousness and their possible influence on or role in how groups of people think about the world.

To undertake the meme typology by reference to their apparent affinities and affinity spaces, we used four prompt questions:

- What is going on here? Who is involved, and how do we know?
- What kinds of people would recognize this meme as a resource for/within, as part of, or as being relevant to some particular affinity space? What is it about the meme that tells us this?
- In what kinds of affinity spaces might this meme most readily be taken up by members, and what is it about the meme that suggests this? What shared purposes, values, interests, or endeavors might be resourced by this meme? What do people "learn" as a consequence of participating in this meme?
- What social practices, or ways of doing, knowing, and using resources, seem to be "part and parcel" of this meme?

Overall, our analytic procedures were designed to give us information about two kinds of research purposes: characteristics of successful online/Internet memes and the types of successful Internet memes in terms of their appeal to people with identifiable shared interests. Our "affinity space" analysis meant returning to our responses to the ideational, relational, and ideological question sets, and reading across them to build a sense of what kinds of groups (defined by their shared interests and identities) seemed to take up and circulate what kinds of memes. This included mapping particular purposes (e.g., promoting manga/anime fanship, to create a hoax, to comment on society in some way), and identifying likely interests shared by those people who were infected by and passed along contagious memes (e.g., in photoshopping, celebrating geek humor, social activism). Accordingly, we traced memes across spaces rather than study the memes of a single space. These analytic questions maintained our focus on *memes-in-use* and usefully kept us from studying memes solely as *texts*.

Worked Example(s) of Doing the Analysis

To explicate our analysis as best we can in the space available, we take an example of a meme and show how we applied some prompt questions and to what outcome. To begin, we set up a simple matrix with the following headings for each column: Meme, Ideational System, Interpersonal System, Ideological/Worldview System, and Affinity Space. The first column—Meme—identified the meme, sometimes including an image of the originating text, details about the origins and spread of the meme when available, and URLs that archived examples of the meme. The remaining columns were then filled in using the prompt questions identified earlier.

The All Your Base Are Belong to Us meme grew out of an introductory scene in a Japanese shooter game, Zero Wing (launched in Japan 1989, and the U.S. market in 1998). This scene established the context for the game: An invading cyborg threatens the entire Earth, and it is up to one hero—the player—to fly a spacecraft and defeat the enemy in an all-out battle. But what really seemed to catch people's attention was this scene's English subtitles, which are full of grammatical errors and mistranslations (e.g., "Someone set us up the bomb," "All your base are belong to us," "What you say?" "For great justice"; for details, see Knobel & Lankshear, 2007; Know Your Meme, 2019). Once the scene made its way to the SomethingAwful photoshopping forums in 2000, the line "All your base are belong to us" was picked up and remixed into still and moving images and other text forms taken from everyday life (e.g., a reworded "Hollywood" sign in Los Angeles, road signs, advertisements, food products, official documents), as well as from popular culture (e.g., remixed as an electronic music track, referencing other cyborgs in television shows, plays on base/bass).

In terms of analyzing the ideational system, the prompt questions engaged us in unpacking what this meme was in the sense of how it came to be and what it comprised in all its various forms. These questions focus on the ostensive content of the meme and resulted in us generating a history of the meme and understanding how introductory scenes worked in video games like Zero Wing. Without access to the game itself, we relied on others' accounts of how it was played. The internet was very different at the time of this study, so we used online searches and available archives to access instances of how "All your base are belong to us" played out in a wide range of remixes and references. In terms of identifying what this meme signified, it seemed that the glitchy English translation of the opening dialogue appealed to what Taylor (2001) referred to as "geek kitsch humor" located at the nexus of a grave situation married to a kind of pidgin English that undermined the seriousness of the threats being conveyed. (Of course, talking about these translations without seeming condescending or patronizing is difficult, but the absurdist humor people found in what was widely referred to at the time as "bad" English translation was crucial to the appeal of this meme.)

Analyzing the interpersonal system of the meme focused our attention on how the originating meme and its various replications signaled a particular kind of social understanding of who viewers of this meme were likely to be. The very banality of many of the images sporting the "All your base" catchphrase generated a shared joke among contributors to (and in conduits for) this meme, concerning an imagined and sudden takeover of the world by an enemy power that is announced via a range of very ordinary media and artifacts (e.g., besides those already listed, cereal packaging, billboards referencing George W. Bush, as a fortune in a cookie, on the packaging of action figures). This emphasis on remixing everyday items with the "All your base are belong to us" catchphrase seems to poke gentle fun at heavy-handed, theatrical threats or bids for power and control.

The ideological system required thinking more broadly about meanings and social practices in relation to this meme. Focusing on worldviews and social groups engaged us in thinking about U.S. popular culture (given where the meme seemed to be most contagious) and what was being valued at the time. This very much included a fascination with Japanese popular culture—everything from manga and anime, to monster movies, martial arts, and food—that was rather nonmainstream back then. The popularity of the All Your Base meme appears to be grounded in this shared passion as well as in a strong appreciation for the absurd. The meme also taps into a common theme in American culture regarding the threat of foreign or alien invasions and hostile takeovers.

Applying the affinity space questions to this meme helped us to identify the spaces in which this meme was popular—such as video game and general discussion boards, photoshopping forums, software programming forums, and the like. Social practices identified include photoshopping the nonsensical as realistically as possible, producing clever and intertextual remixes, participating in a shared joke, hoaxing others, contributing to darkly humorous takes on popular social practices (e.g., being a tourist, "personalizing" consumer products), and so on. This constellation of spaces and practices underscored the ways in which the All Your Base meme seemed to appeal to an absurdist or "geeky" humor.

Finally, we read across all our analytic results to generate a typology of larger social purposes and affinities seemingly served by these memes (see Figure 11.1 later in this chapter).

Results of Data Analysis

Applying this general procedure with the range of prompt questions to address specific aspects of the entire range of memes, we mapped patterns and derived broad categories. This was an exploratory study, seen as provisional from the outset. Consequently, it proceeded more by intuition and direct interpretation at times than by close and detailed induction. Nonetheless, close and detailed induction by means of rigorous coding through multiple phases along the kinds of lines described by Dziuba, Black, and Alexander in Chapter 9 (this volume), would have been ideal and would have given us greater confidence in and better audit trails for our claimed outcomes. Even so, we felt confident claiming the results we did.

These results were of three kinds. They address *characteristics* of successful memes, *types* of successful memes, and meme *practices* in relation to affinities and engagement in particular kinds of affinity spaces. Results also addressed our sense of how the characteristics of memes identified by Dawkins (1976/2006) might be refined or amended to account for the kinds of online memes and practices we examined. We summarize these in turn, as a basis for addressing how we subsequently interpreted them.

Characteristics of Successful Internet Memes

First, we found that humor was the overwhelmingly common feature across the pool. It took different forms, some of it nicely identified as quirky, situational, absurdist kinds of humor, for example, All Your Base, Ellen Feiss, Numa Numa Dance, Oolong the Pancake Bunny, and Every Time you Masturbate . . . God Kills a Kitten. The five politically flavored social commentary memes spanned tongue-in-cheek and sardonic humor through to biting satirical humor, for example, Read My Lips' "Bush-Blair Love Song," JibJab's "This Land," and the Nike Sweatshop Shoes memes.

Second, we found that several memes (e.g., Star Wars Kid, Lost Frog, All Your Base, Flying Spaghetti Monster) were characterized by "rich intertextuality," involving cross-references to a host of popular culture events, artifacts, and practices. Some remixes of the Star Wars Kid meme added music, special effects, and highly recognizable *Star Wars* sounds (e.g., the lightsaber "swoosh-hum") to an original video a schoolboy had made of himself somewhat awkwardly miming a lightsaber fight using a broomstick-like golf ball retriever. Friends found and uploaded the clip. It was viewed by millions and remixed multiple times. Remixes included casting the Kid as Gandalf in *Lord of the Rings*, William Wallace in *Braveheart*, Neo from *The Matrix* movies, and mixing the clip with the Dancing Baby meme in a faux trailer for a Hollywood buddy movie. Cross-references to popular movies, movie genres, and games tap into affinity spaces that recognize and appreciate such intertextuality while blurring lines between ordinary life and the extraordinary lives of characters in movie and game universes. This rich layering of cross-references may have enhanced the fecundity of these memes by encouraging subsequent meme-makers to include their own cross-cultural references, adding dimensions of meaning for "those in the know" to already-humorous contributions.

Third, ten of the memes employed "anomalous juxtaposition" as a hook to maximize the susceptibility of their contagious ideas. The Bert is Evil meme began with a photograph of the Muppet, Bert (from Sesame Street), being photoshopped into a picture of Osama bin Laden and uploaded as a joke to an online photoshop forum. The image was subsequently downloaded and used in Bangladesh on street march banners by bin Laden supporters sometime during 2001. Creators of the banners either did not notice Bert in the picture they downloaded or did not know who Bert was. The banner image caught wide broadcast media attention and rapidly prompted different people to create remixed images that added evidence to the claim that Bert was indeed evil, not a harmless children's television character (see bertisevil.tv). Numerous subsequent remixed images added "evidence" to the "Bert is Evil" claim, through association with Hitler, the Ku Klux Klan, President Kennedy's assassination, the Manson murders, and so on. The juxtaposition of horrible, tragic, or seedy scenarios with an innocuous puppet from a children's television show enacts a kind of gallows humor by presenting documentary evidence that clearly cannot be true.

Anomalous juxtaposition did not always emerge from humorous phenomena. The (notorious) Nevada-tan meme grew out of a child—wearing a hoodie stamped with "Nevada"—killing a classmate at school (in Japan) and included fan art, photoshopped images, and cosplay in a kind of extended and macabre "homage" to the child killer. A young, ordinary-looking girl juxtaposed with a gruesome murder she made no effort to hide created attention hooks that helped turn Nevada-tan's case and persona into a meme within certain affinity spaces based on interest in evil, cruel, macabre, or otherwise chilling events.

Finally, only one of the memes in our data set, Dog Poop Girl, did not display any humor, intertextuality, or anomalous juxtaposition. As mentioned earlier, a young South Korean woman's dog fouled a train carriage, and she refused requests to clean up the mess. A passenger photographed the woman and her dog and posted it to a popular website. It rapidly gained traction, spreading widely online in its original and some faintly remixed poster versions. The woman was identified and her personal information published online to punish her failure to be a responsible citizen. She was hounded online and offline until she posted a contrite apology to an Internet forum. This meme attracted broadcast media attention internationally, due mostly to its vigilante nature and the breaching of the woman's right to personal privacy.

A Provisional Typology of Our Pool of Early Internet Memes

Our analysis suggested that the data set reflects different categories of *kinds* of memes. These differences show up around what seem to be the main purposes the various memes are organized around and the types of memes that spun off these purposes. As reflected in Figure 11.1, we identified four distinct meme purposes in the data set, although the two purposes of social commentary or critique and engaging in absurdist kinds of humor accounted for 17 of the 19 memes.

These broad categories break down into subcategories of interest (or affinity). Most of the memes in our pool seem to appeal to and draw on creative energies of people who enjoy playful and often absurdist ideas. Some of the memes carry little "serious" content, while others carry very serious content in the form of commentary or critique. Across this gulf in substantive purpose, however, the playfulness evident across so many of the memes we studied taps into shared cultural practices and experiences and, in turn, seems to help delineate and partly characterize diverse affinities and affinity spaces (e.g., photoshopper spaces, gamer spaces, left-leaning political spaces, "good community member" spaces, manga/anime spaces, even nihilist spaces) by way of the semiotic nods and winks the memes give to insiders or those "in the know." Outsiders, or those not in the know, may miss the humor in and the point to such memes. Those who pick up on the nods and winks and affiliate with the interests and causes communicated and enacted in and through the memes will often be encouraged to pass them on to kindred spirits or like-minded others and, in some cases, help promote or grow the meme by contributing more variations. Network effects can take over from there in a virtuous circle of further building and consolidating affinities and identities while simultaneously growing meme-ing practices and memes themselves.

Reflections on Dawkins's Original Account of Characteristics of Memes

In relation to Dawkins's (1976/2006) three characteristics of memes, we found that in the case of Internet memes it was better to think in terms of replicability of a meme's core "contagious idea" than in terms of fidelity as a faithful reproduction of that idea because replicability can accommodate variation on a theme. Although the "contagious idea" remained intact in these memes, it often was passed along in ways that changed their "look" when given idiosyncratic spins by participants. And the changed look could be almost total, as in the example previously mentioned of the difference between the original image of "The Lost Frog" flyer and the Error 404 Not Found version.

Such replicability (incorporating digital remix) enhanced a meme's fecundity by hooking others who are participating in affinity spaces where the meme is playing out

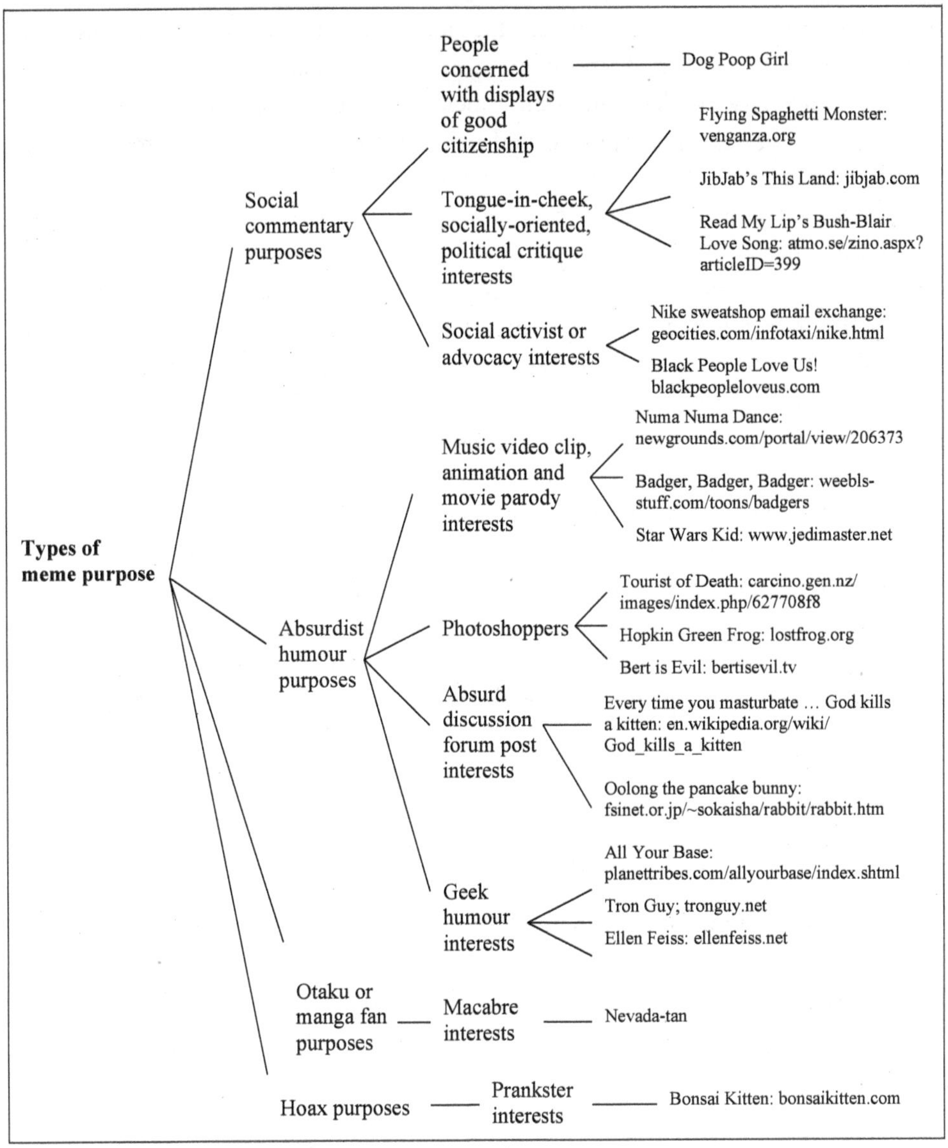

Figure 11.1. Our meme typology

Source: From Knobel, M., & Lankshear, C. (2007). Online memes, affinities and cultural production. In M. Knobel & C. Lankshear (Eds.), *A New Literacies sampler* (pp. 199–227). New York, NY: Peter Lang, p. 218. Used with permission.

into creating their own versions. The scale, reach, and interconnectedness of online networks and relationships among online affinity groups means that a meme could take off, gain traction, generate different versions, and spread rapidly and widely (even in what was then relatively early Internet days). Many participants in a meme are members of multiple online affinities, which means that memes can be projected and "cross over" into multiple affinity spaces. Accordingly, replicability here needs to include remixing as an important practice within much online meme-ing. Remixing ranges over modifying, splicing, bricolaging, superimposing, and reordering original and other images, music, sounds, talk, and so forth.

In terms of longevity, many in our original pool can still be sourced. Some, like "All Your Base," remain alive. For example, Elon Musk contributed "All your patent are belong to us" in 2014, and the phrase "All your base" appeared in a mythical language in a 2017 video game The Legend of Zelda: Breath of the Wild ("All Your Base . . . ," 2019). In terms of the time span of memes in Dawkins's (1976/2006) sense, the kind of life we documented in our meme pool is mere nanoseconds. Nonetheless, writing this chapter now, seeing how easy it was to locate meme archives providing original texts, images, sound, video clips, and other footage and detailed accounts of the origin and spread of these memes and their permutations was interesting. From this perspective, the longevity of memes can, in principle, be as long as archives are preserved and remain locatable, and people maintain interest in the core ideas of such memes. Under current and foreseeable conditions, however, where variety is almost unlimited, trends constantly change, and a sense of history and historical tradition is tenuous, the longevity of specific Internet memes will likely be short, although the ideas they convey may well have much longer shelf lives.

Interpretation

Our approach to interpreting the analytic results of the study simply involved asking, "What might (or do) these results *mean*? What might their *significance* be?" Meaning, however, is always a matter of perspective: "meaning in relation to *what*?" or "meaning *in terms of* what?" In this section, we generated two questions to ask what our results might mean:

1. "What do these results mean in terms of possible significance for literacy education?" This involves interpreting results from the standpoint of our research purpose concerned with trying to help inform (and transform) educational *practice* in potentially useful ways.
2. "What do these results mean in terms of trying to contribute something to our theoretical orientation?" When qualitative researchers undertake research from a Literacy Studies perspective, they draw on theory to help them better understand some social phenomenon—in our case, certain practices of participating in memes. In doing so, however, they also hope to feed back into the *theory* itself by considering how their empirical results about the social phenomenon might tell

us something more about the theory or help us to further refine it in some way.

Interpreting the Meaning of Results in Terms of Possible Significance for Literacy Education

Some educational issues prompted by our study results relate directly to aspects of literacy education that we have become familiar with as a result of our reading and wider research interests. These include the conditions and circumstances under which the characteristics of humor (of various kinds), rich intertextuality, and anomalous juxtaposition are realized in meme generation. Our reading around the topic of memes informed us that Richard Brodie (1996) had argued that we need to pay close attention to the memes that infect us and that we choose to take up, share, or reinvent. Leaving aside the question of "infection" and the extent to which it is to be understood literally or metaphorically, some of the memes in our data set raise troubling questions that go to the heart of literacies as inevitably nonneutral. Our pool includes memes that are not benign and do not constitute constructive and enriching ways of being in the world. This resonates with our long-standing interest in critical literacy.

The Dog Poop Girl meme exhibited extreme vigilantism. The woman was hunted down, identified, and hounded publicly until she apologized. The reach and power of the meme ensured public censure and humiliation on a massive scale, prompting discussion in South Korea where the meme originated about the need to understand the dangers of witch-hunt approaches to castigating individuals: a theme that has been revisited countless times around the world to little apparent effect thus far. Other examples, such as the Star Wars Kid meme and the Lost Frog meme, revealed that the material effects of memes, even when they are not malicious or badly intentioned, are not always beneficial to the "stars" of these memes, and neither do the "stars" necessarily welcome the attention they receive (see Knobel & Lankshear, 2007). Examining memes can provide insights into what the longer range and longer term effects might be of participating in certain memes. As we noted in one report of the original study,

> analyzing meme processes and effects as new forms of social influence can become an important part of revising critical literacy practices in classrooms to better take account of new literacy practices and new ways of transmitting both healthy and toxic ideas rapidly and extensively. Engaging in the serious study of memes can help educators to equip students with important strategies for identifying the memes that infect their minds, and for evaluating the effects these memes have on their (ethical) decision-making, actions and relations with others. (Knobel & Lankshear, 2007, p. 223)

This seems to us to assume genuine urgency at a time when participating in memes has become so thoroughly a part of young people's everyday cultural lives, when the means for such participation are so readily accessible, when the potential to unthinkingly cause hurt or harm to others is so great, and when using media to shame, marginalize, or demean others has become so widespread that it might almost seem "normal" or acceptable to do so.

Interpreting the Meaning of Results in Terms of Trying to Contribute Something to Our Theoretical Orientation

We drew on the results of our study to remix Gee's well-known theoretical constructs of D/discourse and R/reading (cf. Gee, 1996, 2004) and offered up the possibility of thinking about memes in terms of L/literacies (Knobel & Lankshear, 2007). We think of Literacy with a "big *L*" in terms of making meanings in ways that are directly tied to who and what somebody is *being* in the world (cf. Freire, 1972; Street, 1984). In other words, whenever we use language or some other kind of sign (image, sound, animation, icon, emoji, hashtag), we are making some kind of "move" that is intended to realize or bring into being some element or aspect of our world. We are trying to do something, be something, or express something that others will be able to recognize and respond to in one way or another. We think of literacy with a "small *l*" in terms of the actual material processes of using signs and symbols to make the "move." So, for example, if one is modifying an image to create a particular effect, that is "small *l*." But aiming to get that particular effect to realize a purpose in line with who and what one is wanting to be or bring about in the world is "big *L*." L/literacy is always about reading and writing *something*, and this something is always part of a larger pattern of being in the world (Gee, Hull, & Lankshear, 1996).

So how might this help us think about memes and practices of participating in memes? The texts and images we produce or find and pass on, or that we read to participate in a meme, are never freestanding. Instead, they are implicated in and generated out of networks of shared experiences, worldviews and values, interests, habits, and the like that use or pick up on signs in the form of texts, icons, symbols, sounds, images, and all manner of cultural artifacts in particular, distinctive, and often socially particular ways. Take the Pancake Bunny meme as an example. Posting an image of a rabbit with a pancake on its head only makes sense within a context like an online forum where quirky conversation responses are celebrated. As mentioned earlier, the meme began when someone posted an image of a rabbit balancing a pancake on its head to a discussion forum (see kimsal.com/rabbit_pancake.jpg). The image was accompanied by the caption "I have no idea what you are talking about. . . . So here's a bunny with a pancake on its head." The image itself was from a series of "head performance" photographs by Hironori Akutagawa, a Japanese artist who trained his pet rabbit, Oolong, to balance light objects on his head.

These details have crucial implications for how to analyze such memes. They suggest that analyzing the ideational system of a meme such as this needs to be carefully nuanced to appreciate that online memes are often tongue in cheek and/or deeply ironic and that they often reference multiple texts, values, cultural practices, cultural interests, and events. Looking for an absurdist meme of this type to make "sense" in its own right would be to overlook most of what is important. Analyzing the relational or contextual system of memes likewise needs to be carefully nuanced, with close attention paid to their often cumulative, distributed, and collaborative nature (cf. Knobel & Lankshear, 2007, p. 220). Consequently, being the kind of person who responds to online posts in a humorous or ironic waypoints to the "big *L*" Literacy. Creating or modifying the image as the vehicle or means for enacting the role (being or doing something in the world) is the "small *l*" literacy. Like any literacy as a social practice, M/meme-ing involves both.

Conclusion

Since the late 1980s, participating in Internet memes has emerged and evolved as a high-profile cultural phenomenon, albeit one that involves a considerable mutation of Dawkins's (1976/2006) original conception of memes as the unit of cultural evolution. This chapter has spelled out how elements of theory derived from a range of mutually-related and informing sources were used to inform a research design and a methodology for investigating characteristics of successful Internet memes and to identify different types of memes and practices of participating in memes during the period preceding the rise of macro meme generators. These sources included memetics and the study of human cultural evolution; Literacy Studies and the idea of literacies as social practices; a functional language approach to examining meaning-making, communication, and social semiotics; and the closely related concepts of affinities, affinity spaces, and participatory culture. We have described how the concepts of the ideational, interpersonal, and ideological systems for understanding and explaining how meanings are realized can be used to generate prompt questions for analyzing memes as data and how to use these prompt questions in the acts of analyzing memes as data. The chapter has also shown how we used the concepts of affinities and affinity spaces to avoid reducing cultural phenomena to static texts and adopting narrowly text-centric approaches to analyzing the kinds of meanings produced within social-cultural practices. Finally, it has briefly sampled some of the ways we sought to interpret the results of our data analysis in theoretically informed discussion.

Since the study was done, memes and practices of participating in memes have evolved and expanded dramatically. We believe exploring what a similar kind of study might reveal about the contemporary English-language memesphere and the extent to which methodological extensions or refinements might be necessary for undertaking a similar study now would be interesting.

Suggested Further Reading

Gee, J. (2014). *How to do discourse analysis.* New York, NY: Routledge.

Knobel, M., & Lankshear, C. (2019). Language teachers researching and understanding new literacies and language-in-use from a social languages perspective. *The European Journal of Applied Linguistics and TEFL, 8*, 159–174.

Lankshear, C., & Knobel, M. (2019). Memes, macros, meaning and menace: Some trends in internet memes. *The Journal of Communication and Media Studies, 4*(4), 43–57. https://doi.org/10.18848/2470-9247/CGP/v04i04/43-57

References

All your base are belong to use. (2019). In *Wikipedia*. Retrieved from https://en.wikipedia.org/wiki/All_your_base_are_belong_to_us

Brodie, R. (1996). *Virus of the mind: The new science of the meme.* New York, NY: Integral Press.

Burn, A. (2008). The case of Rebellion: Researching multimodal texts. In J. Coiro, M. Knobel, C. Lankshear, & D. Leu (Eds.), *Handbook of research on new literacies* (pp. 151–178). New York, NY: Erlbaum.

Cazden, C. (1988). *Classroom discourse: The language of teaching and learning.* Portsmouth, NH: Heinemann.

Dawkins, R. (2006). *The selfish gene* (2nd ed.). Oxford, England: Oxford University Press. (Original work published 1976)

Dziuba, A., Black, R., & Alexander, J. (2020). Theorizing with (a) difference: Fanfiction, literacy and neurodiversity. In M. Knobel. J. Kalman, & C. Lankshear (Eds.), *Data analysis, interpretation, and theory in literacy studies research: A how-to guide* (pp. 165–180). Gorham, ME: Myers Education Press.

Freire, P. (1972). *Pedagogy of the oppressed.* New York, NY: Seabury Press.

Gee, J. P. (1996). *Social linguistics and literacies: Ideology in discourses.* New York, NY: Routledge.

Gee, J. P. (2004). *Situated language and learning: A critique of traditional schooling.* New York, NY: Routledge.

Gee, J. P. (2012). *How to do discourse analysis: A toolkit.* New York, NY: Routledge.

Gee, J., Hull, G., & Lankshear, C. (1996). *The new work order: Behind the language of the new capitalism.* Boulder, CO: Westview Press.

Halliday, M. (1978). *Language as social semiotic: The social interpretation of language and meaning.* London, England: Edward Arnold.

Halliday, M., & Matthiessen, C. (2004). *An introduction to functional grammar* (3rd ed.). London, England: Routledge.

Jenkins, H., with R. Purushotma, K. Clinton, M. Weigel & A. Robison. (2006). *Confronting the challenge of participatory culture: Media education for the 21st century* (Occasional paper). Boston, MA: MIT/MacArthur Foundation.

Kalman, J., Valdivia, P., & Rendón, V. (2020). Using spreadsheets for analyzing qualitative data. In M. Knobel, J. Kalman, & C. Lankshear (Eds.) *Data analysis, interpretation, and theory in literacy studies research: A how-to guide* (pp. 123–147). Gorham, ME: Myers Education Press.

Knobel, M., & Lankshear, C. (2007). Online memes, affinities and cultural production. In M. Knobel & C. Lankshear (Eds.), *A new literacies sampler* (pp. 199–227). New York, NY: Peter Lang.

Know Your Meme. (2019). All your base are belong to us. Retrieved from https://knowyourmeme.com/memes/all-your-base-are-belong-to-us

Rish, R. (2020). Using mediated discourse analysis to investigate literacy practices. In M. Knobel, J. Kalman, & C. Lankshear (Eds.), *Data analysis, interpretation, and theory in literacy studies research: A how-to guide* (pp. 55–76). Gorham, ME: Myers Education Press.

Scribner, S., & Cole, M. (1981). *The psychology of literacy*. Cambridge, MA: Harvard University Press.

Street, B. (1984). *Literacy in theory and practice*. New York, NY: Cambridge University Press.

Taylor, C. (2001, February 25). All your base are belong to us. *Time*. Retrieved from http://content.time.com/time/magazine/article/0,9171,100525,00.html

Contributors

JONATHAN ALEXANDER is Chancellor's Professor of English and Informatics in the School of Humanities at the University of California, Irvine. His research interests are in writing studies and rhetoric, new media studies and digital rhetoric, genre and popular fiction, life writing, and sexuality studies. E-mail: jfalexan@uci.edu

REBECCA W. BLACK is Associate Professor in the Department of Informatics at the University of California, Irvine. Her research explores on how youth are using new technologies to learn, create, and communicate. E-mail: rwblack@uci.edu

DAVID BLOOME is EHE Distinguished Professor of Teaching and Learning in the Department of Teaching and Learning at The Ohio State University, College of Education and Human Ecology. His research focuses on how people use spoken and written language for learning, to create social relationships, to construct knowledge, and to create communities, social institutions, and shared histories and futures. E-mail: bloome.1@osu.edu

MARIA LUCIA CASTANHEIRA is Professor of Education at the Federal University of Minas Gerais, Brazil. She is particularly interested in examining the social construction of opportunities for learning in diverse classrooms (elementary school and adult education) and literacy practices in and out of school. E-mail: lalu@fae.ufmg.br

ALLISON DZIUBA is a PhD candidate in English at the University of California, Irvine. Her research examines college students' self-sponsored literacy practices, particularly as these students engage in and with feminist activism. E-mail: adziuba@uci.edu

JUDITH L. GREEN is Distinguished Professor Emerita at the University of California, Santa Barbara. Her research focuses on teaching-learning relationships, disciplinary knowledge as socially constructed, and ethnographic research and discourse studies of the patterns of everyday life in classrooms. E-mail: green@education.ucsb.edu

AARON CHIA YUAN HUNG is Associate Professor in the program in educational technology at Adelphi University. His research and publishing focus on communication and collaboration in technology-mediated environments, design thinking, gamification, and game-based learning. E-mail: hung@adelphi.edu

INGRID K. JAKOBSEN is Lecturer in the Department of Education at The Arctic University of Norway. She teaches literature and English-subject pedagogy. Her research interests include multimodality, literacy, picture books in English-language teaching, and digital literature. E-mail: ingrid.jakobsen@uit.no

JUDY KALMAN is Professor in the Department of Educational Research within the Center for Research and Advanced Studies at the Instituto Politécnico Nacional, México. Her research interests center on the social construction of literacy and digital culture. E-mail: jkalman@cinvestav.mx

MICHELE KNOBEL is Professor of Education at Montclair State University (United States). She is especially interested in young people's literacy practices online and offline and how such practices entail shifts in what it means to "be literate" in current times. E-mail: knobelm@montclair.edu

COLIN LANKSHEAR is an independent educational researcher, writer, and teacher based in México and an adjunct professor at Mount Saint Vincent University (Canada). His research and writing focus on cultural practices mediated by new technologies. E-mail: colin.lankshear@msvu.ca

JOANNE LARSON, PhD, is the Michael W. Scandling Professor of Education and Associate Chair of the Center for Urban Education Success at the University of Rochester's Warner Graduate School of Education and Human Development. Her ethnographic research examines how language and literacy practices mediate social and power relations in schools and communities. E-mail: jlarson@warner.rochester.edu

KEVIN LEANDER is Professor of Literacy Education in the Department of Teaching and Learning at Vanderbilt University. His main research interests include Adolescent Literacy, English Education, Literacy and Technology, and Spatial Approaches to Social Science Research. E-mail: kevin.leander@vanderbilt.edu

JASON F. LOVVORN is Associate Professor of English at Belmont University in Nashville, Tennessee, where he teaches composition and rhetoric. His research interests include writing and rhetoric, literacy, new media, service learning, and materialisms. E-mail: jason.lovvorn@belmont.edu

GEORGE MOSES is Executive Director of Freedom School, Sankofa Communiversity-North East Area Development (FSSC-NEAD). His work emphasizes the needs and the innate solutions within diasporas' community development and initiatives and seeks to balance scholarly research with the practical application needed for positive transformation in socially, culturally, and economically challenged communities. E-mail: gmoses@neadrochester.org

VÍCTOR RENDÓN has a PhD in Science from the Department of Educational Research, DIE-CINVESTAV, México, where he is a member of the Laboratory of Education, Technology and Society. His research interests include the relations between young students' literacy practices and new literacies and digital technologies, issues about cultural practices and design of teaching and learning activities, and the link between education inside and outside of school. E-mail: vjrendonc@gmail.com

RYAN RISH is Assistant Professor of New Literacies in the Department of Learning and Instruction at the University at Buffalo (SUNY). His research interests involve the literacy practices of adolescents, especially with regard to how those practices relate to the institutions, social spaces, and geographic places in which they are enacted. E-mail: ryanrish@buffalo.edu

SANGHEE RYU is Research Professor at Korea University. Her research focuses on how multiliteracies can be studied, taught, and assessed within the context of literacy education, with a particular focus on using argumentation as a thinking and communication tool. She also has a special interest in how to theorize and trace social interactions around teaching and learning writing. E-mail: sangheeryu@korea.ac.kr

ELISE SEIP TØNNESSEN is Professor at Department of Nordic and Media Studies, University of Agder in Kristiansand, Norway. Her research focuses on reading, writing, and multimodality. She is interested in texts ranging from literature to data visualizations, mainly for children, in various genres and contexts, including education and popular media culture. E-mail: elise.s.tonnessen@uia.no

PATRICIA VALDIVIA is a master's student in the Department of Educational Research, DIE- CINVESTAV, México, and a member of the Laboratory of Education, Technology and Society. Her research interests center on literacy in the social world, the appropriation processes of digital technologies in precarious contexts, and the relations between literacy practices and the uses of digital technologies. E-mail: cp.valdivia91@gmail.com

BETH V. YEAGER, PhD, is currently a consultant with Rio School District in Oxnard, California. Her research focuses on practitioner inquiry, literacy, disciplinary practices and identities, and transdisciplinary inquiry-based instructional design, with/for linguistically, culturally, socially, and academically diverse students. E-mail: eyeager76@gmail.com

Name Index

J

K

L

M

N

P

R

S

T

V

W

Y

Z

Subject Index

R

S

T

U

V

X